PRAISE FOR Charlie Walker

"Thanks for your very kind letter of July 3. It was a real pleasure hearing from you…. We were very happy to have you visit Montgomery. I count it a real personal privilege of having the opportunity of meeting you. I hope that we will be able to renew this fellowship at a later date, and that I will see you again when I am not so busy with other things. Please give my best regards to all of my friends along the Philadelphia area."

> —**Martin Luther King Jr,** letter to Charles Walker

"Charles [Walker] was a significant figure in the civil rights movement. I was privileged to know him well. This pamphlet was widely used at the time. Although the technology of protest has changed, the wisdom here is timeless, and the current moment in politics makes its thrust seem particularly relevant."

> —**Robert Dockhorn**, former editor of *Friends Journal,* regarding Charlie Walker's handbook, *Organizing for Nonviolent Direct Action,* republished November 2016 by Brenda Walker Beadenkopf

PRAISE FOR *A Quaker Behind the Dream*

"This is a very important book. Charlie Walker was a great visionary ahead of his time, who did not get the credit he deserves."

> —**Reverend James Lawson**, described as "The Architect of the Civil Rights Movement" by Congressman John Lewis

"Charlie Walker played a critical role in working with Martin Luther King in building a powerful freedom movement to help change the course of American history. Read this important book to find out more."

> —**David Hartsough**, author of *Waging Peace: Global Adventures of a Lifelong Activist* and Co-founder of Nonviolent Peaceforce and World Beyond War

"For Brenda … who shares the Dream."

> —**Edythe Scott Bagley**, Coretta Scott King's sister

"Charlie and I were good friends and comrades. I have read the manuscript with fascination and am impressed with the research you have done. You are doing a very good work on your father. He would be proud of you. You have done a skillful job of writing and it is very readable. You have done your Dad a great service and the movement too. Charlie comes through with flying colors."

—**George Houser**, Co-founder of Congress of Racial Equality (CORE)

A Quaker Behind the Dream

Charlie Walker and the Civil Rights Movement

Volume 1 1920–1955

Brenda Walker Beadenkopf

ISBN: 978-1-945975-86-8

Published by EA Books Publishing a division of
Living Parables of Central Florida, Inc. a 501c3
EABooksPublishing.com

Cover photo by Theodore Hetzel, Charlie Walker speaking at 1965 rally in front of Philadelphia City Hall with statue of William Penn in background.

Dedication

To my mother, Marian Walker,
without whom this book would not have been written.

Contents

Preface...iii

Prologue: March on Washington, 1963 1

Chapter 1: Childhood Days 13

Chapter 2: College Years...45

Chapter 3: Conscience during the War Years, 1940–1945 91

Photographs 144

Chapter 4: Postwar Years, 1946–1948 162

Chapter 5: Working for the FOR, MLK Encounter, Late 1940s ...190

Chapter 6: Taking Up Race Issues, Early 1950s..................213

Chapter 7: Supreme Court Decision of 1954 254

Author's Note..273

About the Author...275

Endnotes...276

Abbreviations Appendix 301

Index ....

....303

Preface

Several years ago, after Dad had been ill for some time, I visited the family home near Philadelphia from my home in the Midwest. My mother, Marian, showed me her recreation room and my father's office, quite full of boxes of papers, tapes, magazine articles, old typewriters, pamphlets, monographs, and books.

"Someone needs to write a book about your father's life," she declared. "And it needs to be done soon, or all this will be lost." She swept her arm toward the piles, indicating the scope of the task, and it looked daunting. I nodded.

My Quaker father, Charles Coates Walker, had become an expert in nonviolence, rising in the American civil rights movement to work with many of its distinguished leaders. He taught the principles of nonviolence—its theories and strategies—which were longtime Quaker principles.

Having been raised in a Philadelphia Quaker household, I had been expected to stand on picket lines for justice, the environment, and civil rights. I remembered visiting the extraordinary Dr. A. J. Muste, and having such guests at our home as Bayard Rustin and Glenn Smiley. Even though I had marched with Dr. King in the thrilling 1963 March on Washington, I went on with my life as a Midwest journalist.

The next time I visited my parents, my mother made the same comments, and I agreed someone needed to write the story, but it was not until the third or fourth time I felt God saying to me, You know this is your task, don't you?

"Me?" I protested. "My siblings can write, and they live here, which I do not."

But none of my siblings felt led to write it. I was a writer and senior editor of a local newspaper—had the skills and background—but still argued with God.

Even so, He kept nudging me, gently pushing me out of my ruts. He convinced me this was my task, by eventually countering my many objections. When God refutes all your excuses, there is nothing left to say but, "Yes, God." And it was one of the best decisions of my life—as well as one of the most adventurous.

As I sought guidance about how to approach my father's story, suddenly—as if watching a movie with radiant colors—I envisioned a happy, carefree, ten-year-old Charlie, dashing out the door of his brick elementary school in 1931, stack of books in hand, running up the hill toward home. Blond with beautiful hazel eyes, athletic but bookish, the farm boy then stands breathless and hungry at a glassine case of penny candies, wishing his family weren't so poor. Deciding to not let it get him down, he continues his happy mood until he reaches home—to receive shocking news. I felt God showed me in Technicolor how to write this book.

The image of Charlie as one of the organizers of the 1963 March on Washington came to me in similar sounds, smells, and emotions. I knew then I had to make the tale of this dreamer, doer, and organizer come alive. Not just a listing of times, dates, and events, but the real-life story of a brilliant farm boy from Lancaster County, Pennsylvania, who made a difference in our nation's history.

The title of the book came largely from a sweet note written to me from a meeting I had with Edythe Scott Bagley, Coretta Scott's King's sister, in March of 2002 in Pennsylvania. My mother, Marian Walker, and Edythe were great friends and neighbors, and I asked my Mom if I could meet her. Mom took me to the Bagley home, where Edythe, Mom and I had a lovely talk about Charlie Walker and "Martin," whom she called a wonderfully handsome man!

My father knew Rev. Martin Luther King and worked with him on the nonviolence aspects of the civil rights movement. He corresponded with Rev. King, who called Walker "a man of skill and understanding," and praised him for his "Christian generosity and moral support." He also expressed the belief that Walker was working on "a more adequate understanding of the structure and dynamics of nonviolent movements."

While visiting Edythe, I received some gifts from her—some enlightening tapes of Martin Luther King's sermons to encourage me in writing this book about my father, who had been her friend and a friend to the Kings. She also presented me with a new book (at the time) by Christine King Farris, *Through It All*. Edythe wrote on one of the inside pages, "For Brenda, who shares the Dream. Edythe Scott Bagley. March 28, 2009."

Because of this, my motto has become, "Sharing the Dream." Charlie Walker was not a Quaker in front of the Dream, or beside the Dream, but behind Martin Luther King's Dream that persons should not be judged by the color of their skin, but by the strength of their character. Passionate about racial justice, Walker not only backed the Dream but also the most successful means to bringing about that Dream—nonviolence—the teachings of Jesus in a practical form.

I wrote this book to establish Charlie Walker as a bona fide historic figure. But I also penned it as narrative so it would be engaging and memorable. I worked to bring Charlie and Marian's story to life and make it an easy read. I felt it necessary to tell the story of nonviolence, along with Quaker history and civil rights movement history, as they wove together in Charlie Walker's life—the story of a visionary, a Quaker icon, a selfless servant of the cause of human dignity everywhere.

To explain some terms: African Americans were called Negroes in the 1950s and first half of the 1960s. I did not change quotes that included those terms, because I wanted to be correct for the times. Also, for the sake of simplicity, I more often used the terms black and white, rather than African American and Caucasian American.

To assure the reader this is an accurate and well-researched volume, I included a vast number of endnotes. I often took material from personal interviews, plus Charlie's written archival organizational reports to his bosses, and his articles, papers, books, and letters to the editor, and merely put quote marks around them or fashioned them into conversations. For instance, the prologue is almost entirely taken from an article Charlie wrote, reporting his firsthand experiences of the 1963 March on Washington. As a trained journalist and newspaper editor, I took copious notes and made meticulous attributions, because I knew people would look at this book with a critical eye, since it was written by his daughter. A disadvantage, yes, because people could think that as his daughter I might stretch the truth, but the true advantage is that I knew this man, talked with him, saw him happy and sad, busy at work in his element—training, organizing, explaining, and teaching this dynamic force called nonviolence.

These extensive notes are placed at the end to distract less from the narrative. Because many of the physical sources cannot be found on the internet, I placed where necessary, abbreviations for them: (CORE) stands for the Congress of Racial Equality archives at the University of Wisconsin, Madison; (SCPC) stands for the Fellowship of Reconciliation archives at Swarthmore College Peace Collection, Swarthmore College; (AFSC) stands for the American Friends Service Committee archives at Friends Center, Philadelphia; and (CCW) means that I found this material in Charlie's personal papers. An index has been included to make quick and easy reference for those who wish to look up events, organizations, or people.

Placing Charlie Walker quotes at the beginning of each chapter seemed a fitting bonus—many authors quote varied famous icons. But I had a more than ample treasure trove of beautiful, intelligent, and moving quotes from Charlie himself, so moving that sometimes I sat at my computer with tears streaming down my face.

God never said He would write the book for me, but I felt certain He would provide what was needed. A wealth of help materialized. My mother introduced me to people my father had worked with—Rev. James Lawson, Edythe Scott Bagley, and many others. She took me to visit Quaker institutions such as Pendle Hill, Swarthmore College, Arch Street Meeting House, and Concord Quarterly Meeting; and she showed me Elizabethtown College, where she and Dad met and fell in love. I cannot thank her enough for her dedication and enthusiasm.

I also thank my siblings: my sister Valerie, the family historian, who explained Walker history as the Quaker founders of Valley Forge and as conductors and stationmasters on the Pennsylvania Underground Railroad; my sister Gloria, who took me to visit Pennsbury (William Penn's Manor) and tirelessly helped sort, catalogue, and copy mountains of material; my sister Winifred, who took me to the Congress of Racial Equality (CORE) Archives in Wisconsin; and my brothers, Allan and Larry, who contributed their own memories of Dad. All my siblings remain cheerfully supportive of my efforts to set down our father's life for posterity. I additionally thank my uncle, William Walker, for his extensive information on Dad's childhood.

I especially thank my editor, Allen Reeder, for the long hours, dedication, and professionalism he put into this book. Deep appreciation must be expressed for George Houser for agreeing to write the Foreword, but, sadly, passed on before he could.

Thanks are in order to Wendy Chmielewski, curator of the Swarthmore Peace Collection; Donald Davis, curator of the American Friends Service Committee archives; to people I interviewed in Gap such as Viola Baker, Marshall Walker Jr., Carolyn Neuhauser Keneagy, and Lee Coates; Charlie's many Quaker friends in the Philadelphia area such as Chel Avery, Thomas Swain and Robert Dockhorn; and Charlie's buddies from

Elizabethtown College: Ernest W. Lefever, Wilmer Fridinger, Lowell Ridenbaugh, Ross Coulson and William Willoughby. Thanks also to John Griffith, George Lakey, John Ewbank, Peter Blood, William Frysinger, Walter Naegle, George and Lillian Willoughby, Lyle Tatum, Karen Harris, the Theodore Hetzel archives, any others I left out, and lastly to Martin Luther King Jr., Charlie's brother in the great struggle for human dignity and freedom.

Prologue

March on Washington, 1963

The August 28th March on Washington will surely stand as an important and memorable achievement in the work of building a more democratic America.... It represents a significant landmark in the struggle for civil rights in this country.... The spirit of the occasion will be long remembered and cherished.

–Charles C. Walker[1]

Sweat trickled down Charlie Walker's forehead and ran in a small stream down his back. He stood on the National Mall, where Americans had turned their attention for that day's event with either dread or hope. While over 200,000 people poured into the nation's capital, few people watching it on television had an inkling of the herculean amount of preparation involved.

Although three-fourths of the demonstrators were black, one-fourth, including Charlie, were white.

It sure is hot! Charlie wiped his damp forehead with a handkerchief. He removed his suit jacket and tossed it over his shoulder, revealing the shirt and tie required for all marshals. But although the thermometer read close to 100 degrees, even 130-degree heat could not have kept him from that day—the March on Washington for Jobs and Freedom, one of the most memorable marches in US history. He had worked on it for months. Planners had chosen the end of August partly as an antidote for the racial violence that typically erupted in late summer.

Some of the sweat on his brow was due to his heavy responsibility in keeping the march nonviolent. Almost three thousand Washington, DC, police were on hand, as well as two thousand National Guard troops, and one thousand police officers in nearby suburbs stood at the ready, with army units trained in riot control stationed close to the capital. Charlie hoped they would not be needed.

Prior to that day, a firestorm of nonviolent actions had swept through the South, making momentous changes, starting with the famous student sit-ins and Freedom Rides of the early 1960s. Then came boycotts of department stores, restaurants, and lunch counters. Prayerful demonstrators marched through city streets. African Americans demanded and received promises for (but not implementation of) equal facilities in such places as restrooms, parks, schools, buses, and waiting rooms. Tremendous strides had been made in Nashville, Birmingham, and Albany. The nation was poised for sweeping, concrete national reforms.

A Philadelphia Quaker, Charlie had worked for twenty years in race relations and the civil rights movement, organizing and training for nonviolent direct action. The man behind the scenes, he worked to assure a smooth demonstration, sit-in, boycott, or march without violence. Since graduating from college in 1941, he had dedicated his life to searching for nonviolent ways—peaceful ways—to conduct human affairs.

Charlie waited with citizen safety marshals to greet the first arrivals.

Yellow buses pulled in, jolting Charlie into a high state of alertness. A wave of cheerful expectancy flowed over him as he strode to meet travelers who would soon stream onto the grassy area near the Washington Monument, where the march was to begin.

Charlie greeted marchers from the first bus he encountered, his excitement growing as each eager face looked to him for instruction. He directed everyone toward the rest of the participants gathering to line up. While other marshals took over the greeting process and Charlie saw it was going well, he headed toward the beginning of the march. Under his arm a portfolio of notebooks contained lists to check off to make sure the demonstration took place as planned.

"I woke up this morning with my mind set on freedom!" a singer's clear voice resonated over loudspeakers as people assembled.

Charlie's longtime friend, Bayard Rustin of Philadelphia, had been appointed chief organizer of the march because of his stellar organizing ability. Bayard, a tall African American intellectual in his fifties, spoke with a British accent so distinguished that people often mistook him for African royalty. Bayard and Charlie had often worked together, challenging segregation and organizing marches and campaigns.

Charlie, in his early forties, was also brilliant, but not as tall as Bayard.

Although slightly overweight with wavy brown hair that was starting to thin, Charlie still kept the good looks, high energy, and drive of his youth. With his strong chin, high forehead, clear hazel eyes and erect bearing, he struck a handsome figure as he strode purposefully with the marchers.

A seasoned veteran of civil rights activism, Charlie had helped plan previous marches like this as either chief or second in organizing large numbers of buses and trains from Philadelphia.[2] In this march he had helped with training of marshals and urged Philadelphians to go to Washington. A. Philip Randolph was director of the march[3] with Bayard second in command, Randolph's deputy director. Charlie's title was deputy coordinator, Philadelphia area.[4]

During the course of the march, Josh White, Joan Baez, and other renowned musicians led inspirational freedom songs over the public address system, such as "Oh, Freedom!"

Bayard, a well-known proponent of nonviolence, with Charlie Walker's help, had headed up three previous demonstrations in Washington in the late 1950s. Then in 1962 Bayard had drawn up a memorandum proposing a large demonstration aimed at dramatizing the need for jobs for African Americans, along with government sanction to help provide those jobs.[5]

We were expecting a hundred thousand people, but it's easily shaping up to be twice as many, Charlie thought. *This is going to be massive!*

The crowd cooperated beautifully. Marchers gathered in the streets. Assisting other marshals Charlie lined them up as planned, black and white interspersed in orderly rows across two parallel streets—Independence and Constitution Avenues.

I couldn't have asked for a better assembly.

Charlie moved through the marchers, directing them authoritatively and respectfully, noting they were well mannered, friendly, and self-controlled.[6]

He stopped to pull out a notebook to check his lists and headed to inspect rows of toilet trucks and outdoor toilets. The leaders had ordered one hundred twenty units. Charlie knew from experience that demonstrations could be shut down for lack of suitable toilet facilities. He checked to ensure the sixteen medical tents were ready, as well as food stations and drinking fountains.

Charlie hoped the emergency medical preparations made by Bayard's staff would not be needed. Hospital patients in the area had been moved to make a special allotment of beds available. Forty doctors and eighty nurses had been placed on special assignment. Ambulances stood by, with traffic rerouted and stores closed for the day. Bayard had even made plans in case of a terrible thunderstorm.

Bayard and the staff had spent most of the previous week in Washington, making sure permits were procured, parade routes were provided to the police, and copies of speeches were given to the authorities. No stone was unturned in preparation for the big day. There could be no option for violence.

Charlie Walker looked around in vain for Dycke Moses, a young neighbor he had heard would be in attendance. The Moseses were his neighbors in an interracial housing development (a rare occurrence in the 1960s) in Cheyney, Pennsylvania. Charlie had moved his family into integrated housing a few years before as part of an ongoing determination to live his life in accordance with his beliefs.

The march was too massive to spot one young man, so Charlie gave up and hurried to check on the two thousand volunteer citizen marshals, trained earlier in the week on the tactics of nonviolence. His rush had been unnecessary, as they were effectively making order out of the friendly chaos in the streets. Among the marshals were 1,500 black policemen from New York City, who volunteered as private citizens on their day off.

Lines of people formed quickly in the hot sun, scarcely containing their urgency to make a powerful statement—anxious to show the world they could, through peaceful assembly, cause a dramatic appeal for redress of grievances and call for urgent action throughout the land.[7]

———

It was 11:30 a.m. The march was to begin at noon.

Charlie fought conflicting emotions of elation and apprehension as he hurried to the front. Another half hour yet.

A few minutes later an urgent call pulled him away from his checklist.

"Charlie!" Bayard, who by choice had stayed at headquarters to oversee the parade, shouted over a portable radio. "Quick! They've started to move!"

It was only 11:40 a.m., but some marchers had started down Constitution Avenue on their own. Charlie sprang into action, helping to assemble the seven march leaders, who had been meeting with President Kennedy, as close to the beginning of the advancing line as possible.

Photographers stepped in and took pictures as if it were the head of the march as twin rivers of humanity moved slowly down the two major arteries of the nation's capital.[8]

That was symbolic. Charlie chuckled to himself.

Just as the march had started without its leaders, he believed the movement had been started by the people, not by puppeteers at the top or outsiders, as critics claimed.[9]

He snorted with disgust as he remembered the previous night's television news interview with former President Harry Truman, who had declared, "I know President Kennedy will kick every last one of them out of Washington if there's any trouble!" If Charlie had his way, there would be no trouble. An expert in his field, he had worked too hard to make this massive display of nonviolent direct action a reality.[10]

At first, only the so-called Big Six planned the march: the National Association for the Advancement of Colored People (NAACP), National Urban League (NUL), Congress of Racial Equality (CORE), Southern Christian Leadership Conference (SCLC), Student Nonviolent Coordinating Committee (SNCC), and Negro American Labor Council (NALC). Then, Walter Reuther, a top labor leader, and three religious leaders—Catholic, Protestant, and Jewish—became cochairmen along with officials from the Big Six.

I don't need my name on the marquee. Charlie walked in the hot sun, mindful he must stay near the beginning of the line, so he could help organize the afternoon's program on the dais. *I'm just glad everything's running smoothly. Look at all the people we have here. Look at all the people who came here nonviolently!*

Hearing applause from another sector, Charlie saw a man who had roller-skated from Chicago, all 671 miles on those little wheels.

Bayard's plan was to have the marchers in Washington by 9 a.m. and out of the city by sundown. Things had gone well so far. Charlie walked at the edge of the column of marchers, watching the crowd, looking for signs of violence. If trouble showed in any way, he was prepared to stop any disturbances before they started. No matter how calm the crowd seemed, he would not let down his vigilance.

"Freedom! Now!" the marchers chanted in antiphonal fashion. "Freedom! Now!"

Charlie herded the crowd skillfully around Washington policemen who were long practiced in handling large demonstrations and presidential inaugurations. Even so, he reminded himself that law enforcement departments had been hard pressed to complete plans for the huge march. He was afraid local police might not be happy that all leaves had been canceled. The mass protesters made little attempt at military marching.

One reporter commented, "Americans don't know how to march … Thank God."[11]

Charlie marveled at the formidable organizational tasks Bayard's staff had faced and completed for this day. Special planes had flown delegations from the West Coast. Fifteen hundred chartered buses and forty special trains had been hired for the event. Railroads soon ran out of special trains, and bus companies could not make enough chartered buses available. Organizers had hired buses to transport marchers from Washington's Union Station to the start of the march.

Television networks positioned themselves everywhere to broadcast all day. March organizers, Charlie among them, had prepared the media well with comprehensive press releases informing them of parade routes, general plans, and human-interest stories.

"Well, I'll be doggoned!" Charlie laughed out loud. Having spotted a small group who had trudged 243 miles in the summer heat from New York to DC for this special event, he stopped to offer congratulations.

"Marshal! Over here!"

Charlie jumped into action, at once seeing in the marching crowd one of his worst fears. A portly elderly woman had fainted from heat exhaustion into the arms of friends and family. Panic showed on their faces as they held on to her against the press of the crowd.

The goodwill and ingenuity that marked the day came to the fore. Multitudes of human beings effortlessly lifted her hand over hand to the street, where others carried her safely to one of the first-aid stations. Someone had the foresight to attach spouts to provide drinking water at all the fire hydrants, which helped the woman rehydrate.

At times the crowd became impassably dense, but patience remained abundant.

"We shall overcome. We shall overcome some day. Deep in my heart, I do believe, we shall overcome some day." The people repeatedly sang what had become the movement's anthem. The lilting melody was incredibly beautiful and the harmonies of the old Negro spiritual infinitely powerful. Hope charged the air in this exhibition of love and brotherhood in the nation's capital by thousands of integrated Americans.

"Black and white together," they sang. Side by side, blacks and whites lifted their faces to heaven and prayed in song and action to the God who had brought them this far. Black and white hands held fast to each other as marchers clung to the hope that this would be the turning point in their long struggle for freedom.

The year 1963 marked exactly one hundred years since the Emancipation Proclamation, President Abraham Lincoln's order freeing enslaved people in the South during the Civil War. Black Americans were chagrined to see whites planning commemorations to celebrate this event. Governors of states and mayors of cities were trying to use the milestone to foster their political images by naming commissions, issuing statements, planning state pageants, and sponsoring elaborate dinners.

African American civil rights leader Dr. Martin Luther King Jr. pointed out that this anniversary only served to remind Negros they were not free. They still lived in a form of disguised slavery. In the South, discrimination faced blacks in glaring and obvious forms. In the North, it confronted them in subtle and hidden camouflage. King saw his people as living on a "lonely island of economic insecurity in the midst of a vast ocean of material prosperity."[12]

As Vice President Lyndon Johnson had said, "Emancipation was a proclamation but not a fact."[13]

However, African Americans had not responded to this situation by seeking revenge. Dr. King described a philosophy worthy of the goals of the civil rights movement—nonviolence. "Nonviolent direct action did not originate in America," King wrote, "but it found its natural home in this land where refusal to cooperate with injustice was an ancient and honorable tradition and where Christian forgiveness was written into the minds and hearts of good men. Nonviolent resistance had become, by 1963, the logical force in the greatest mass-action crusade for freedom that has ever occurred in American History."[14]

A powerful preacher firmly rooted in the teachings of the Southern Christian Negro church, Dr. King had reminded his followers that early Christians' nonviolent resistance had constituted a moral offensive of such overriding power it shook the Roman Empire. He proclaimed, "There is something in the American ethos that responds to the strength of moral force."[15]

In Birmingham, Alabama, through persistence and the power of love, black demonstrators had brought the forces of bigotry in the most segregated city in America to their knees and turned the tide from ingrained prejudice to justice for all Americans. They had won their demands to desegregate public facilities and hiring practices in Birmingham, and they had done so nonviolently.

Nonviolent direct action was a force to be reckoned with, and Charlie had known it for a long time, at least twenty years. A Quaker, he had dedicated much of his adult life to nonviolence training. Most Quakers were pacifists (opposed to all wars), and Charlie had gone to prison rather than support the war effort in World War II. Dr. King and James Farmer, head of CORE, although pacifists, did not ask their followers to be pacifists. It was enough that they commit themselves to the strategy of nonviolence. And that was enough for Charlie.

Although civil rights leaders accepted help from Northern whites on matters of training, they kept them mostly in the background for very good reasons. African Americans did not trust whites. They were afraid they would subvert or take over the movement.

Another reason to keep whites in the background was because the civil rights movement was often accused of being run by "outside agitators." Charlie, however, knew this was truly a movement of the people.

It was collective leadership at its best. The mass media sought out King, but he pointed to his coworkers and to the people walking the hot streets and dusty roads. This was no phony act of humility. Charlie reflected on the famous bus boycott as he walked in the scorching sun. Montgomery was a participatory movement.[16]

Marchers turned toward the Lincoln Memorial. Charlie hurried to the speakers' platform. Television crews set up cameras. Another of his areas of expertise, he would answer the media's questions, ready to help in any way needed. A nuts-and-bolts man. The crowd settled.

Then came introductions, songs, and speeches. A. Philip Randolph, respected elder statesman among African American leaders and head of the Brotherhood of Sleeping Car Porters, presided over the program with impressive calm and dignity. The program would be long, with varied speaking styles. Randolph set the tone in his opening talk.

"Let the nation and the world know the meaning of our numbers," the seventy-four-year-old Randolph announced. "We are not a pressure group.

We are not an organization nor a group of organizations. We are not a mob. We are the advance guard of a massive moral revolution for jobs and freedom. This revolution reverberates throughout the land touching every city, every town, every village where black men are segregated, oppressed and exploited."

Randolph's dignified voice rang out. "But this civil rights revolution is not confined to Negroes, nor is it confined to civil rights. Our white allies know they cannot be free when we are not.... We must destroy that notion that Mrs. Murphy's property rights include the right to humiliate me because of the color of my skin. The March on Washington is not a climax to our struggle but a new beginning." Randolph paused. "Not only for the Negro but for all Americans, for personal freedoms and a better life."[17]

Charlie stood on the dais, watching the crowd for any signs of violence.[18]

Eugene Carson Blake, leading Protestant spokesman from the National Council of Churches who had been arrested in civil rights demonstrations in Baltimore, spoke soberly. "We come late, late we come—in the reconciling and repentant spirit in which Abraham Lincoln once replied to a delegation of morally arrogant churches: 'Never say God is on our side, rather pray that we may be found on God's side.'"[19]

Charlie, a troubleshooter, could not bask in the glory of the speeches. His job continued as the speeches went on: watching every inch, every corner, every face, to detect the smallest trace of a problem. He stayed on highest alert.

Joachim Prinz, president of the American Jewish Congress and a rabbi in the Jewish community in Berlin under the Hitler regime, said, "Bigotry and hatred are not the most urgent problem. The most urgent, the most disgraceful, the most shameful and the most tragic problem is silence. A great people who had created a great civilization had become a nation of onlookers. They remained silent in the face of hate, in the face of brutality and in the face of mass murder. America must not become a nation of onlookers. America must not remain silent."[20]

Next, CORE's Floyd McKissick read from an epistle that Charlie's friend Jim Farmer wrote from a Louisiana prison: "You have said to the world by your presence here, as our successful direct action in numberless cities has said, ... violence is outmoded for the solution of the problems of men. It is a truth that needs to be shouted loudly. And no one anywhere else is saying it as well as the American Negro through nonviolent action."[21]

Charlie looked for his wife, Marian, and five of his six children, adding their young voices to the throng. Marian had driven to Washington from Cheyney with Larry, 17, Allan, 14, Valerie, 12, and Gloria, 8. Brenda, 15, had traveled to Washington with a busload of students from Westtown School, a Quaker school near her home. Winnie, 20, had to work and could not attend, but later desperately wished she had found a way.

Charlie could see Larry in the front of the crowd. Knowing his dad would be near the speakers, he had navigated his way to the front to see the proceedings firsthand. He was all Charlie saw of the rest of the family that day.

––––––––––

About halfway down the reflecting pool from the Lincoln Memorial, Brenda thrilled with the festive mood of the marchers. Many in her group had brought coolers of food. When they could not see action on the podium, they sat down on the grass to listen to the speeches and ate their lunches. Brenda spent fifty cents on one of the eighty thousand box lunches made up for the occasion by the National Council of Churches. (The NCC donated thirty thousand leftover lunches to the Salvation Army; people had conscientiously followed instructions to bring their own food.) When other marchers took off their shoes and cooled their hot feet in the refreshing water of the reflecting pool, she followed suit. It seemed like a grand picnic.

An aspiring folk singer, Brenda felt elated when she heard Joan Baez and also Peter, Paul and Mary sing to the crowd. But nothing she had experienced so far compared to the excitement when Martin Luther King took the podium. People around Brenda stood up and went wild. She stood up, too.

King proclaimed in his rich Georgia accent, "I have a dream today!"

Currents of what felt like electricity pulsed up and down her spine. His voice boomed over the loudspeaker, streamed across the water, reached over the crowd, and electrified her brain. Never had she felt anything like it! Never before had she heard a voice like his—one that could drive into a person's heart and mind to inspire a vision!

King's dream became her dream that day, as it did for many young people, African American and white, in a nonviolent army, whose only weapon according to Dr. King, was love.[22]

Exhilarated with the day's success so far, Charlie still could not relax. However, he looked forward to King's speech. He knew they had saved the best for last. He had heard King speak before and felt "none surpassed the great orator in grasping and voicing the universal themes and evoking responses of the 'better angels of our nature.'" For Charlie, King was "the most effective speaker in evoking Negro lore—history, songs, daily experience, imagery and examples that plumbed the depths of memory and aspiration."[23]

King took the mike. "There will be neither rest nor tranquility in America until the Negro is granted his citizenship rights." He paused. "The whirlwinds of revolt will continue to shake the foundations of our nation until the bright day of justice emerges.... In the process of gaining our rightful place we must not be guilty of wrongful deeds. Again and again we must rise to the majestic heights of meeting physical force with soul force."[24]

When he referred to soul force, King quoted the famous spiritual leader of India, Mahatma Gandhi, who had led his people on successful nonviolent campaigns for twenty-six years in the beginning of the century, until India dealt a blow to the caste system and gained her independence from Britain. As a student at Crozer Theological Seminary near Philadelphia, King had studied Gandhi's remarkable movement, and march leaders wore the white "Nehru" or "Gandhi" hats on the podium to show their utter commitment to nonviolence.

Over the throng, King's powerful oratory continued, "Continue to work in the faith that unearned suffering is redemptive. Even though we face the difficulties of today and tomorrow, I still have a dream. I have a dream that one day this nation will rise up and live out the true meaning of its creed: 'We hold these truths to be self-evident, that all men are created equal.'"[25]

The crowd again roared its approval.

Charlie harkened back to his own special contribution to the civil rights movement—a step-by-step manual published in 1961, *Organizing For Nonviolent Direct Action*. It had been used to train CORE and SNCC leaders, students on the Freedom Rides and now this monumental March on Washington. That manual had been read by many influential people in the movement and used to train leaders. It influenced everything later written

on the subject of nonviolence training all over the world. Charlie had
brought it all together. Having had tremendous success with actions and
events in which he was deeply involved, Charlie had often been called upon
to conduct workshops based on the manual.

Behind him. . .

"I have a dream," King concluded, "that on the red hills of Georgia
the sons of former slaves and the sons of former slave owners will sit down
together at the table of brotherhood.… Go back to Mississippi, go back to
Alabama, go back to Louisiana, go back to the slums and ghettos of the
northern cities, knowing that somehow this situation can and will be
changed.… With this faith we shall be able to hew out of the mountain of
despair a stone of hope."

The audience cheered with wild enthusiasm, and Charlie noticed they
were still unmistakably disciplined and self-restrained.

A potent combination![26]

President Kennedy afterward issued a statement of warm praise for
the conduct of the demonstration.[27] It was a proud moment for African
Americans in particular and Americans in general.

As the march concluded, those around Charlie started packing up. He
breathed a sigh of relief. Millions of people, through seeing the march and
hearing its spokesmen, gained a clearer idea of what the African American
people were saying and doing. America had been put on notice that action
on civil rights must be sped up.

What African Americans demanded for themselves could be rightfully
demanded by all. Problems that African Americans faced—lack of jobs,
education, and housing—acutely affected the country as a whole. And racial
injustice merely added another great burden to an already formidable task.
African Americans were in no mood for tokenism or gradualism.

Charlie maneuvered carefully past the many volunteers Bayard had
organized to clean up around the Lincoln Memorial. That night, as quiet
began to envelop the city, Charlie stayed with others from the Quaker
youth conference who had participated in the march. And the following
day, as he headed out of Washington, DC, Charlie thought of Dr. King.

Keep on walking down the freedom road, Martin. God be with you.

Chapter 1

Childhood Days

Each child comes into the world new born with hope and unique potential, each to this special and unrepeatable moment; another messenger from creation.

—Charles C. Walker[1]

On Route 30 from Philadelphia toward Lancaster, Pennsylvania, after Coatesville, the road heads down a long grade into the small town of Gap. Spread out to the right lies a spectacular view of Amish and modern farms—lush, charming Lancaster County. Charles Coates Walker was born September 15, 1920, at the Walker family farm a mile south of the "Gap-in-the-hills." Charlie's childhood shows how many-colored threads of historic fiber weave together to shape the mind and heart of a visionary.

Joe and Mina Walker's Boys

After the ring of the dismissal bell, Charlie dashed out the boys' entrance of Gap Consolidated Elementary School. Though it was labeled "Boys," girls exited there as well, ignoring the hope of school planners to keep the genders separated.[2]

Full of energy, Charlie kept a good run all the way up Harmony Hill[3] toward the Walker farm, despite the weight of many books under his arm. The beginning of May heralded beautiful days, and Charlie could feel the cool wind in his blond hair and the fresh breath of spring on his young face. New leaves on the trees and sweet flower fragrances filled him with an unexplained exuberance.

The year was 1930. Charlie felt as if he could run on his nine-year-old legs all day. Hesitating as he passed Marsh's store, he felt tempted to run in and look at the candy in the glass case, but he had not even a penny to buy a treat. His farm family always seemed poor. Casting that thought aside, he continued his joyful run to the top of the hill.

A brilliant boy, Charlie was in fifth grade and would start sixth in the fall at only ten. He always read when not burdened with farm chores. He devoured anything he could get his hands on. Never enamored with agrarian life, he longed for the day when he could leave the grueling, difficult life of the farmer. He read to escape a future in farming. The townspeople chuckled and shook their heads at how smart young Charlie was. He had an answer for every question and, despite skipping a grade, always remained head of his class.

Turning right at the Methodist Church, he headed slightly downhill toward the Gap Town Clock and Rutter's dry goods store. Charlie loved that town clock and slowed down to look up at it. As he stared into the blue sky at the impressive bell tower, he drew comfort from its tall, fatherly presence watching over the tiny town. He appreciated its ring every hour, no matter what he was doing.

Behind the clock he could see the William Penn Spring House, and on the other side of the square stood the famous William Penn Rock. Isaac Walker Sr., Charlie's great-great-grandfather, had built the spring house over the Penn Spring.

Governor Penn, who used to own two hundred acres in Gap, including the Walker's farm, had eaten on this rock and drank from the nearby spring. It was even said that when he visited Gap in 1701, he danced with Indian maidens in the Shawnee Gardens and may have slept in one of the caves underground. Mr. Penn went without a gun or rifle among the Indians, because Quakers, or Friends as they call themselves, believe every man has the Light of God in him. And that included people with different-colored skins[4] like Dan and Maggie London, the Walkers' hired hand and his wife and all fourteen of their children, whose ancestors were slaves.

They are free now, Charlie mused. *They work for us of their own free will.*

Charlie knew the Walker family attended the Methodist church in town, as his mother wanted. But James Madison Walker, his grandfather and father of Joseph Walker, Charlie's own father, was a Friend and all his family were Quakers way back to Lewis Walker, who left England around 1684 and came over to Pennsylvania from Wales in 1687. That was only five years after William Penn himself arrived. Lewis soon bought a thousand acres from Penn, with James Logan, Penn's man in charge of real estate, signing the deed. Penn even visited Lewis Walker, the first settler at Valley Forge, at his new home.

Charlie suddenly noticed he had been staring at the town clock in a reverie. The other children had passed him, and he was alone on the road. He left the clock at a jog but slowed at the William Penn Spring House up the road. Knowing he might be late getting to his farm chores, he nevertheless leaned over to peer at the writing on the little spring house down in a depression.

"Whatcha doin', Charlie?" came a young lady's voice behind him. His much-older first cousin, Christine Walker, who had grown up in the house next to the spring, put her hands on his shoulders and looked down at the four-sided cupola, perched on the famous spring house. "Are you reading the names?"

"Is that what they are?" Charlie asked. "Names?"

"Yes, they're the names of three Indian chiefs William Penn met by this rock. I probably have them memorized by now."

Charlie and Christine walked around the cupola reading together, "Pomoyojoogh, Napathatha, and Lo-may-tungh."[5]

"Lo-may-tungh?" Charlie said impishly. "Low-my-tongue! That must be the guy who took the dare to lick the outside water pump in the middle of winter and got his tongue stuck to the metal. When the other Indians stopped to ask what he was doing, all he could say was, 'Low-my-tongue! Low-my-tongue!'"

"Indians didn't have water pumps!" Christine said indignantly, but Charlie laughed and ran across the bridge to Mine Road.[6] He took a left onto Gap Road and jogged the winding hill toward home. Crossing Walker Lane, he headed around the bend to the Walker farm.

Joe met Charlie at the door, which surprised him, since his father would usually be plowing at this time of day.

"Charlie, your mother's not feeling well, and I'm taking her to Lancaster General Hospital. Here's some money to take your little brother and go buy some treats. I'll be back to fix you a late supper, so you may stay out till about dark. Don't worry."

Charlie put down his heavy pile of books, took five-year-old Herbie's hand, and started back down the road toward town. What had seemed so bright an afternoon now filled with clouds of sadness. Charlie worried about his mother, fun-loving Mina Pearl Walker, who always had a laugh and a smile for everyone.

They passed farm after farm along the way. Despite his desire to leave it, Charlie strongly loved the beauty of the rolling green hills and grand panorama of black-and-white Holstein cows grazing in golden sunshine.

The two boys walked slowly back the way Charlie had come running only minutes before. They crossed the railroad bridge and the trolley tracks,[7] then passed the town clock.[8]

"Let's go get some candy at Hess's store," Charlie suggested. "We can each get a big bag for five cents."

They carefully crossed the four sets of railroad tracks to the opposite side. Charlie resisted the temptation to play in the old jail, where many a group of town boys passed the time, but he knew his mother disapproved. They passed the Walker Feed Mill in the Walker Block, the part of town their grandfather Walker had settled.

The boys entered Hess's store with its divine smells. Mina sometimes came here with the boys to purchase food they could not grow on the farm—flour, sugar, coffee, and rice. The clerk weighed each order while people waited, putting them in brown bags tied with a piece of string from a metal canister hanging from the ceiling.[9] She never bought eggs, because she raised her own chickens and guinea hens on the farm.

Charlie bought Herbie and himself each a bag of candy and asked the clerk to get some cookies from the glassine containers. What a change from an hour before when he had been wishing he had a penny for candy. They bought chewing gum, and Charlie put the baseball cards in his pocket to trade with the boys at school.

"Let's go watch Mr. Ruth." Charlie steered Herbie down Belleview Avenue and across the turnpike, to the shop of William Ruth. "I hear they're going to build this into a two-lane highway this summer and call it the Lincoln Highway,"[10] he began as they crossed the street. "We call it the Philadelphia-Lancaster Turnpike. The Quakers' idea, it was the first private turnpike in the whole country![11]

"Westbound pioneers came through here from Philadelphia and Delaware. This was a stage coach and wagon trail for those heading through the Cumberland Gap and a route for pioneers heading south to Kentucky. They stopped here on their way to Lancaster to buy Conestoga wagons and needed supplies, because it was about one day's journey from Philadelphia or Delaware."

Herbie kept up the pace as they walked along.

"Lots of famous people came along this road," Charlie continued. "General Lafayette stayed in Gap at the Rising Sun Hotel over there, and so did President Andrew Jackson and General Winfield Scott. And President James Buchanan, the only president from Pennsylvania, gave a campaign speech from the porch of the Mansion House near where we live.[12] Even General George Washington and his wife, Martha, stayed the night a few miles north at the White Horse Inn.[13]

"How come y' know so much?" Herbie asked.

"I guess it's 'cause I read so much. I wish I could read every book in the library." Charlie paused. "Y' know, Herbie, this road used to be a wagon trail for pioneers heading to Kentucky. Conestoga wagons were named for the Conestoga River that goes through Lancaster."[14] Then he rambled on about pioneers to keep their minds off whatever was wrong with Mother.

Soon they found the machinist's shop and went in.

"Hello, Mr. Ruth," Charlie said politely to the African American. "I brought my little brother, Herbie, to watch you work."

Mr. Ruth smiled. "Come in and make yourselves at home."

"Could you tell Herbie how you learned to be an inventor?"

"Well, Herbie, my father couldn't understand why a kid would want to take things apart and put them together again. I didn't always understand it myself. One day he gave me a bicycle air pump, so I tried combining it with an old jack. I was trying to lift a loaded wagon with it when it buckled and fell. It knocked me on the head, and boy, did that hurt. I just kept working, though. I think it stirred up my brains to do better."[15]

"Really?" Herbie asked, his eyes wide.

"One winter day in the middle of a snowstorm, I saw people trying to head up the Gap hill, and they were slipping and sliding all over the place. I decided I could use a machine to spread cinders. By the time of the next blizzard, I was up on the hill testing my new invention, and now the Pennsylvania Department of Highways is looking to buy lots of them!"

Charlie asked, "What are you working on now?"

"This is an automatic tie for a hay baler," he explained. "It has eighty-seven parts, and since the patent people say that's too many, I'm still perfecting it."[16]

The boys watched the inventor for a while before Charlie decided it was time to head back. They put on a couple of cigar bands found by the road, pretending they were expensive rings worn by the fashionable men in the Sears and Roebuck catalogs.

Charlie turned to Herbie. "It's after five and the town men have closed up their shops and are practicing out at the ball field on Newport Pike. Let's go watch."

Herbie liked the idea, so they walked over to watch Pete and Lee Walker, Roy Trout, Ray Acker, and Warren Ammon practicing on the ball diamond.[17] Every year when spring rolled around, Charlie felt an unexplainable excitement. He smelled baseball in the air. He loved the sound of baseballs smacking leather mitts, teammates talking to each other and the pitcher, or calling out a friendly, "Hey, batter, batter, batter!"

"Maybe I'll be a baseball player when I grow up," Charlie mused. "They play ball on Saturdays instead of working on farms and they live in big cities."

"Aw, that'll never happen." Herbie shook his head with conviction. "Farmers stay on their farms."

"We'll see about that," Charlie answered, his hazel eyes narrowing. "We'll just see."

The town clock rang out seven times as the boys headed back toward the farm. It was way past suppertime and getting darker when they wearily rounded the bend to the Walker homestead. The two trudged slowly past the barn to their right and turned left to head up the steps to the front door. Then headlights glared behind them in the growing darkness, as their father pulled the old Model T into the drive and parked in his usual spot by the barn.

Their mother was not with him.

"Where's Mother?" Charlie inquired nervously, not sure he wanted to hear the answer.

"Your mother's okay, but she has to stay in the hospital a few more days.[18] Then she'll be comin' home. Now, get inside and wash up, boys. Did you have a good time in town?"

"You bet, Dad!" Charlie nodded, grinning.

"Yef," Herbie managed to speak through a mouth full of oatmeal cookie.

———————

Almost a week later, Charlie bolted eagerly through the front door of his home. His father had assured them Mother would be home by late afternoon.

Herbie stood inside waiting for Charlie. "Guess what?" said Herbie. Charlie brushed him aside and headed toward his mother. Dashing into the living room, he ran to hug her.

"Guess what, Charlie?" Herbie followed him, almost shouting. As Charlie reached out to his mother, he found something in the way. Wrapped in a white blanket, a baby whimpered slightly at being wakened.

Seated in a soft chair, Mina spoke gently and held out the baby for inspection. "Charles, this is your new baby brother, Billy. His name is William Harold Walker.[19]" With a face very red and hair very black, he had to be the smallest baby Charlie had ever seen.

"Mother, did you have to pay the people at the hospital for this baby, or did you get him for free?" Charlie felt concerned about the cost, with family finances so tight.

"Shush, Charles, don't ask such questions. Get to your chores, and when you're done I'll let you sit on the rocking chair and hold him a while."

Dumbfounded at his mother's lack of an answer, Charlie headed out to the wash room to change out of the knickers and good shirt and shoes he wore to school. Donning his galoshes and raggedy work clothes, he stepped out the back door to help his father bring in the cows for milking.

———

One spring day a couple of years later, Mina helped Joe in the milking parlor by placing a strainer in the top of the large milk can and pouring the steaming milk through the mesh. In the barn Charlie forked hay to the front of the cows, while Joe scooped up manure at the other end. As bovines chewed contentedly in their stanchions, Charlie wiped his hot forehead with a dirty sleeve. He tried not to notice the strainer filled with drowning, black flies. Farmers should not be squeamish, but it turned his stomach anyway.

Mina was in a good mood. "There's a dance tonight in town," she proposed to Joe in a pleasant tone, "and I'd dearly love to go. We need to get out a little bit and have some fun."

"No, I'm tired and my back hurts. I don't feel like dancing."

"Your back always hurts. I just want to kick up my heels a little and spend some time with my girl friends. Farmwork can get to ya' after a while. Please, Joe?"

"I'm sorry. Let's just forget it."

"You're not sorry," Mina charged, exasperated. "You only want to sit around and read in the evenings or go to bed early. You never want to have any fun. You never want to go to the beach, or a drama or anything. You'll just turn into an old man with an attitude like that!"

"To me, those things are not fun. They're frivolous."

"If I listened to you, I'd never have any friends. If you're not coming to the dance, I'll go by myself!"

"You go ahead. I'm tired. I want to go to bed."

"Go to bed then." Mina was angry. "Good night!"

They would not argue like that in front of a child, but Charlie had gone after some fresh hay, and they thought he could not hear. But he did. He hated to overhear his parents arguing. Stopping just outside the door, he waited until Mina stalked past him before heading into the barn.

"Dad, why don't you go dancing with Mother?"

"Don't tell me how to run my marriage!"

Charlie became quiet. He believed a good bit of the trouble between Mina and Joe was because of the difference in their ages. When they married, Joe was thirty-nine, while Mina had only reached a tender nineteen. Her parents, Charles Thomas Coates (for whom Charlie was named) and Elizabeth (Lizzy) Kreider, had opposed such a union, but Mina had always been headstrong, and she had made up her mind.

Mina was twenty-four when Charlie was born, while Joe was forty-four.

Now it was 1932. Mina was thirty-six, Joe fifty-six, and they no longer meshed together like they did at twenty and forty. Charlie never remembered sitting on Joe's lap or being read to by his dad, whereas his mother was very affectionate. She was full of life and fiercely resisted turning old before her time.[20]

Charlie angrily forked more hay, frustrated and sad.

When I get married, I'm going to marry somebody my own age, Charlie determined silently. *Somebody who likes to do the things I like to do.*

Childhood Lost

When twelve-year-old Charlie awoke on a bitter winter night later in 1932, something felt wrong. Fear stuck like needles up his neck and into his scalp. In the dead of night he heard voices and whispering. His mother was crying and Dad spoke in urgent tones. Something ominous in the air told him not to get up. Shivering under the blankets and homemade quilts in his upstairs room, he wondered if seven-year-old Herbie and two-and-a half-year-old Billy were awake, too.

Finally, the door opened and Joe came into the dark room, bringing in a welcome beam of lantern light. He sat on Charlie's bed.

"Charlie, I'm taking your mother to the hospital, and I need your help. Get Herbie up, dress Billy and take him to the London house. Maggie London will take care of him. Fix breakfast for Herbie and yourself and get the two of you to school. Now, don't miss the school bus, because I won't be able to give you a ride."

"You aren't going to take the milk to the creamery?" Charlie's voice trembled.

"No, son, Dan London will take care of the milking. Take Herbie with you on your paper route this afternoon, because I don't think anyone will be home until supper. Make supper if we're not home when you get back. I have to go now. Your mother needs me."

Charlie waited until he saw headlights vanish down the road before he got up to wake the boys. But they were alert and wide-eyed.

"Dad had to take Mother to the hospital," Charlie whispered to Herbie, though the need for hushed tones had passed. "I have to take Billy to the London's, and then I'll come back and get you something to eat."

Herbie's eyes glazed with terror at being left alone. "Let me come with you, Charlie!" Soon the three of them headed across snowy fields in swirling darkness with the wind at their backs, one brother in Charlie's arms and the other in tow. Shadowy woods stood off to his right. The freezing night wind howled and yanked at the trees, tossing them about violently. They seemed like prim old ladies angrily trying to keep their skirts down in a winter storm.

On the way back, Charlie and Herbie fought against the howling, mournful winds that tore at their clothes. They wrapped their winter jackets more tightly around their bodies, bracing themselves against the frightening tempest. The blast now at their fronts, they walked backwards until they arrived at the farmhouse door. Charlie managed to find cold baloney, butter and bread, and the two gulped this makeshift breakfast, washing it down quickly with milk. There was always plenty of milk and butter, even if they were short on other things.

The "school bus" (a pick-up truck with folding chairs in it) dropped Charlie and Herbie at Gap Elementary School. Charlie now attended eighth grade. The education of many boys and girls ended at eighth grade, but

Charlie had shown himself to be an exceptional student who dearly longed to attend high school.[21]

———————

"Y' know, Charlie, I think Mom's coming home with another baby," Herbie mused a week later as they walked Charlie's newspaper delivery route for the *Lancaster New Era* around town. "Dad said she's coming home today."

"You think so? I suppose you're right, but I hope she brings home a girl this time."

"A sister?" Herbie was taken aback. "Why do you want a sister?"

"I think Mother would like a girl. She had a little girl when I was very young and named her Mildred after her sister, our Aunt Mildred. But the baby died of influenza."

"Mom also had another boy, Jimmy," Herbie added, "but he died before either of us was born. I think she remembers him sometimes."

"I know she does, Herbie. Y' know, she told me one time he was too brilliant to live. What could it mean when somebody is too brilliant to live?"

"I don't suppose she'd ever think that of me," Herbie answered, "but people call you brilliant."

"Oh, don't go saying stuff like that, Herbie. You're plenty smart. And we're both going to live to be old, old men and brilliant, too."

"You're the boss," Herbie smiled.

"Anyway, I want Mother to have a girl to help her around the house with the laundry, the cooking, cleaning, canning, washing dishes—all that stuff I don't like."

"Okay then, it's a girl! I don't like doin' that kind of work either. Charlie, I've been thinking, do y' know where babies come from?"

"No, Herbie. Whenever I try to ask about it, I get shushed. I heard Carolyn Neuhauser and the other girls whispering on the bus today about where babies come from. Even they don't know the answers. I don't know why we're not supposed to know."[22]

Herbie delivered the last paper. "Maybe we'll find out today," he grinned. Despite the snow and ice on the road, he challenged Charlie to race him the last stretch to the farm. The two boys rushed into the house, prepared for good news. They were shushed, but not for what they had expected. Mina was not holding a baby. She lay on the parlor couch sleeping and very pale.

"Your mother's had what they call a heart attack," Joe told Charlie and Herbie soberly, as they sat around the kitchen table. "The doctors say it's a really strange thing to happen to a woman only thirty-seven years old. So you boys are going to have to keep the house quiet. Try to keep Billy from making noise. Your mother needs bed rest and it needs to be like Grant's tomb around here. Do you understand?"

"Yes, Dad," they said in chorus.

"And Charlie, you'll have to take on more responsibilities around here. You'll need to do most of the cooking, cleaning and laundry on top of your farm chores."

"But, Dad, how am I going to do that? I have my paper route after school. I'm at the top of my class, and I have a lot of reading to do, and...."

"You'll just have to find a way, Charlie. Nobody ever made a success of himself by complaining."[23]

Growing Up in the Great Depression

"Charlie, you didn't wash the pots and pans well enough last night!" Joe came inside after milking his cows. Removing his heavy coat, he had seen black pots on the counter. "I told you to boil them in water."

"But Dad," Charlie objected as he stirred a pot of oatmeal on the stove, "when I do that, the burned stuff gets burned on even worse."

"Just do as I say, Son. Why isn't breakfast ready? The milking's done, and I need to eat and get back out for the other chores."

"I'm sorry, Dad. It was hard to get Herbie up this morning, and I just sent Billy down to the cellar to get some butter. There he comes now. Just set it on the table, Billy. Thanks."

Two-year-old Billy had a wet sleeve. "Charlie, it's hard for me to reach the butter, and I slipped and got my sleeve wet in the dairy trough." [24]

"Maybe you should send Herbie to do errands in the cellar instead, Charlie," Joe snapped.

"But Herbie was still getting changed from helping you with the milking, and I was dressing Billy, getting the fire started to cook the oatmeal and getting raisins from the pantry." Hurriedly tossing raisins in the steaming cereal, he hoped his dad would not complain he was using up the last of the raisins or that they contained seeds that made oatmeal difficult to eat quickly.[25] Because of its slimy consistency, Charlie could not stand plain oatmeal, but butter and raisins made it more palatable. They could not afford the sugar some people ate with their hot cereal.

23

A knock startled them all. They looked out the door and saw a tramp outside. At the man's polite request for breakfast, Joe let him in and said he could sit by the fire. The year was 1933, and the sight of a homeless man on a wintry road had become quite common. The Great Depression had taken over. The Roaring Twenties had turned into the Depressing Thirties, and townspeople and farm folks alike struggled to get by. Fifteen million Americans were unemployed. Charlie and his brothers had no fear of cold, hungry hobos who came to their door. Everyone let unfortunates warm by the fire and have a bite of bread or stew. Even town women, not just country women, welcomed them. Sometimes men worked to pay for what they ate by chopping wood or helping out in some other way. Joe gave the man some oatmeal and weak coffee.

Joe had made his usual morning coffee by adding another tablespoon of grounds to yesterday's grounds and running another pot of water through it. Tomorrow, he would add another tablespoon and do the same. The grounds would be thrown out only at the end of the week. Charlie loved the aromatic smell of the perking coffee and sometimes sneaked a cup with cream after Joe left the house.

After the hobo headed down the lane, Joe said, "I'll drop you and Herbie off near school on the way to the creamery today."

As the three bounced along the snowy Gap Road in the old Model T, Joe insisted: "Charlie, you've got to come straight home after your paper route to do your chores. Your mother can't do what she did before on the farm. They say she'll be in bed at least a year and will be weak after that."

"But Dad, this afternoon, the kids are skating on Kauffman's Pond, and this evening some of the town kids are going sledding on Creamery Road.[26] I hear the big boys are getting out their fourteen-person bobsled. With that kind of weight on it, they can sail clear from the top of Old Strasburg Road, down Route 41,[27] go across the railroad tracks, take a sharp left and go all the way to Lincoln Highway!"

"Charlie, you're not a town boy, you're a farm boy. You have to come home for the chores. This farm is your life. It's been my life. This land is your inheritance. Consider yourself lucky, when so many are homeless and out of work."

"I know I should be grateful, Dad, but I just don't think I want to be a farmer."

"But most of the Walkers have been farmers. In fact, one of your ancestors back in England, John Walker,[28] introduced the practice of fallowing fields. But, to be fair, my father was a lawyer some of the time, and my grandfather, James Madison Walker, was a Lancaster County historian as well as a farmer. He loved to study, and he sure loved to write. But farming is a good occupation, Son.

"Dad, where does the name Walker comes from?"

"The first Walker we know of, Anthony Walker, walked the king's forest in England. He was a keeper of the forest, making sure nobody stole deer and that everybody paid tolls for using the king's roads."

"Doesn't sound like he was a farmer," Charlie muttered slyly as he jumped off the running board and waited for Herbie to climb out from between milk jugs.

"See you after school," Joe called. He started down the road to deliver his cans of milk to the town creamery. In the summer he pulled the milk by horse in an old spring wagon,[29] but was glad to have the Model T for use in cold weather.

Heart Attack Changes Life

"It's your turn," Charlie told eight-year-old Herbie. He and his brother played marbles on the dining room rug on a Saturday afternoon in February of 1933. The circular design in the middle provided the perfect place for Charlie to hone his championship marbles game. A chicken wing used for dusting had been placed in the door to keep away the youngest brother, Billy. For some reason the duster scared the youngster, and, typical of brothers, the older two didn't want a pesky three-year-old messing up their marbles game.

"Mom! Charlie put the chicken wing in the door again!" Billy yelled.

"Charlie, stop teasing your little brother. You're forgetting it's your job to keep him quiet," Mina called from a downstairs room, which had been converted into a bedroom.[30] "Billy, come in here. I've got a box of clothes from your cousin, and I want to try them on you." Billy obediently trotted into Mina's bedroom to see the clothes passed along by Aunt Mabel.

New clothes were hard to come by during the Great Depression. Charlie received hand-me-downs from a cousin or Mina ordered him clothes from Sears or Montgomery Ward's catalogs. When Charlie outgrew them, they became Herbie's. Worn out and holey after Herbie had finished with them, most of the clothes at that point had become unfit for Billy to wear, so he received hand-me-downs from his cousin, Freeman "Freedy"

Walker. Charlie thought the cousins in that family had unusual nicknames. Freedy's older brother was nicknamed Juney, from his given name, Marshall Walker Junior.

"Why can't I have new clothes?" Herbie complained softly to Charlie. "The only thing I might get would be a new pair of knickers. I'm tired of wearing your hand-me-downs."

"Yeah, I guess I wear out my knickers from playing baseball and stuff," Charlie answered thoughtfully.

Mina called again, "Charlie, you're supposed to be doing the laundry. Stop playing marbles and go check and see if the washboiler water is hot."

Grumbling, Charlie sauntered to the kitchen to check the fire in the wood stove and the water heating on top. Since they did not have a separate summer kitchen in which to do the weekly laundry, Charlie did it in the house. Separate large tubs sat around for soaking and boiling, while smaller pans on chairs contained Fels Naphtha soap, starch, bleach for whitening, and bluing to prevent yellowing. Laundry would take all day.[31]

"Mother, do y' think we could buy a washing machine some day? I hear you can buy what they call an immersible heater to heat the water, instead of warming it on the stove."

"When we can afford it, I think we should do that, Charlie, but I hear they take a long time to heat a load of water."

"Well, I think it'd still be better than this," Charlie urged. "Herbie, would y' please come and hang up these clothes? I need to do the next batch of laundry. Please add some wood to the fire, too." Soon, several clothes lines in the kitchen steamed with drying laundry. Joe entered the house from doing chores and complained about the strong soap odors.

"You'll have to wait another month before we can hang it outside," Mina reminded him. He became quiet, because he did not want to upset her. Because of his bad back, before her heart attack she had done almost as much farmwork as a man. And he felt guilty about it. At fifty-seven he was no longer a young man. With hard times had come an even greater strain on their marriage.

"If you were a better farmer, we'd be out of debt now," Mina said from her bed.

"I'm having to do everything myself, now. And the boys aren't men yet."

"Are you blaming *me* for having a heart attack?" Mina countered.

26

"No, only you criticize me all the time without helping any. And Charlie acts like he can't stand farmwork and argues with me. You don't know what it's like!"

"I don't know anything, is that it?" Mina tried to sit up. "If I could get out of this bed, I'd show you how to run a farm."

Charlie, who had been listening, ran out the front door and kept running, far up the hill to a secret spot in which he liked to spend time alone. He was in tears, miserable and frustrated. Angrily he folded his arms and leaned against a tree trunk.

"I hate this place." He looked up into the blue sky through bare branches. "I can't wait till I can get away from it. I will never be a farmer, and my children will never be stuck on a farm. I'm going to college somehow. I have to get perfect grades, 'cause I'll need a full scholarship." Charlie's anger turned into resolution, and after a while, he went back to the house to do cleanup.[32]

Christiana Resistance

One evening that summer, Herbie poked his head inside. "Charlie, Dad wants you out in the barn."

Charlie changed into his barn clothes, grabbed a warm sweater and dashed outdoors, taking with him Mehitabel, the Walker boys' pet sheep. Most boys had pet dogs, but the Walker boys had a pet sheep, to the neighbors' amusement. She liked being petted and talked to, like any domestic animal. He found his dad and his friend, Ed London, leaning over a horse stall fence.

"Charlie," Joe looked up. "Ed's going to stay up with Chestnut until she gives birth, probably some time tonight. Would you stay with him and keep him company?"

"Sure! Can I go back into the house and get some cards to while away the time?" At his father's assent, Charlie left and returned with a deck of cards. He and Ed pulled some milking stools up to a large tree stump that had been rolled into the stable area for a makeshift barn table. Soon they were playing canasta and pinochle and enjoying each other's company. They were best friends and thought nothing of racial differences. Mehitabel curled up at Charlie's feet.

"Charlie," Ed said after they had laughed and joked together for a while, "I don't see how you and I are any different deep down. Here in town, people treat me fine, but when I go places outside of Gap, they look at me like I'm not quite a person. I don't know what to do about it except stay out of people's way."

"Yeah, I've read about that kind of stuff, Ed, that people with dark skin are treated bad. Even though the Civil War was fought to free people like you, in some places lots of people are still almost slaves. They can't vote or get good jobs or own property. And I hear they're called disgusting names. My cousin, Pete, told me when he went to the South in the service, he saw a sign in a town near Fort Benning, Georgia, that said, 'Coffee, 10 cents. N------ and Yankees, 15 cents.' That should cover both of us, shouldn't it, Ed?"

Ed chuckled. "I swear, Charlie, you're good at making me laugh. But, do tell, my mother says there was a battle fought near here that people say was the first battle of the Civil War. It stirred up a heck of a lot of trouble, because a white man was killed by some colored people, and they got off scot-free. Unheard of!"

"Yes, it happened a couple miles from here in Christiana," Charlie said. "The Christiana Riot, Christiana Rebellion or Christiana Resistance depending on your point of view. I found some books on it in the Christiana Library. It happened ten years before the Civil War, and people all over the country started taking sides because of it."

Charlie explained that on September 11, 1851,[33] a family of slave holders from Maryland came up to Christiana to retrieve some of their "property" at the house of a black man named William Parker, who was hiding the former slaves in his house. Charlie leaned back, elbows out and his hands behind his head.

"Parker himself had escaped from a Maryland plantation a few years earlier and had lived right here at this very farm as a tenant of my great-grandfather, Isaac Walker. At the time of the raid, William Parker rented a little two-story stone house from Levi and Sarah Pownall—a Quaker couple I'm related to way back."

Charlie had read that when Mrs. Pownall heard of a coming conflict, she tried to convince the group to escape to Canada. But Parker believed the laws for personal protection were not made for him and his friends, and he was not bound to obey them. He hoped the whites would stay away, saying the whites "have a country and may obey the laws. But we have no country."[34]

Parker and his friends armed themselves, hoping they would not need to use the weapons. At dawn, a confrontation occurred when an armed Edward Gorsuch and his party demanded the return of his property.

Charlie continued, "Parker told Gorsuch he could go through the downstairs rooms and that if he saw any chairs, beds or bureaus that were his, he could take them. When Gorsuch threatened to burn down the house, Parker called him a coward and quoted Bible verses. The Negroes kept saying they did not want to shed blood, but the whites fired. So Mrs. Parker blew a horn from an upstairs window to signal their African American neighbors, who showed up and stood in the cornfield across from the house."

Mehitabel shifted a bit at Charlie's feet and then fell back to sleep.

"Sounds like a big pot ready to boil over. What happened next?"

"Well, Edward Gorsuch and William Parker argued with each other, citing the Bible. Gorsuch invoked the 'Servants obey your masters' passage, while Parker asked, 'Do you see it in Scripture that a man should traffic in his brother's blood?'"[35]

In the meantime, two white men from the community, Elijah Lewis, who was a Quaker, and Castner Hanway, not a Quaker but hoping to stop a fight, showed up, along with more colored folks, till they numbered about forty. Hanway had not felt well that morning, so he rode his horse. The Negroes inside the house cheered what they saw as reinforcements, and the southerners outside became uneasy.

"I'm glad the neighbors came to help." Ed's eyes gleamed.

Charlie detailed how the Quaker and his friend tried for a short time to keep the Negroes in the fields at bay, then they left the scene. The Marylanders bolted and ran, with the exception of Gorsuch and his son. The son pleaded with his father to leave the premises or he would be murdered, but the older man became enraged and shouted, "I've not had breakfast. My property I'll have or eat my breakfast in hell!"[36]

That turned out to be prophetic, because William Parker, with the other men behind him, came down and stood in the doorway. He begged the Southern men again to leave the premises. Gorsuch fired on Parker and missed, so Parker knocked the pistol out of the older man's hand. He clubbed the Southerner with the butt of his rifle but fired no shots. Fighting broke out, and in the bedlam Edward Gorsuch was killed, and Dickenson Gorsuch badly hurt. The Pownalls nursed the younger Dickenson back to health, where he later declared he hoped William Parker had escaped to

Canada.[37] It was believed by many to be a "slave insurrection," and in the aftermath, many blacks were arrested and held in jail in Lancaster.

Parker had a friend in Maryland who had been a slave, too, by the name of Frederick Augustus Washington Bailey. He escaped slavery before Parker did. Parker fled north, stopping on the way in Rochester, New York, which gave him the chance to see his friend, later known as Frederick Douglass, the great abolitionist orator. Douglass helped Parker escape to Canada.[38]

"Hanway and Lewis were charged with treason," Charlie said. "And so were the Negroes. The trial was held at Philadelphia's Independence Hall, with high-powered lawyers on both sides. The national press covered it. Northern newspapers said Negro people should be allowed to defend themselves in a free state, but the Southern papers naturally took the side of the slaveholders."

"Naturally," Ed added.

"It was a really big trial, Ed, the largest treason trial in the history of our country, because forty-one people were charged with 'wickedly and traitorously intending to levy war against the United States.'"[39]

Charlie described how a famous Quaker, Lucretia Mott, attended the trial with her Quaker lady friends. They sat quietly knitting, and when the Negroes were led into the courtroom, the defendants wore brand new gray suits with red, white and blue scarves, knitted by the Quaker ladies. Thaddeus Stevens, the famous lawyer from Lancaster, played the most important role, with Maryland's attorney general leading the prosecution, which angered the Northerners.

Castner Hanway's lawyer had declared, "Leveling [sic] war against the United States? Sir, did you hear it? That these three harmless, nonresisting Quakers and eight and thirty wretched, miserable, penniless Negroes, armed with corn cutters, clubs and a few muskets, and headed by a miller in a felt hat, without a coat, without arms, and mounted on a sorrel nag, levied war against the United States. Blessed be God that our Union has survived the shock.'"[40]

Charlie and Ed howled with laughter.

"And that was how the defense brought down the case," Charlie concluded. "Hanway was acquitted and everyone else let off, too!"

"What a story, Charlie!" Ed's eyes sparkled. He thought for a moment and then asked, "Why do people call it the first battle of the Civil War?"

"As I hear it, lots of people believe the Christiana Rebellion was one of the main events leading to the War Between the States. It left such a sour taste in the mouths of Southerners, that when General Robert E. Lee invaded Pennsylvania and headed to Gettysburg, he asked where Christiana was, so he could burn it down!"[41]

A personal account of William Parker's story appeared in the *Atlantic Monthly* fifteen years later in 1866, which drew national attention to the injustices of slavery.[42]

"Listen to this," Charlie added. "Edward Gorsuch's younger son, Tom, who never came to Christiana, had a college roommate he told this story to. Tom talked bitterly about the abolitionists who had viciously murdered his father but were freed by a 'Yankee jury.' In a speech in 1860, this roommate spoke of the riot and the 'inaction of the authorities to punish the guilty.' He felt this injustice called for revenge. Can you guess who this college friend was?"

"No, who was it?"

"John Wilkes Booth, the man who later killed President Abraham Lincoln!"[43]

"You don't say!" Ed, taken aback, was silent a few minutes. "Charlie, I was thinking about what you said on account of how the colored people didn't think they had a country, because the laws did not apply to them. You know, the laws still don't apply to us. We still don't have a country that treats us like citizens."

A loud moan sounded from behind them, as Chestnut neared her time to deliver. The two boys left their conversation and turned to help the graceful creature in her time of need.

Later Charlie said, shaking his head as he looked at the new colt lying in the hay, "Well, I'll be doggoned! So, that's where babies come from!"[44]

———

Between the ages of eleven and thirteen, most children have the biggest growth spurt of their lives. At fourteen in the spring of 1935, Charlie had grown into a strong, athletic young man with medium height and lean build. The straight platinum blond hair of his childhood became darker and wavier with years. His handsome profile and beautiful hazel eyes made him a topic of conversation with the girls.

"Charlie, it's time to make supper," Mina reminded her oldest son, after he had hung the last batch of laundry. She was still too weak to do chores and remained bedridden most of the time. He reluctantly stoked the fire and took out saltine crackers. He heated several cups of milk and melted butter in it, then carefully poured it over crackers he had placed in bowls on the table. After serving his mother he called the men of the family to eat. With gusto they wolfed down the buttery white stuff, a favorite supper during the Great Depression.

An urgent knock on the door startled them all. Charlie's father opened the door to a wide-eyed girl about Charlie's age: his cousin Verna Walker, Uncle Blaine Walker's daughter from across the street and down Walker Lane.

"Momma's ailin' and I need to call Dr. Hershey right away," she said, breathlessly. Joe led the child to a large, wooden phone on the wall. He cranked it and, after the operator answered, asked for the doctor. Then he gave the ear piece to the girl.

The three brothers got ready to do the supper dishes. Charlie washed, little Billy rinsed while standing on a chair, and Herbie dried. Herbie, in a teasing mood, threatened to kick the chair out from under Billy. But Joe, hearing the conversation, angrily swatted Herbie hard from behind, knocking the boy several feet.

Herbie squalled in pain. Joe, at once worried at the noise, felt sorry he had hit him so hard. "Herbie, did I hurt ya'?" He ran up and lifted Herbie off the floor.

Verna, on the phone, could not hear the doctor, so started yelling into the receiver, and Mina called from her room about all the commotion. Joe beat a hasty retreat outside, taking Charlie with him to finish farm chores, leaving Herbie to put away the clean dishes.

Charlie became thoughtful as he helped his father. First, he resolved not to strike his own children in anger. Additionally, although he had nothing against Verna, he wished one of her brothers had come to the house. Stuck on the farm, he hardly had anyone but Herbie and Ed London to play with. Verna's many brothers were also tied to their farm, the biggest reason farm boys rarely played with their neighbors. Again, he wished he lived in town.

Charlie's childhood had left him the day Mina left for the hospital. He had fought this abrupt change in his life, but it came just the same. As he sat down at the kitchen table after the others had gone to bed, Charlie thought wearily, *I sure wish Mother'd had a girl instead of this blamed heart attack.*

Regardless of the late hour, he decided to read a book he had borrowed from the Christiana library, *All Quiet on the Western Front*, a tale of German soldiers in the great world war.

By the soft glow of a kerosene lamp Charlie read its gruesome lines from the viewpoint of ordinary German soldiers, simple German soldiers, starving and miserable in foxholes, trying to understand why they fought this war. The author, Erich Remarque, surmised through his characters that simple laborers, workmen and clerks do not want war. He believed war resulted from choices of national leaders and factory-owners who benefit from war.

Charlie suddenly became aware of voices in the night. Their conversation pulled him from his book, and he realized his parents were arguing about him.

"Charles is brilliant. He must have the opportunity to go to college," Mina urged in low tones. Still bedridden, she assumed Charlie was upstairs asleep. "We need to decide whether he should take the college preparatory class at Paradise High School next year."

"No. We cannot afford it, and I really need his help on the farm," argued Joe. "Besides, Charlie must get used to the idea that he will be a farmer. If you send boys off to college, you almost never find them coming back to the farm. Mina, Amish don't educate their young ones past eighth grade, mainly so they can keep them on the farms."

"You and I went to college, Joe. We haven't always been farmers. Remember, I was a teacher for a while. We should not deny our son a college education. He wants it so badly."

"My college money was wasted, since I ended up taking care of a farm all my life."

"No, Joe, we must let Charlie find his own way in the world. He loves books and learning. I'm sure with his excellent grades he can get a good scholarship. His destiny is beyond the village of Gap."

"I disagree. I won't encourage him in his idealistic notions. I won't allow him to leave the family homestead."

Mina started to cry, but it became a forceful, painful cough. Joe instantly knelt down beside Mina, took her hand and told her how sorry he was. Mina kept coughing and crying. Frightened that Mina would have another heart attack, Joe decided to take back what he had said.

"All right. All right, Mina. Charlie can go to college," he agreed desperately.

"You promise?"

"Yes, I promise," Joe answered, and Mina began to calm down. Joe begged Mina to rest and go to sleep. He assured her he would try harder to keep the house quiet, although he was not sure what more he could do. Billy had already been spending his summers at her sister Mai's farm in Cochranville.[45]

The house became silent once again, and Charlie turned back to his book, but could not help thinking about his mother's words, *His destiny is beyond the village of Gap.*

Stepping Away from Farmwork

The summer sun shone hot on Charlie's back as he plowed the field on top of the hill. Lancaster County, "America's Garden Spot," was and still is one of the most fertile areas in the world. Farmers often put young boys behind the plow, because gentle, well-trained work horses could almost operate plows by themselves. Mehitabel walked behind him.

All of a sudden the plow hit a rock, and the clumsy plow jumped several feet in the air. The horses stopped in their tracks. Charlie was not hurt, but it took a great deal of hard work to get the farm implement back into the row. He sweated and shook with effort. His hands trembled, but he finished the row.

Herbie called from the house. "Charlie, come in here. Mom wants ya'" The younger boys called her Mom, while Charlie called her Mother.

His mother was displeased. "Charles, I had to pay your newspaper boss the money from your paper route again. That bill is yours to pay. You're supposed to collect the money from your customers, pay your boss first and then pay yourself. I know you're taking that money and playing pool with it in town. You know most townsfolk consider pool halls 'dens of iniquity.'"

"Yes, I know, Mother, but they're really not bad places at all. Pool is a skill and I like it. Besides, Warren Ammon lets me rack balls for him in exchange for playing a few games in his pool hall in the basement of the Bellevue Hotel."

"Charles, why don't you have any regard for money? You're old enough," Mina sputtered.

"I don't know, Mother, I just don't care about such things."

"What *do* you care about, Charles?"

"I know I really care about the world being a safe place to live in and about whether certain laws are fair or unfair. I care about keeping peace in our world and not allowing wars like the last one."

"You like to sing. How about joining the church choir?"

"Sure, Mother, and I'd like to learn to play piano, too."

"Piano? We don't have a piano or the money to buy one."

"Aunt Mildred has one. I could go over there to practice. Please, Mother."

"Well, okay, if you keep up with your chores *and* the newspaper bill." In the next room, Herbie wondered why Charlie always got what he wanted. Charlie was Mother's favorite. He idolized Charlie yet never seemed to harbor jealousy.

After that, Charlie spent as much time as he could in town at Aunt Mildred Zimmerman's, teaching himself to play on her piano and visiting his cousins, Patsy and Lois. He became better and faster, memorizing classics such as Handel's "Largo" and Beethoven's *Moonlight Sonata*. He improved his pool game by practicing at home with oranges and a broomstick on the kitchen table.[47]

Disaster on the Farm

Uncle Rhea and Aunt Mai Albright hurried up the Gap Road. The car swayed around the curves, as ahead of them an evil, black swirl billowed into the sky. Friends had called, telling them the Walkers' barn had burned to the ground. It was late August of 1935, right before Charlie's fifteenth birthday. They and their daughter, twenty-three-year-old Pearl, had just finished milking, and they dashed over as soon as they cranked up the car.

"Is it real bad, Dad?" Pearl asked anxiously. "Was anyone hurt?"

"I didn't hear of anyone being injured," Uncle Rhea answered, "but I think it is real bad."

They rounded the bend and pulled over to the side of the road near the house. Charlie's uncle dared park no closer to the pockets of small infernos still raging. A cluster of men had joined Joe on the hill across from the barn. Rhea pulled off his jacket and strode over to help the men put out the flames, while Mai sought out her sister, Mina, to make sure she was all right.

Pearl heard Joe tell her father, "We called the fire department, and the siren on the engine house signaled four blasts to indicate the fire was out of town. But by the time the volunteers got here with the fire engine, it was too late to save the barn. We herded our cattle out, and a neighbor said he'd keep them for the time being. But the poultry died and our brand new car was destroyed."

Herbie, ten, hung on to Mina, who sat on the hill facing the fire. Billy had been taken to a neighbor's. Pearl did not see Charlie. She cautiously picked her way around the farm, keeping a watchful eye on the fire while searching for her fourteen-year-old cousin. Then, she heard a low moan. Upon closer investigation, she found Charlie under the grape arbor on the other side of the house, away from the inferno. He sobbed uncontrollably, face blackened with soot and clothes ragged with burn holes. Kneeling, she attempted to console him.

"All that work gone!" he groaned. "All that hay in the barn and all those days plowing and planting, harvesting and storing. It's all gone, Pearl! What are we going to do?"

Pearl held the young teen in her arms and assured him it would be rebuilt. The neighbors would have a barn raising and he'd have a beautiful, new barn in no time. She took a clean handkerchief out of her pocket and wiped his face, but he just cried harder.

"I tried to stop it, I did, Pearl! But it was too far gone!"

Pearl held him until he stopped weeping, and they stayed in the shelter of the grape arbor until the scene outside started calming down.

"Come on, Charlie, people will start to miss you," Pearl urged, so the two went to see what they could do. Charred to a crisp, only the stone walls of the barn still stood. At least no people had been hurt.

Charlie thought his heart would break as he looked at the smoking wreckage, but he remembered Pearl's comforting words. The community would hold a barn raising, and everything would be all right again.

But things never were right again.

In a year, the Walkers had a new barn, but Joe had spent all his money on materials for rebuilding, since they had no insurance. Their cows returned, but the chickens and guineas lost in the blaze were not replaced. The Great Depression continued. Money remained scarce, and life became even harder for the Walker family.[48]

Thoreau and Emerson

By the fall of 1935, Mina remained bedridden much of the time. Now that Charlie was college bound, she encouraged him to study hard, so he could get a scholarship. *One more year,* he thought, *at Salisbury High School, and then I'll head to Paradise High School for twelfth grade.* [49] Charlie had spent his ninth, tenth and eleventh grades at Salisbury High School, where eleventh graders were considered seniors, after which public education ended.

"Mom says your teachers think you're really smart, Charlie," Herbie commented as the brothers did barn chores together after school.

Charlie chuckled. "Well, my favorite teacher is Mr. Charles Parmer. He brings in classical music and plays it on a Victrola record player. I especially love Beethoven and Mozart. Mr. Parmer talks about things going on in the world and tries to get the class to talk about them, too. I'm the only one who seems to be really interested, though. Well, I'd better go in and make supper."

Charlie headed in from the barn, stoked the fire and started frying some baloney for gravy. While the sweet and spicy, Amish-style Lebanon baloney fried in the iron skillet and filled the house with luscious smells, Charlie sat down at the kitchen table to read some new books he had obtained from the back shelves of the schoolroom at Salisbury High in White Horse. Mr. Parmer had suggested he read Ralph Waldo Emerson and Henry David Thoreau.

Thoreau lived from 1817 to 1862 in New England, and published his essay, *Civil Disobedience*, his most famous piece of writing, in 1849. Fascinated, Charlie read Thoreau's assertion, "Under a government which *imprisons* any *unjustly,* the true *place for a just man* is *also a prison.*"[50] Marking the passage, he took the book to his mother's bedroom, where Mina listened to music from her radio, a special gift from her sister, Mildred, to comfort her while bedridden. She was not sickly all the time, but often still took to her bed because of her weak heart. "Listen to this, Mother." Charlie read her the passage. "What do you think?"

Mina thought for a moment. "Well, Charlie, many good people have gone to prison for what they believed, including the Quakers…. Don't let that meat burn!"

"Yes, Mother!" Charlie stood quickly and tended to the stove. The meat had fried crisp but not burnt. He added milk and flour and began stirring slowly, allowing the flavors to blend just right. Charlie had always been told that Lancaster County hard baloney was far superior to the mild stuff found elsewhere.

While he waited for the meal to cook, Charlie sat at the table and read Ralph Waldo Emerson's peace classic, written in 1838, an essay called *War*. "The cause of peace is not the cause of cowardice.... If peace is to be maintained, it must be by brave men."[51]

Herbie pushed open the screen door, and an excited Charlie read him some of Emerson's essay while Herbie leaned against the door jamb. "'History teaches the wise men to put trust in ideas, and not in circumstances. We have all grown up in the sight of frigates and navy yards, or armed forts and islands, of arsenals and militia.... It is really a thought that built this portentous war establishment, and a thought shall also melt it away.'"[52]

Herbie crossed his arms. "Charlie, maybe you believe the military is an awful monster that just goes around killing people, but I don't agree. I think it defends and protects us."

"But, Herbie, listen to this: 'But when a truth appears—as, for instance, a perception in the wit of one Columbus that there is land in the Western Sea; though he alone of all men has that thought, and they all jeer, it will build fleets; it will carry over half Spain and half England; it will plant a colony, a state, nation and half a globe full of men.'"[53]

His brother came into the room and faced him. "Charlie, what if I went into the military? Would you think I was just following some evil person's thoughts?"

"But, Herbie, Ralph Waldo Emerson says thoughts are important and we have to think thoughts of peace instead of war."

"I think it's what a person *does* that's important." Herbie turned, unimpressed, to wash up for supper.

Charlie went back to the stove to finish cooking the evening meal.

Can just one man change the world? Charlie asked himself. *I wonder.*

"Charlie, you're on!" whispered play director Arline Herr as she stood behind the curtain and motioned to him. Dressed as hotel owner Obediah Macklin, Charlie stepped onto the stage in the Salisbury High senior class presentation of *The Blue Bag*. The play was part of his eleventh-grade commencement exercises in 1936. As was traditional, the top student landed the starring role, and this year he had won the honor. June Bair played his wife in the drama situated in a small Pennsylvania town.[54] He smiled, walked authoritatively behind the registration desk and began to say his lines. Now past initial stage fright, he started warming up to the part.

Charlie liked this kind of dramatic performance, fast moving with a nice mystery to it. Out in the audience, he could see his father, Herbie and Billy. Pleased that most of his family could come, the young actor nevertheless wished his mother had been well enough to attend. Little Billy had his own seat. Joe never took his children on his lap.

"Charlie's the best actor on the stage," Herbie whispered to his father, who nodded. Joe grudgingly admitted to himself that his oldest son certainly had a flair for drama and said his lines with relish. Charlie was fifteen, a year younger than the others in the class, having skipped a grade. He received gifts of money and a Schaeffer pen and pencil set from the school, as class valedictorian.

The Underground Railroad

Late one evening, Charlie went to Mina's room and sat on her bed.

"When I talked to Ed London a while ago, we discussed the Christiana Rebellion and the Civil War," Charlie began. "I told him William Parker had lived here on our farm as a tenant of Great-Grandfather Isaac Walker."

"Did you tell Ed about Lindley Coates on *my* side of the family, a conductor on the Underground Railroad?" Mina asked. "Lindley lived on a farm near here on the north end of Christiana and belonged to the American Anti-Slavery Society as early as 1833. You can still see his house there. You must have walked past it many times on the way to Christiana, which was settled primarily by Quakers. Lindley was a Quaker lawyer and they said he was eagle-faced, gaunt and erect. In 1850, someone burned his barn to the ground, and they said it was because of his work on the Underground Railroad."[55]

Mina continued, "The Quakers in our area treated the runaway slaves so well that many of them stayed in Christiana and Gap instead of heading on to Canada."

In fact, most of the Underground Railroad was run by the Friends, who had denounced slavery as early as 1688, when Germantown Friends Meeting, near Philadelphia, wrote the very first written protest against the hated institution. In 1780 Pennsylvania was the first state to abolish slavery, and Quakers were the first sect to ban slavery in their midst. By 1800 it had become a "disownable" offense for a Quaker to own slaves.

"Lindley, an excellent debater, became very good at cross-questioning anti-abolitionists," Mina said. "Lindley especially opposed greed, which he felt caused people to wrong each other. He was a member of Sadsbury Friends Meeting."[56]

Mina added, "Runaway slaves came to Lindley from Caleb Hood, Daniel Gibbons, Thomas Whitson and many other Quakers in this area."

The aftermath of the Christiana Resistance became a terror-filled time in the whole valley, because government officials arrested anybody and everybody. Fugitives from the Resistance came to Lindley's house for safety. The Coateses felt sure that recently-deputized officials would come and search the property, since they were searching all abolitionists' houses to arrest any colored people they could lay their hands on. So the Coateses hid fugitives in Lindley's cornfield under the shocks, where it was safer.

Mina said, "In a few days, sure enough, constables showed up and searched high and low, but couldn't find anything. Lindley, absent on business, had hired a carpenter to work at the barn. This man walked to the house and asked the 'special constables' if they had a search warrant. When they said they didn't, the carpenter gave them a piece of his mind about their 'unlawful search.'"[57]

"I can just picture that, Mother!" Charlie laughed.

"A colored girl living with the Coates' at the time hid out in the corn," Mina continued. "She was engaged to one of the slaves Gorsuch had been looking for. The fugitive had gone on to Toronto and wrote his fiancée to meet him there. She joined her love in Canada, and they were married."

"That's a happy ending for a love story," Charlie said.

"Your famous relative also helped form the Clarkson Anti-Slavery Society[58] in the United States before the American Society was even formed, and advocated immediate emancipation of the slaves before hardly anyone had heard of William Lloyd Garrison. When the American Anti-Slavery Society began in New York in 1840, Lindley was chosen as its president. When he resigned, William Lloyd Garrison took his place."[59]

"I've heard about the American Anti-Slavery Society, but I didn't know my ancestor helped found it," Charlie said.

"Yes he did, and Lindley was also a member of Pennsylvania's Constitutional Convention of 1837. He, Thaddeus Stevens and Thomas Earle worked very hard to stop the Pennsylvania Constitution from including only 'white' citizens in the suffrage laws, but it didn't work."[60]

"That's too bad," Charlie said.

"People just weren't willing to change." Mina shrugged. "We're related to others who aided in the Underground Railroad: Caleb Hood and his brother Joseph Hood, who aided fugitives from the Christiana Resistance; Joseph Brinton of Salisbury Township, Jeremiah Moore of Christiana, Joseph Moore of Sadsbury Township, Levi Coates near Cochranville, Charles Jackson of West Grove, Charles Moore of Lionville and James Moore of Lancaster County. Others were Truman and Jeremiah Cooper and Thomas and John Hood. But, even though most white people who helped fugitives gain their freedom were Quakers,[61] the Society of Friends as a whole refused to allow anti-slavery meetings in their meetinghouses, and some Meetings even kicked out their members who worked in the Underground Railroad."[62]

"Is that a fact?" Charlie had a difficult time comprehending such polarities within one group.

"It was not an easy life for those who followed their convictions." Mina, emphatically nodded her head. "Charlie, you have an ancestry to be proud of."

"Mother, I'm so glad you told me all that, but if the Quakers have such a great past, then why are we Methodists?"

"I like singing in the Methodist choir, and Quaker Meetings don't have choirs. I'm also busy in the Women's Christian Temperance Union at the church. And you've liked the young people's version of the WCTU."

"Well, I never had much interest in liquor." Charlie was not satisfied with his mother's answer about Methodists, but he was realizing there were many things parents just did not talk about.

———————

In the summer of 1936, the Walker men rode up the hilly, rutted roads toward the farm after visiting Mina's father's[63] house in Gap. She recently purchased it after Charles Coates' sudden early death. They would move there as soon as they could arrange to sell the farm, which was still a losing enterprise. It would be two more years before they actually moved.

The boys felt excited about moving to town, especially Charlie.

He had been deeply affected by all his mother had told him about the Underground Railroad and how the Coateses had helped hide slaves in Christiana after the rebellion. He could not get the conversation out of his mind, and on the trek up the hill told Joe all about it.

"I'll bet you she didn't tell you about how the Walkers helped runaway slaves, did she?" Joe grinned.

"No, she didn't," Charlie answered, a bit puzzled.

"Your Grandfather James Madison Walker sewed money into his clothes and went to Canada to help fugitives from slavery to get resettled. And right here in Gap, white residents helped colored folks from the South who ran away from plantations. I've heard stories of fugitives hidden in caves below the town clock until it was safe to move them on. There are lots of caves down there, because of the many springs in the hillside. Sometimes we kids would crawl down and play in them, pretending there was a posse after us, and we were runaway slaves. We did it in secret, though, because our parents would have whipped us if they'd known."

"Dad, really? That sounds like fun!"

"Those caves aren't safe anymore," Joe hastened to add, "and I don't want you or Herbie going down into one. I've heard other stories of free colored people in town helping hide fugitives, too, maybe in a secret room under the kitchen or parlor. There would be a signal, such as a chair scraping or a foot moving a certain way, to tell the slaves they'd better make their getaway through an escape route—a cave tunnel or a secret stairway behind the house."

Charlie pondered this. "You know, most accounts of the Underground Railroad seem to only talk about what white people did to help fugitives, and that was important. But, in general, they seem to have left out the things many free Negroes did, like William Parker and the folks you just talked about."[64]

"Yes, that's true," Joe realized, as he often had, that his son questioned everything and wanted to soak up as much learning as possible. He had one more year of school, considered another senior year, and this time at the high school in Paradise for college-bound students. Joe had agreed Charlie should go to college but regretted making that promise to Mina when he thought she was dying. Glad Mina's health had improved, he nonetheless wondered what he'd do in two years without Charlie's help on the farm.

When Mina had been well, everyone said she worked as hard as a farm hand. She still did, when well enough, because there was so much to do. With back troubles, Joe found it more difficult than ever to maintain the farm.[65]

When they arrived home, Mina, in bed again, seemed angry at Joe for something he had done or not done. She called him into her room, and soon Charlie heard her accusing, "It was your fault the barn burned down. Those types of hay fires are produced from improperly stacked hay."

Charlie knew if hay is stacked when too wet, it can become combustible. Farmers have to use their judgment on when to cut hay and how long to let it cure. Mina seemed to think Joe had bad judgment.

Charlie spent his senior year perfecting his grades, his pool game, his piano-playing and his baseball game. He had even begun learning a new skill—legerdemain, the skill of a magician. He loved performing before an audience and hearing them ooh! and aah! when he executed a particularly neat trick. Joe had given up making Charlie do the bulk of the farmwork. So, winter afternoons after school found the young man delivering papers and spending his profits in the pool hall. When spring arrived, Charlie donned a catcher's uniform along with protective gear and headed to the baseball fields.

"Charlie, come help me and Billy pick potato beetles,"[66] Herbie called. Charlie sat on the porch in the warmth of a spring sun, studying. Herb stepped onto the porch and threw a book down next to Charlie. "Hey, I found this on the back porch. You leave stuff all over the place. You're getting a reputation for forgetting things!"

Charlie ignored Herb's remark. "I can't help with beetles. I've got to help Mother with supper, and I need to prepare for an important test tomorrow."

"Look, Charlie." Herbie leaned down into his brother's face. "I know you spend your time reading while you're making supper. And yesterday, you played pool instead of hoeing the potato field. You don't seem to care about the farm any more. You just want to read about making peace, and you leave me and Billy to do the work."

"Herbie, I'm working real hard on my studies so I can get a scholarship for college, and Dad can't complain about me. I'm getting out of here. I don't want to be a farmer. And I can't stand being around people who argue all the time and make each other miserable."

"But, Charlie, where does that leave me? And Billy?"

"I don't know. But I'm going to do something different with my life."

That spring, at sixteen, he graduated at the top of his class at Paradise.

Valedictorian of the class of 1937! It gave him great satisfaction and hope for the future. Mina had become well enough to attend his graduation, and her huge grin as he received his diploma thrilled him like summer rains on parched land. He had been accepted at Elizabethtown College, a Church of the Brethren school west of Lancaster toward Harrisburg, and *he had additionally earned a full tuition scholarship.* Charlie's dreams were coming true!

"Joe, I know I've been sick lately, but I'm going to the Coates family reunion this year," Mina called.

Joe had just come from the barn and was washing up. "That's not a good idea, Mina. I can drop the boys off at the picnic and come back, but I think you should stay home."

"I'm not staying here! You can stay home if you want. Now, if you won't take me, I'll get someone who will," Mina huffed.

"No, Mina, you need to rest. You've been unsteady lately."

"Charlie, get my sister Mai on the phone."

Feeling squeezed in the middle of their argument, he reluctantly telephoned his aunt, who still took care of Billy during the summers.

"Tell her I want a ride to the reunion," Mina ordered Charlie. While Charlie waited for someone to answer the phone, Mina asked, "Are you attending the reunion this year, Charlie? Last year, you went to that Epworth League Conference on peace instead."

"Yes, I'm coming this year, Mother. Now that I'm sixteen I can drive Herbie, you and me in the old jalopy." But Mina wanted the Albrights to pick her up.

She attended the festivities, sitting in a chair the entire time.[67]

As he strode to join the men on the cow field for a game of baseball, Charlie knew he would soon be leaving this farm life behind. By fall he'd be in college, starting classes at the tender age of sixteen.

He sincerely hoped life in college would be better. In high school he had been primarily a loner, not making many close friends, but he felt secure in his ability to succeed in the classroom. With the innocence and passion of youth, Charlie felt poised to take on the world.

Chapter 2

College Years

I am torn between two idealists—an emperor who says, "Get to the top and crush anyone who gets in your path," while the other says pleading from the depths of the Holy of Holies, "Help the needy."

–Charles C. Walker, handwritten in 1940 in Elizabethtown College yearbook

In the fall of 1937 Charlie began attending Elizabethtown College, nicknamed Etown, founded in 1900 by the Church of the Brethren, a division of Anabaptists—a religious movement of the 1600s that protested widespread corruption in Europe's monarch-led governments and state-recognized churches. The two other main US Anabaptist branches are Mennonites and their more conservative offshoot, the Amish.[1]

Quakers (officially The Religious Society of Friends), along with Brethren and Mennonites, are recognized as the three historic peace churches in the United States. The American public often wrongly confuses Quakers with Amish. Although Quakers have similar views to Amish on the peace testimony, separation of church and state, not bearing arms and refusing to take oaths, the two sects differ greatly.

Freshmen Buddies

So this is it! Charlie surveyed the bustling campus. The buildings sparkled under a warm September sun as Charlie stepped briskly up the sidewalk toward the boy's dorm, Fairview Hall,[2] his home for the next four years. Trying not to feel self-conscious about his overstuffed, battered suitcase, he gazed approvingly over an emerald-green lawn, sometimes used as a golf course. Scattered with tall trees, it followed a gentle slope up to the looming Alpha Hall, where he had been told young women were housed—at this point only a vague interest. At this moment Charlie felt more curious about the dining hall. After Depression food and his own cooking, he was eager to try the college's culinary offerings.

Mina had driven him from Gap in their old Model T. She had helped him register as one of the five full-tuition scholarship students.[3] She had fought for this day—prayed he could leave the farm life he hated. Even so, he was only sixteen and it had not been easy to let him go. She left him with a flurry of last-minute instructions and hugs. Charlie sighed, trying to let go of the past. It was time to move on.

The Church of the Brethren had founded the college in 1899, opening to students in 1900 despite objections from certain Brethren who believed higher education was a threat to their nonconformist way of life.[4] Charlie was familiar with nonconformist churches. Pennsylvania was home to several persecuted religious groups that William Penn had deliberately invited to the New World to take part in his Holy Experiment. These groups had formed a cohesive, vigorous society, tolerant of differences, and it was partly their trustworthiness and honesty combined with ability to work with many different groups that had hastened the colony's economic growth. Quakers had established the "fair price," doing away with haggling over the cost of goods, and were known for high-quality work.

Some female teachers still wore white caps on the backs of their heads, evidence of the "plain" faiths, which in the 1800s were largely Amish, Mennonites, Quakers and Brethren. But in the 1900s this began to change and now Elizabethtown students mostly wore modern clothing, although Mennonite girls still wore traditional caps and dresses with built-in capes. Plain dress among Brethren young people was on the way out.

All his life, Charlie had seen people in plain attire. In the culturally diverse farm area between Coatesville and Lancaster, he sat in classrooms with Amish, Mennonite and Brethren children wearing different types of clothing and speaking in various accents. Charlie's father and other conservatives believed "plain dress" and behavior helped keep the young within their faith, while others felt "plain people" raised their children in a type of pious ignorance.[5]

As Charlie entered Fairview Hall, he met two tall young men with heavily-browed features, dark hair and friendly faces. They put down their bulging bags, and the nearest one held out his hand. "Hello, I'm Ern Lefever, and this is my older brother, Herb."

Charlie grinned, "Charlie Walker from Gap."

As they chatted, Charlie learned the brothers had hitchhiked together, thumbing automobile rides from nearby York, and had been thankful for nice weather along the way. Herb was in his second year, but Ern was a new student. Charlie liked the fact that Herb would join him on the baseball team in the spring. "I love baseball. It's my best sport," Charlie remarked, then mentioned he had been captain of the Salisbury Township High School baseball team.

"Herb has condescended to be my roommate my freshman year," Ern grinned. "We're heading up to Room 202. Why don't you come with us and we'll help you find your room?" Charlie gratefully accepted and grabbed his beat-up bag, relieved that the brothers carried old suitcases and were not ashamed of worn shoes.

Charlie continued conversing as they headed up the dorm stairs. "I'm majoring in Liberal Arts. What about you, Ern?"

"Secondary education, but I really believe I'm here to prepare for a life of service, as the Etown motto says." Ern spoke seriously, his large brows bristling. "I'm of the Brethren faith and hope I can someday serve abroad." Herb opened a door and led the way down the hall.

Charlie said, "I'm a Methodist, and many Methodists are talking about peace as war continues to build in Europe. There is strong Quakerism in my father's background, though."

"Are you a pacifist, then, Charlie?" Herb inquired.

"Quakers have always been religious pacifists, totally against war," Charlie answered, "but Methodists generally follow the Just War Doctrine. It defends war under three specific circumstances. One, the intention must be just; two, the violence must be in proportion to the evil opposed to it; and three, if violence is used, the possibilities for justice will be enhanced."

Ern jumped into the conversation. "I understand the Just War idea. It must be used only with good motives, such as to save my country. The second part is to only want to throw back the evil. I don't want to do to you what you were trying to do to me. And as for the third criteria, there must be an element of reconciliation."[6]

The hallway became progressively more crowded with students as the young men conversed while heading upstairs. Entering the second floor, they heard their footsteps echoing down the long hall. They finally turned into Room 202, the Lefevers' new home.

"Welcome to our humble abode, Charlie," Herb beamed. Charlie sat on one of the beds and looked around. The walls had been freshly painted and the room felt airy and cheerful.

"Charlie, you said your family was Quaker before they became Methodists." Ern placed his few items of clothing in the drawers and hung a suit in the closet. "Our mother came from five generations of pious Mennonites, who believe all war is wrong."

Herb piped up that their direct ancestor on their father's side was Isaac LeFevre, a French Huguenot persecuted by Louis XIV. His forcible conversion of "heretics" to Catholicism resulted in the killing of Isaac's uncle, three sisters and three brothers. Isaac was only sixteen when he was forced to escape to Bavaria carrying the family Bible in a loaf of bread.

Charlie thought it must have been a really big loaf of bread.[7]

Herb's bureau was next to a window, and he took a moment to look out onto the campus. Happy to be back at college, he sighed deeply. He told Charlie that Isaac had come to the New World from London in 1708, purchasing 2,000 acres from William Penn, making him and his family the first settlers in the town of Paradise.

"Paradise? That's just down the road from Gap!" Charlie said. "Do your parents still live there?"

"No, we live in York." Ern added, "The spelling of LeFevre was changed to Lefever during the French and Indian War, when it wasn't too popular to be French."

"Ah, yes," Charlie agreed. "I'm glad we never had to change Walker. My mother's background was Quaker, too. Her maiden name is Coates."

Recognizing the name, Ern asked, "Was Coatesville named for your family, Charlie?"

"Yes, Moses Coates Jr., my direct ancestor, founded Coatesville. And his father, Moses Coates Sr., was the first settler in Phoenixville. We believe Benedict Arnold stayed at his house for a week after the battle of Saratoga. That was before Arnold turned traitor, of course."

"We all seem to be related to pioneers, don't we?" Ern grinned. "Perhaps we'll be pioneers of a different sort."

Charlie stood to go, since the Lefevers had finished putting away their belongings and offered again to help Charlie find his room.

The older Lefever was full of advice as the brothers led Charlie to the door of the room where he'd stay the next nine months. "Freshman Week is full of fun activities, Charlie," Herb offered. "Why don't you go with Ern to the freshman picnic supper tonight?"

Charlie perked up at the thought of a picnic and a chance to meet people. "Great!"

"Sounds good to me," Ern echoed. "I'll come over tonight and pick you up."

Later that evening, Charlie opened the door as Ern was just about to knock. "I heard your footsteps coming down the hall!" Charlie laughed, enjoying Ern's surprise. "They really need to put rugs in the halls." They headed down to Lake Placida, a large pond, where college staff had placed a generous picnic. Tables and benches began filling up with freshmen.

Charlie and Ern grabbed plates and served themselves fried chicken. "I understand this is Etown's biggest freshman class ever," Ern said. "Sixty-six of us!"[8]

Charlie assented. "There are fifteen faculty and 200 students overall."

The two sat down at a table with several other young men. One of them held out his hand to Charlie.

"I'm Aaron Herr."

"John Glass," waved another.

"Charlie Walker." Charlie grasped Herr's outstretched fingers.

"Nice to meet you," Glass said. "What are you studying, Charlie?"

"Liberal Arts," Charlie answered. "I'd like to be a philologist, but most people don't know what a philologist is."

"I do," Ern said eagerly. "It's a wordsmith. Someone who likes and knows how to use words, primarily big ones."

"If you want to meet someone who likes big words, go talk to that guy over there," Herr said, pointing to a handsome, cleft-chinned young freshman conversing two tables away. "That's Bill Willoughby. You probably won't understand a thing he says," he laughed.

"I could go talk to Willoughby," Glass said, "but I'd really like to talk to that redhead over there," nodding his head toward a young woman at an adjoining table. They all chuckled.

"Go talk to her, then," Charlie urged.

"Never was real good with girls." Glass hid his awkwardness with a big gulp of lemonade. The others nodded in reluctant agreement.

"This food is great." Charlie dug in. "It doesn't take any big words to say that!" The whole table laughed.

His first day at college and already he had made friends. They talked about war, pacifism and evolution until dusk.

As he and Ern headed back to their rooms, Charlie asked, "Do you have any sisters, Ern?"

"No, I just have brothers. Herb, Tim, Don and John."

"I only have brothers, too—a brother Herb, like you, and a brother Bill." He already felt at home at this school, having found people similar to him in background, personality and intelligence. It felt good …very good.

E-A to the Fifth Club

It was comfortingly dark in the dorm room, as one dim lamp illuminated six young men sprawled about Room 202. Walker, Glass, Herr, Willoughby, and the two Lefevers, at various times, had discussed topics from the fourth dimension to the virgin birth.

"Why are we even talking about girls?" Ern sounded frustrated. "They're ignoring us. Besides, I'd really rather talk about the state of the world than the length of girls' skirts."

"The unexamined life is not worth living, according to Plato," Glass said.

"Most definitely, I'd rather do ten pages of math than try to figure out what makes a girl tick," Herb added.

"I'd rather spend an evening reading Beowulf out loud," Willoughby agreed.

"I'd rather study philosophy,"[9] Herr countered.

"But you read your whole philosophy text the first week," Charlie teased. "What is there left to read?"

"True, but Walker, you aren't any better," Herr countered. "Instead of asking a girl for a date, you'd rather type with two fingers on that old typewriter, sending out *Harper's Magazine* articles to everyone you know."

"We're all pathetic," Herb said.

"No, we're ascetic," Willoughby countered loftily. "We're shy with girls because we have higher principles in mind, denying ourselves for the sake of our beliefs."

"Aw, Willoughby!" the guys laughed.

"We're adherents to ascetic agamy, which, by the way, means asexuality. Even better, the ethereal agglutination of agnostic adherents to ascetic agamy," Willoughby said with a flourish.

His friends groaned. "What are you talking about?

Herb the mathematician asked, "What does ethereal agglutination mean, Willoughby? And why agnostic? We all believe in God."

"Agnostics because we are skeptics, not in our belief in God, but in various religious tenets. For example, Ern and I still believe in the Brethren tenets and others here pretty well line up with Quaker or Mennonite beliefs, but we don't all agree on, say, the virgin birth. Ethereal agglutination is a spiritual unity," Willoughby smiled, "a spiritual unity of skeptical bachelor guys who don't date girls because of lofty principles."

"Ethereal Agglutination of Agnostic Adherents to Ascetic Agamy. Hmm, Willoughby," Charlie mused, "it does have a certain alliterative ring to it. How about starting a club right here and now?"

"Here, Here! So be it," the guys agreed and tried to pronounce the club's verbose name.

"Willoughby, that's just too long," Glass finally said.

Willoughby thought a minute. "How about E-A to the Fifth Club?"[10] he suggested and was met with a chorus of agreement and congratulations.

"E-A to the Fifth Club it is!!"[11]

———

"It's Baby Walker's birthday today!" John Glass announced to the E-A to the Fifth Club fellows in the dining hall.

"Really! How old are you, Charlie?" Herr asked.

"I turn seventeen today," Charlie answered, "September 15 is my birthday."

"Then, they should be providing birthday cake today for dessert," Ern remarked, "but instead they're serving mincemeat pie. Charlie, you may be a year younger than the rest of us, but we don't notice it. At least I don't."

E-A to the Fifth members sang "Happy Birthday" to Charlie, then dug into their pie. As Ern got up to leave, he stuffed an extra piece of pie in his pants pocket.

As Charlie and Ern headed back to Fairview Hall, the skies shone a robin's egg blue and the day felt sunny and warm. Other students passed them, headed for activities, practice, or work duty. Girls looked shyly at the boys, while young men glanced slyly at the girls. The campus bustled with purposeful activity.

Ern explained he had no time for girls. He had to work his way through college since he had no financial help from his mother and father. And his studies had suffered.

"Your parents can't help with room and board?" Charlie asked, walking briskly.

"No," Ern responded awkwardly. "And I realize all you fellows in the

E-A to the Fifth Club are great academics, but I make up for my lack of brilliance with zeal to change the world." Ern's eyes brightened with youthful idealism.

Charlie had to smile. "You seem brilliant to me, Ern." He gazed at the beauty around them. "As brilliant as the sky is today."

Ern thought that even though they were both somewhat shy, Charlie was more openly joyful than he, and had more basic confidence. The two ran laughing up to Room 202, talked about their futures and shared Ern's pilfered piece of pie.

Soon, feeling lazy and full, Charlie asked, "Ern, don't you feel you were drawn to this college? Do you believe in predestination? What do you think of determinism? Was it all planned out for us fellows to meet here? Or do you believe we have freedom of choice?"

Ern looked at him seriously. "Charlie, I wrote a paper called *I Do Not Choose* based on Calvin Coolidge's remark, 'I do not choose to run.' I think man has very little freedom. He is determined by genetics and synapses and environment."

"Don't you think a person has some freedom of choice, though?" Charlie asked. "Some people agonize that it's all planned out and that we might as well not try to struggle, while others think nothing is planned at all, and it's all up to us."

"What freedom we have may be limited," Ern admitted, "but it is important to exercise what choice we have within the framework in which we find ourselves."[12]

Charlie became excited as an idea came to him. "Then don't you suppose it could be a clever combination of both? That certain things are predestined, but they can be superseded by choice? That we change them by our acts of will? How free is a person, really, Ern? What is freedom?"

"Maybe we're not free at all, Charlie."

"But what if freedom is the responsibility to learn from mistakes or poor choices, Ern?"

"Maybe we're only puppets on a string," Ern persisted in playing the devil's advocate.

"I can't accept that, Ern," Charlie declared between bites. "And if it's true, who pulls the strings? Who creates the set...?"

The two talked on into the night, joined later by Herb Lefever, Glass and Willoughby, and ended only when it was time for bed. Charlie left the room, knowing he would have to stay up late to finish his assignments, but was glad for the chance to expand his mind.

Gap Farm Sold

When Charlie arrived home at the Gap farm for Christmas break in 1937, Herbie ran outside to meet him on the porch.

"Guess what, Charlie?" he asked angrily, bracing himself against the cold. It was the same thing he had said when Billy was born, but this time it was not good news. "You got your wish. Mom and Dad will be selling the farm in March and we'll move to the house in town in April."

Joe and his boys (and Mina when she was well enough) had tried to make a go of it, but the farm was a failure. Their barn having burned down during the Depression was more than they could take. Even though they were not rich before the barn burned, Joe felt like a failure, and Mina would not let him feel otherwise. An Amish man named Beiler bought the hundred-acre farm.

This turned out to be the fate of many a Quaker farm. Amish money was intact after the stock market crash of 1929 because the Amish did not take part in the stock market. The Amish instead put their money into real estate and had bought much of the land in the Conestoga Valley at the beginning of the Depression. Quakers, however, who believed in investing, lost money, and were easy pickings for the Amish. This was one of the factors which caused the Quakers to lose economic power and influence in Pennsylvania.

Charlie stepped inside, took off his winter coat and looked around questioningly. Mina and Joe asked the boys to sit down while they explained the situation.

Mina began, "Herb and Billy, we'll move to the Henderson Place in the spring after we sign the papers to sell the farm. Charlie, on school breaks, you'll live there, too."

"We've already sold the herd and other animals, but there will be hay, straw and potato crops," Joe explained. "It's too bad Charlie cannot help with the move, but I'll need you younger boys to help with the remaining farm chores until it's all final." The meeting broke up and Mina talked quietly with Joe.[13]

Charlie ran to his room upstairs in shock. He felt the hollowness of an unknown future but did not feel guilty about losing the farm.[14]

In fact, some part inside him was relieved he no longer had the burden of it. When he took his next college break in the summer, the family would have moved to town.

Music, Sports, and a New Friend

With Christmas break over, Elizabethtown was busy once again. The new year 1938 had arrived during the holidays and the campus nestled under a blanket of snow. Freshman Charlie was eager to continue his studies and make his family proud.

Winters in Pennsylvania can bring a chill to the spirit as well as the body, but students at Elizabethtown, in warm coats, scarves and hats, tingled with excitement. Gathering in happy clusters on the frigid sidewalks, they laughed at their frosty breath suspended in the air. At that time of year, the sun goes down early, and darkness descends at dinner time. But college students are undeterred by such tricks of nature, and these young people enjoyed such night life as the institution allowed.

Inside Alpha Hall one evening, the lilting strains of piano music could be heard. Having just entered the building, Charlie's friend Willoughby crossed the spacious lobby, smiling at the sight of a blond, wavy-haired young man peering into the Social Room. The freshman's eyes widened as he watched Charlie's fingers dance over the ivory keys playing "I'm Looking Over a Four-Leafed Clover."

"Hey, Wilbur, I hear you can play piano like Walker," Willoughby opened up the conversation.

"The name is Wilmer, Wilmer Fridinger," he answered with a look of frustration, "and I really don't play much at all, certainly not like Walker there." Willoughby and Fridinger entered the Social Room and sat down on some chairs near the back. Although some students conversed in couples, others just sat and listened to Charlie, now playing "Red Sails in the Sunset."

"Doesn't he use any sheet music?" Fridinger was amazed.

"No, it's all memorized. Do you really want to be called Wilmer?" Willoughby asked.

"No, Fridy's better."

"Not Friday, but Fridy?"

"Yes, I like it."

"I Cover the Waterfront" sounded in the background as they talked quietly. The two young men compared notes on courses and teachers, until Willoughby finally looked at his watch and called to the pianist, "Walker, it's seven-thirty. Social time is over. Let's go." Willoughby and his friends usually waited until after Charlie's evening performance to do their studying.

Charlie turned, slid his legs around the piano stool with an athletic flair and propelled himself to a standing position. Together they headed back to the men's dorm.

"This is Fridy, Walker," said Willoughby.

"I really enjoyed your piano playing, Walker," Fridy said, extending his hand.

"Oh, it's not much. I just memorized some pieces." Charlie shook Fridy's hand warmly. "What's your major?"

"Commercial Education, but I'm really just a farm boy from York who likes sports."

"You should talk to Herb Lefever," Charlie grinned. "He's from York! What kind of sports? Baseball? Basketball?"

"I play basketball now and then," Fridy answered, "but farmwork and sports don't mix well. In high school, I didn't have time to perfect anything."

Willoughby cut in. "Don't let him fool you. His uncle is the dean, A.C. Baugher. And he's even younger than you are. Won't turn seventeen until February. He skipped a grade like you. Must be the two youngest members of the class. Mere children."[15]

———

"Who among us feels Etown is a dull, pious village?" Ern asked one night in Room 202. It was March the same year, as Ern, Charlie and Willoughby anticipated the coming of spring. It had been getting a little warmer, and with increasing daylight hours had come greater enthusiasm for E-A to the Fifth Club. Their informal meetings often became a dialogue between faith and reason.

"This campus is far too subdued for my taste," Ern persisted. "No social dancing, no parties, what is there to do? Especially on weekends."

"We could all go downtown and split a Farmer's Special at the drug store," Charlie offered. "Five scoops of ice cream for twenty cents seems like fun to me! Who among us knows how to dance, anyway?"

So they decided on the Farmer's Special, one of the few fun activities for young people at a nonpartying college. Their shoes echoed on the sidewalk, and fresh, clean air from a new rain caressed their faces. Such a welcome harbinger of spring!

"What did you think of that visit by Senator Nye of North Dakota to our campus this week?" Ern asked. "How did you feel when he said modern wars are caused by merchants of death who sell armaments to all sides of a conflict?"

"He declared that what is happening overseas is Europe's war, didn't he, and he accused President Roosevelt of trying to drag us into it?" Charlie added.

"Yes, he did. I went up to him afterwards and asked him if letters to senators made any difference. You know what his answer was? He said thoughtful letters do make a difference! It was exciting to talk with a real senator!"

"That's great, Ern!" Willoughby exclaimed.

"Fantastic!" Charlie agreed.

Ern pulled some papers out of his pocket and handed them around. "I made up some leaflets afterwards—mimeographed them myself. Here, I saved some for you."

Willoughby read Ern's tract. "As a pacifist I agree we should stay out of an overseas war. We should write our congressmen and urge them to oppose the new Navy appropriations bill."

Ern nodded. "I already did, and mailed postcards to that effect to several church members at home in York."[16]

"I hear our class is trying something new this year," Charlie said to Fridy one morning on their way to classes. Forsythia, daffodil and hyacinth blossoms exploded into effusive color and fragrance, spreading a heady feel in the air.

"Something new?" Fridy asked.

"Every year it's customary for sophomores to crash the freshman party. The college administration doesn't like it, since it often results in property damage. The Dean of Men, Dr. Musick, had a meeting with the presidents of the two classes and proposed a change. We'll see what happens."

A few weeks later, E-A to the Fifth Club members sat at a table waiting for the freshman party to begin. They were eager to find out if sophomores would crash the party or whether the new plan would win out.

"Let's see if this plan of passive resistance will work," Ern said hopefully.

"If something can be turned into a peaceful resolution, I'm all for it," Charlie agreed.

A disturbance at the entrance interrupted their conversation, and all eyes turned to a group of sophomores forming at the edge of the party. Were the smiles on their faces malicious? What did they have in their hands? When they entered en masse unobstructed, at once it became clear they were carrying their own refreshments!

"I believe those are smiles of triumph," Charlie exclaimed, "triumph over enmity! They're making a peace offering to us!"

"Hallelujah!" Glass and Herr shouted together, and all the young men at the table raised their paper lemonade cups to the sophomores in a happy salute.

Once the "crashers" had eaten, they left the party as quickly as they had entered it, amid a feeling of victory and friendship.[17]

"I've witnessed an historic event," Charlie observed, his eyes twinkling. "What a great day for this college."

———

It was the last day of school before his first college summer break, and Charlie had his new yearbook in hand, *The Etonian* (1937-38). He'd just learned that the yearbook only came out every two years, so he treasured this one. He'd get another at the end of his junior year, but none for his senior year. He was signing other classmates' volumes and getting signatures from his friends in return. He saw a familiar figure coming from the opposite direction.

"Ern come sign my yearbook!" he called.

Ern wrote on Charlie's yearbook, while Charlie scribbled on Ern's: "Psychologically, your doctrine of predestination is O.K.; religiously it's junk. Sorry if you don't believe in the 4th dimension[18]—happy if you do. We've had some good bull sessions; I've gotten a kick out of them. Don't get in the red as I am."

Ern congratulated him on the article about the successful varsity baseball team. Charlie kneeled in the team picture, his hat creating a shadow down to his nose in the dazzling sunshine. At the yearbook's writing, Elizabethtown had been tied for the league lead. The article mentioned two freshman pitchers, Stan Disney and Curtis Day, along with Herb Lefever on third base.

Knowing he was one of four freshman starters, Charlie turned to Freshman Class History which pointed out, "the freshmen were also well represented on the varsity baseball team by Charles Walker behind the bat." It also referred to the class keeping their five, full-scholarship students, including that 'wit and philologist from Gap.'"[19]

Charlie laughed. "We did have a good season." Then he became serious, as they switched yearbooks once again. "Ern, you didn't once come to any of Herb's and my games."[20]

"Well, that's true," Ern admitted guiltily. "I've been too busy with the YMCA, the International Relations Club and Student Volunteers."

"I was in two of those clubs, and that didn't stop me from going to your events," Charlie chided. "You were occupied with sending out postcards against the war and trying to convert everybody to being pacifist."

"Charlie, I'm sorry," Ern said. "I'll do better next year. But you have to admit, I've almost convinced you to be a pacifist."

Charlie flashed his famous, quick smile. "So you have, Ern. So you have."

First Summer Off

As soon as Charlie arrived home on his first summer break from Etown, Charlie's mother and father gathered their three boys together at the Henderson Place to explain the situation to them. "Your mother and I are going our separate ways," Joe began soberly. "We already have separate bedrooms. I will be moving out as soon as I can get a room elsewhere."

"You're not staying with us?" Herbie asked, incredulous. Eight-year-old Billy started crying.

"No, I'll be leaving soon," Joe said bitterly. "Be good and help your mother with the chores."

"Where will you go?" Charlie inquired.

"I'll still be in town. I think your Aunt Mildred Zimmerman might have a room available for me in a few months."

Mina tried to reassure the siblings. "You boys will be fine with me." But thirteen-year-old Herbie fought back tears, while Billy sobbed.

Charlie sat by himself, wondering anew about the future. He did not know how his brothers and mother would manage without his father in the picture, but despite her poor health, his mother was a strong woman. He believed they would manage.[21]

Charlie never spent much time at the house in Gap during his college years, finding ways to fill his summers away from his new home. But that first break from Etown, short on cash, he stayed and worked with his father and brothers.

"Right this way, boys," Joe Walker called to his three sons. They left the old Model T next to a corn field and headed toward the beginning of the first rows. The hot sun baked the backs of their necks, even though it was still morning.

White cirrus clouds streaked across an otherwise clear sky overhead. Green corn rows stretched as far as Charlie could see, bordered by hedgerows consisting of thick trees and bushes. The Pennsylvania farm field was large, and at first the job looked tremendous.

Charlie's father worked with the Agricultural Adjustment Administration. The boys could each receive ten cents a day if they helped him survey the fields for the US government.[22]

"We're making sure that when the farmer says he's *not* planting a certain amount of acreage, he's telling the government the truth," Joe explained.

Charlie quickly learned how long his own stride was to the very inch, so he could walk down a long row and tell exactly how many feet it was. This would come in handy later in life for measuring gardens and fields.

Charlie was now seventeen, Herb thirteen and Billy eight. All three were intelligent and handsome with brown wavy hair, strong, masculine faces and striking hazel eyes.

"I'm glad you're home this summer and are working with us." Herb smiled at Charlie as the two tackled adjacent rows quite a ways from Joe and Billy.

"I figured I'd better earn some money somehow, until I know what other opportunities are out there." Charlie grinned. He told Herb about college life and his new friends on campus.

Charlie's chatter and laughing at his own jokes saddened Herb. "Unlike you, I liked being a farmer. I love the outdoors and the smell of the earth when it's newly turned behind the plow. Town life is not for me."

"I feel just the opposite." Charlie marked another row and stood to pace it off. "I like the bustle of a town, with things happening and transportation to just about everywhere. But I gather you're not happy here."

Rather quietly, Herb said things were not going well at all.

"I'm sorry. What's the matter?"

"Well, Dad isn't around much; he's got this new job. And Mom's gone during the week, living at jobs where she takes care of old people. That leaves Billy and me by ourselves all day and night. She comes home on weekends and cleans up a bit and buys groceries, but we eat cereal for supper most of the time. I work at Uncle Warren's bowling alley in Christiana in the evenings, setting pins to make some money. I have to hitchhike each way from Gap. Sometimes it's real snowy and cold, but folks know me and are generous in giving me rides. Unfortunately, that leaves Billy alone in the house till I get home around eleven o'clock at night. He eats cereal for supper, but it's not much of a life for a little kid. He has to carry two heavy buckets of water every day from the town spring to the house. He carries all that water over four sets of railroad tracks!"

Charlie was shocked.

"Why doesn't Mother stay home and take care of you?"

"She says she can't get any other work since the Depression hit, Charlie. With you gone, the Henderson Place is real cold and dark. I miss you."[23]

"Why do they call it the Henderson Place, anyway?" Charlie asked.

"Well, some people named Henderson lived there awhile. I don't think it makes sense, because the Coateses and Walkers seem to have the most history there. I heard a story about how it was purchased by our Great-Aunt Mary Louisa Walker. She was a nurse who's a heroine in the South, 'cause she bought medical supplies from Canada and all by herself made a 500-mile dogsled ride over the St. Lawrence to get them out of Canada. Then she ran a blockade to get them into Texas."

"She did this for the South?" Charlie's surprise was evident.

"Yeah, she'd gone to school down there and was convicted with the cause of states' rights. But here's the thing—if she hadn't been pardoned after the war by Governor Gordon of Georgia, she'd never have been able to buy the house we live in, 'cause rebels were forbidden to own property."[24]

Charlie became very quiet. He loved to hear stories of strong Quaker women, and he admired his great-aunt, despite being on the wrong side, for her courage in face of great odds to provide medical supplies for the wounded and suffering.

Although fascinated by the history of their new house, he knew it was not a happy place for his family. What could he do for his brothers? What could he do to help his mother? Helping his father and brothers with the surveying job was a start, but everyone in the area was still very poor and doing what they could to survive. He wondered about returning home to help, but he knew Mother would not stand for it, and she'd probably insist he could help most by doing his best in college.

Sophomore Year

Back at college in the fall of 1938, Ern had a new roommate, Oscar Wise. As Charlie and Ern headed toward the dorm, Charlie smiled. "Congratulations on your new column in the school paper, Ern. I saw your *Catty Tales*—what a name for campus gossip—which made reference to the Walker, Willoughby and Wise bull-slinging combination, Station W.W.W.!"

"Yes, I challenged any campus trio to attain and maintain a higher batting average in that subject than you fellows." Ern grinned.

"How about Lefever, Herr and Glass?"

"No, no one can compete with you three in a war of words, especially you and Willoughby."[25]

They chortled, and Ern noticed that when Charlie laughed heartily, his eyes danced, darting here and there in an almost nervous fashion. With every belly laugh his eyebrows gleefully leapt up and down. Their mood calmed as they continued walking.

"I understand congratulations are also in order for your election as our new class president, Ern. Why is it that people consistently elect you president of clubs and organizations?"

"I'm not sure. I was elected chair of three Brethren Youth offices this year—chairman of the District of Southern Pennsylvania, chairman of the Eastern Region of the US and chairman of the National Youth in Elgin, Illinois. It's odd, because even though I'm lacking in the social skills, people just seem to look to me for leadership."

"I also heard you went to a seminar last month, Ern."

"Yes, I attended the national conference of Fellowship of Reconciliation at Bound Brook, New Jersey."[26]

"What do they do at the Fellowship of Reconciliation?"

"They are religious pacifists from many denominations who work in war prevention and peace building. I'll get you some pamphlets."

One afternoon after classes Charlie turned to Fridy as they headed down the sidewalk enjoying brilliant fall colors. "Why not try out for the basketball team this year, Fridy? You've got the build to be a good forward."

"I don't know, Walker."

"Well, let's find out. I'll meet you in the gym tonight at seven, and we'll go through some plays. You'll like it. I was manager last year and it was great! We can even try out for the team together."

Later that night, the two were playing one-on-one in the gymnasium.

"Come on, Fridy, try to steal the ball from me! You can do it!" Fridy swiped at the ball, but Charlie faked and jumped for a clean basket.

Fridy stood dejectedly watching Charlie deftly dribble back to the free-throw line. "I'm just not very good, Walker."

"It's all in your mind, Fridy. Try again." They kept at it, until Fridy started to get competitive. Charlie pushed him with friendly teasing, but not so much as to make him give up.

"Let's go play ping-pong for a while," Charlie finally said, dripping with sweat. "Or you'll start beating me."

Fridy laughed as they headed to the showers.

A late autumn sunbeam made its way through Charlie's dorm window and onto the newspaper, as he opened the latest issue of *The Etownian* and spread it on his desk. His eyes intent on the pages, he stopped at an editorial geared to the upcoming Armistice Day, November 11. Headlined "Armistice Day Peace Call," it was a reprinted message from the National Student Federation of the USA.

> Students of the United States, twenty years ago the first world war ended! Will this coming year go down in history as the beginning of a new and greater conflagration?... War rages still in Spain and China; Czechoslovakia is dismembered.
>
> Whatever may be our own wishes, we cannot, when there is trouble elsewhere, expect to remain unaffected. When destruction, impoverishment, and starvation afflict other areas, we cannot, no matter how hard we may try, escape impairment of our own economic well-being. When freedom is destroyed over increasing areas elsewhere, our ideals for individual liberty and our most cherished political and social institutions are jeopardized.[28]

Charlie read further, riveted by the recommendations made by the article. It suggested a limited and progressive reduction of armaments, economic reconstruction with assurance of justice to all peoples, adherence to the basic principles of international law, observance of treaties freely entered into, and abstention from the use of force in pursuit of national policies. It recognized that equality of all people and races is basic to securing a peaceful world order.[29]

Charlie sat studying the paper for a long time. Then, he set up his typewriter, got out some white paper and dark blue carbon paper and with two fingers began typing "Peace Talk."

The next morning, Charlie stopped in Room 202 after breakfast to see if Ern wanted to walk to class with him. Ern's roommate, Oscar Wise, answered the door and dashed out past Charlie after offering a quick, "Mornin.'"

Ern was still asleep. "Get up, Ern! You missed breakfast." Charlie rolled Ern's long, inert body, which started to moan.

"Who needs breakfast?" Ern finally sat up on his bed in his underwear, yawning.

"Those who have been raised on a farm know the importance of breakfast," Charlie said. "It gets you ready for the day. Speaking of getting ready, you'd better get moving."

Ern looked up, startled into realization. "Wait a second!" He reached for his bureau drawer.

Ern dressed hastily, and the two men jogged to class.

"You've got to quit putting things off." Charlie talked easily while jogging. "Procrastination is the thief of time, you know."

"If procrastination is the thief of time, I've been robbed!"[30] Ern lamented.

Charlie rolled his eyes at Ern's dramatics, but enjoyed his ready wit. "How's your new roommate, Ern?"

"Oscar? He's a good egg. I've been working on him, trying to convert him to pacifism."

"What does he think?" Charlie was interested. "I heard him say he's a pacifist, except he might change his view if the US were to declare war on Germany."

"I told him a pacifist between wars is like a vegetarian between meals,"[31] Ern said haltingly. Not having eaten made exertion even more arduous.

"I like that!" Charlie laughed, glad sports kept him in shape. "A pacifist between wars is like a vegetarian between meals."

Spring Again

Another Christmas break had passed, and the year was 1939. Times were hard and many Elizabethtown students looked to earn spending money. Charlie planned to raise a little cash by selling his favorite treat—chocolate.

Fridy looked up from his schoolwork as Charlie knocked and entered his room holding a flat box in his hand. He let go of the front door knob and grasped the inside knob to close the door. Suddenly, he yelped and jumped into the air. Grabbing the box top quickly, he barely prevented the contents from being scattered.

"Good God, Fridy, what do you have here, giving all your friends an electric shock?"

"Uh, I guess my roommate wired the door knob again." Fridy rose quickly. "I'm sorry."

"I've heard rumors about Fridy's Execution Chamber[32] in Fairview Hall."

"I didn't have anything to do with it!"

"Really? Why should I believe you?"

"I'm only a farm boy, not an engineering student!"

"Okay, okay. Anyway, I came to see if you were interested in my newest money-making project, selling chocolate bars. Care for a few? I'll sell them to you at a bargain."

Charlie bought them at the new chocolate factory in town at reduced rates. "Here, I'll give you one to sample."

"These are delicious, Charlie, I'll buy five. That's a clever idea to give me one for free."

Charlie pocketed the money, left Fridy's room and went on to the next customer. Ern, too, was studying. He bought some candy, although he had almost no money.

"Ern, I hear you had a busy Christmas break."

"Yes, I started a peace study group at my church and spoke in church against the war." He and Charlie both chewed on chocolate.

"What did you say to them?"

"I was talking about how the Germans have just built a new artillery piece that can fire a shell for seventy miles with great accuracy. War has become unthinkable, Charlie!"[33]

"Yes, it has. Unthinkable. Uh, oh. I just did the unthinkable, Ern. I just ate up my profits!"

"Then, you'd better get to studying, so you can make up for lack of money. But, on a different subject, what are you going to do this summer?"

"I have a job with Sears, Roebuck and Company in Chicago," Charlie said. "How about you?"

"I've been talking with Willoughby about hitchhiking down through the South."

Juniors' Worries about War and Peace

Charlie and his friends were now juniors. The class of '41 had dwindled by half, from sixty-six strong to a tenacious thirty-three. The campus felt like home now, especially with his friends there.

Freshman Week was beginning, and upperclassmen had been asked to help welcome new students with fun and games. YMCA members were in charge of planning Freshman Week, so Willoughby did not feel surprised to see Charlie in front of a group of people in the Alpha Hall Social Room. Wearing a comical costume of overstuffed, plaid and polka-dotted clothing and a long, black, curly wig, Charlie entertained freshmen with his magic craft—legerdemain, or sleight of hand.

"There are three walnut half shells on the table with a bean beneath only one of them," Charlie said in a mesmerizing tone, as he began moving the shells. "Watch my hands carefully and do not let your eyes deceive you. Watch the walnut shells and do not lose sight of which one carries the legume."

Charlie smiled graciously and asked, "Who can tell me where the bean is?"

Someone from the audience ventured a guess, at which Charlie lifted the shell. No bean. Exclamations from the audience. Charlie moved the walnut shells again. Someone else thought she knew where it was, but also was proven wrong. More mutterings of wonderment from the audience. Then he revealed the walnut shell with the bean, and the crowd clapped and roared with delight.

A classmate, Harry Berberian, started heckling, saying Charlie had rigged the walnuts, but the magician ignored him and continued with his show. For a little change-up he juggled some colorful balls.

Willoughby admired Charlie's coolness under pressure. Someone else in the audience felt intrigued by the handsome junior—pretty freshman Marian Groff. After that magic show, she never changed her high opinion of him. Charlie was the man she liked above all others, but it took him quite a while to truly notice her.

Charlie hailed his audience. "Who here has a dollar to spare a poor magician for a trick?" A student reached into his pocket, fished out a greenback, and handed it to the outrageously-dressed entertainer.

"I will change this dollar into...." Charlie continued fooling the audience with various moves, then finally pulled the dollar from the student's ear. He handed it back to the student amid much applause.

After the show was over, Willoughby helped Charlie pack up his props. "That was inimitably entertaining, Charlie. Is it all self taught?"

"Every bit of it," Charlie assured his friend. "I enjoy playing to the crowd and fending off hecklers."

Willoughby smiled. "I heard you worked this summer for Sears, Roebuck and Company. How'd it go?"

"Shears, Sawbucks and Cutlery?" Charlie answered facetiously, hoisting a heavy trunk onto his shoulder and heading with his friend to the men's dorm.

"It was all right, but the best part was that I was able to spend some time at Bethany, the Brethren biblical seminary in Chicago.[34] I love studying new things, even on summer vacation." Charlie avoided spending his summers in Gap. No one was ever home. Joe, Mina and Herb worked constantly, and Billy spent his summers on the Albright farm.

Charlie hailed Ern Lefever coming from a different direction, who promptly fell into step with them. "How about you two telling me more about your famous trip through the South over the summer?"

Willoughby was eager to tell of their adventure. "We went through sixteen states in sixteen days for sixteen dollars. Ern had heard of the unrest of Negroes and other poor in the South. FDR[35] called them ill-fed, ill-clothed and ill-housed, and we wanted to see for ourselves."

On August 22, the two students had met in Philadelphia, hitchhiked to Washington, DC, and bummed a ride with a Quaker relief worker to

Jacksonville, Florida. Splitting up at times, they rode the rails when auto rides had not materialized.

"I was most shocked to see Negro prisoners working along the highway with their legs in chains," Ern said. "I was actually more shocked at that than finding out Hitler and Stalin signed a pact."

"And we were in jail in McComb, Mississippi, when we found out Hitler had started a blitzkrieg against Poland, and that Germany and Russia were carving up Poland between them," Willoughby added.

"The war had started," Ern said animatedly, "while I slept on one of four filthy mattresses with drunks on the other three. Willoughby took the concrete floor, because it was cleaner!"

"What did they arrest you for?" Charlie asked.

"Oh, they were alcohol-reeking policemen who thought we were vagrants. When they looked into my briefcase, which had YMCA correspondence, fig bars and marshmallows, I think they decided we were neither hoboes nor health nuts!"[36]

Laughing at Ern's comment, the three college juniors entered the now familiar Room 202 of Fairview Hall, where Ern and Charlie now roomed together. They deposited Charlie's magic props and sat down on beds and chairs to talk.

Charlie spoke first. "So, do you think the South is on the brink of revolt, Ern?"

"No, I don't think it's ready for revolution, and I still believe, as I did at the outset, that hope is stronger than despair in the South, even though there is widespread and very deep poverty."[37]

"Your hope for the South sounds good to me, because I can only stand one war at a time," Charlie said. "I have decided I will protest all wars, at home or abroad. I am approaching the pure pacifist stance that all war is evil. If they have a draft, I will be a conscientious objector."

The others voiced their agreement and support of Charlie's decision. Charlie pulled out a piece of green paper on which he had handwritten the heading "Peace Talk" over a typed essay. "When I read that England and France had declared war on Germany, I typed this."

> There have been Neutrality Laws, disarmament conferences, farcical attempts to take the profits out of war,....Yet war will not be ended only by such measures. It will be ended only when the plain people of all lands lay down their weapons and say resolutely: "Once and for all, I am through with war."

"You're right, Charlie," Ern agreed. "The common people don't want war."

"I truly believe that," Charlie said, and continued reading:

The people want peace. The common man, the laborer, the layman, looks around him perplexed, does a little figuring, and then concludes in his simple manner, "Well, if war is the trouble, why not get rid of it?" Immediately the intellectual, the realist, the politician, the expert—all rush up and try to soothe him: "Yes, yes, of course. A worthy goal, no doubt. But it is impossible, you see. There must always be war. Why, even the Bible says that. We must protect our interests and our trade and our honor, yes, even if it means your—pardon me—our lives. You can't change human nature; you should know that.

Those are always their arguments," Willoughby interjected. "They say the pacifist position is unrealistic and utopian."

"They constantly say the common people are not intellectually prepared to make such decisions, that the ruling classes know best," Charlie agreed. Then he finished reading:

The plain man, awed by the doctor's degrees, the pomp and circumstance, the columns of figures, and the high, silk hats, no longer trusts his own judgment. For don't the experts have the facts?.... Hasn't the scholar studied much history and economics? And of course, one should know better than to hope that there is any simple solution to such a complicated problem. So he reluctantly bids goodbye to his work and his dream and goes off to war.

He may have the insight to see that a lasting peace cannot be made by treaties, or legislated in impressive halls or called into being by a diplomatic wand.

It will come when men realize peace cannot be maintained on the basis of power politics or on mutual self-interest or by "keeping aggressors in their place." There is one basis upon which peace can last: brotherhood. The people have it in their power to write their own emancipation proclamation. May that day be hastened![38]

"Charlie, that's good writing, very impressive," Willoughby said. "Can I have a copy?"

Charlie had a few carbon copies of the paper to hand out. They spent the evening discussing war and the obligation of a conscientious objector to make his views known.

————

On September 17, 1939, two days after Charlie's nineteenth birthday, Russia invaded Poland. Ern and Charlie had formed a Peace Team, which others in the E-A to the Fifth joined, along with Mark Ebersole. The team fostered peace discussions at the college, went to hear speakers in Lancaster and Philadelphia and talked about earning money so members could attend peace conferences.

Willoughby hung out in Charlie and Ern's room. Willoughby did not live on campus, but it seemed like he did. He paid for board so he could eat, but could not afford a room at the college. He spent many hours in Room 202 and with other fellows in the E-A to the Fifth Club. Hitchhiking to school every day, no matter rain, sleet or snow, he sometimes spent nights in the campus attic where a few cots were set up for day students and used communal bathrooms for an occasional shower. Willoughby was affectionately called a "hobo" by his fellow students.[39]

————

One shining October day in 1939, Charlie headed for the chapel, hurrying across the campus with its foliage rust and gold. Charlie often balked at compulsory chapel, but Ern had been invited to speak, and Charlie was glad to support him as a member of the Peace Team. He entered the chapel and sat behind some freshmen girls. Ern was introduced to the students and started speaking, true to his name, in earnest. "Do you condone war?" he asked in a booming voice.

"What does 'condone' mean?" one of the girls whispered, and the others shrugged.

Charlie smiled, remembering how inexperienced he had been as a freshman two years previously. Ern passed out questionnaires to the students, asking what they would do in certain situations, whether they opposed the draft and other pertinent questions.

"Ern Lefever uses such big words," Marian Groff quipped as the girls left chapel. The rest giggled in agreement.[40]

While helping Ern collect the questionnaires, Charlie told Ern about the freshman girls and Marian's comment at the end. "They all think you use big words, Ern," Charlie teased.

"No, I don't," Ern objected, "I just talk normally."

Undaunted by Ern's big words, within a few weeks Marian joined the Peace Team, the only female in the group. She also joined the International Relations Club and the YWCA (Young Women's Christian Association). Charlie belonged to the YMCA (Young Men's Christian Association). The YMCA, started in Britain in 1844, was a public club for boys, although girls were included in many of its activities. Many Ys had been formed to include blacks, Native Americans and other minorities.

Marian had wavy, almost black hair, worn in the bobbed style of the times. She smiled often, had the brightest blue eyes imaginable, and faced life with a shy but friendly manner. Why was she interested in peace? The Methodist church she attended had always been strong on peace. Her ancestors were persecuted Mennonites, who, at William Penn's invitation, came from the German-speaking section of Switzerland.

And it turned out she was an unusual young lady in other respects as well.

"What did you say we were going to do, in order to raise money for the Peace Team?" Marian gasped.

"We're going to trap muskrats for their fur around Lake Placida and sell them at one dollar per pelt," Willoughby repeated. "I did it when I grew up on a farm in New Mexico, and I know where to sell them. Do you have a problem with this? Perhaps you have a better idea?"

"That's a disgusting thought, killing animals for fur or anything else," Marian said.

"Well, you eat them, don't you?" Willoughby charged.

"No, I don't. I'm a vegetarian!" Marian's blue eyes widened in her heart-shaped face. "I've been a vegetarian since I was nine years old."

"Oh." Willoughby backed off. "I apologize. But do you have a better idea?"

"No."

"We could sell chocolates to students," Charlie piped up.

"I heard about your money-making project, but you ate the profits, Walker," Willoughby pointed out. "Let's think of something else."

"Go ahead and trap your muskrats, but don't expect me to help." Marian's dark curls shaking with indignation.

After the meeting broke up, Charlie asked Marian about being a vegetarian. "Nine years old is young to make such a decision. How did that come about?"

"Well, I was visiting my Aunt Loretta and Uncle Charles where they lived at the farm of General Hand, a famous American Revolutionary general,[41] when they butchered a pig. They killed it and dragged it out of the barn and below my window into the kitchen. I watched them dragging that dead thing in the dirt and it made me ill. I decided I would not eat anything killed like that, and I resolved, then and there, to never eat pork again. I took away other meats later. My family gave me trouble over it, claiming I would get sick and die if I did not eat meat, but they could never change my mind."

Those who listened to the story could not help marveling at Marian's spunk.

Now, that's a person with determination, Charlie mused.

————————

While Willoughby worked on putting together the school newspaper, Charlie came to talk. "I'm glad you're the editor of *The Etownian*," Charlie smiled warmly. "I was circulation manager of the paper last year, but I'm looking to do more this year. I'm associate editor of the yearbook, but do you have anything in the way of a promotion on the newspaper?"

"I'm sorry, but advertising manager is the only position open. Would you be interested?"

"I guess so, but I want to do some writing. As president of the International Relations Club, maybe I could write up some of how the students feel about the country heading toward war."

"I'd be happy to print what you submit, Walker. I think we can raise the consciousness of this student body. Ern Lefever is going to write a column on national and world affairs, and I'll be writing editorials on campus issues."

After talking for a while on journalistic subjects, Willoughby said, "By the way, Walker, we've been catching quite a few muskrats and have made a tidy sum. We'll have enough money for the Peace Team to go to the Penn State peace conference this fall."

"That's swell!"

"Yes! And we'll need to make special arrangements for Marian to stay on the girls' side of the big cabin."

"Did she ever go out and help check the traps?" Charlie asked.

"Once, but she was so disgusted she never helped again. She's an interesting person, isn't she?"

"Yes, she is."

The *Etownian* and Hitchhiking during Christmas Break

Ern, Charlie, and Willoughby sat in the *Etownian* office working on the next issue of the newspaper, which came out every two weeks. Charlie brought up a disagreement between students and faculty and suggested a faculty member might be under pressure to resign.

Ern wagged a finger. "You can get rid of people who disagree with you, but others usually rise in their place if you don't change the conditions which created the disagreement. If Hitler were to be removed from power in Germany, the forces which brought him into being would probably create another Hitler. Remember my poll in the last issue? Twice as many students feel Hitler is responsible for this war, as opposed to those who feel he is not. But how can one person be to blame? If Hitler is crushed and Germany is wiped off the map, the bulldog will be gone and his kennel will be destroyed. Then will the world have peace? Wasn't that the purpose of the last war? To crush Germany? Thirty-five students in the poll said war is inevitable, but the same thing was said about the institution of slavery. Let's think about this here!"[42]

Charlie agreed. "The three historic peace churches believe war is wrong and not inevitable.

Does this talk of religious subjects bother you, Ern?" Charlie couldn't resist a playful dig. "I remember your article slamming the 'religious man' last year. It's around here somewhere. Let's see, here it is. You called him a 'perky peacock as he struts abroad, a featherer of his own nest, a caretaker of number-one, a dog in the manger, who is self-righteous, un-Christian, self-admiring, arrogant, self-esteemed, egotistical and sanctimonious as he mounts his high horse and proudly raises his saintly head.' Furthermore, you said 'from this elevated position he looks down upon the low, ill-bred, vulgar, vile, polluted, defiled, uncivilized barbarians who are rushing headfirst into hell where they rightly belong.'"[43]

Red-faced, Ern hastened to defend himself. "That was about self-seekers who use religion to feed their arrogance. It does not pertain to sincere religious persons who strive to truly practice what they preach. I did mean it, though, when I said many of those who profess to be religious are wolves in sheep's clothing and goodly apples rotten at the heart who don't practice what they preach, nor what Jesus preached for that matter. They are men who find it easier to be on their knees than to rise to good action."

"Here, here, Ern," Willoughby clapped. "Truly spoken. But don't you acknowledge there are true saints in the world who actually try to live as Jesus and other godly men lived?" Ern agreed there were such. Charlie concurred and the three went back to work.

Inspired by Ern and Willoughby's summer trip through the South, Charlie, Fridy, Herb Lefever and another student named Charles Wilson decided to hitchhike to Florida over Christmas break. They split into groups of two: Charlie buddied with Fridy while Herb and Wilson traveled together. Through rain, bad drivers and having to sit on each other's laps, they persevered and finally joined up with the other two in Jacksonville, Florida.

A seven-cent breakfast of one egg, grits, and coffee, helped make a happy reunion for greenhorn, country-born, college boys who had never strayed far from home. They returned to Pennsylvania without incident, and Fridy and the others headed home for the last day or two of Christmas vacation.[44] Charlie opted to go to Elizabethtown, instead of the cold, dark Henderson Place in Gap.

He arrived on campus so late at night, he could not find a way into the dormitory. After curfew, the college truly came under lock and key.

Very early next morning, a surprised Willoughby, who had stayed on campus over the holidays, found Charlie sleeping on a campus park bench. He woke up the cold "hobo" and invited him inside to a warm room.

While Charlie slept under a warm blanket, Willoughby got out a piece of paper and penned a cartoon for the yearbook—a young man with only a jacket on for warmth, uncomfortably snoozing on a wooden bench, hands behind his head and elbows spread like a big bird. Charlie's face revealed a peaceful expression, his youthful face turned to the sky.

As the bench was too short to stretch out on, Charlie's knees were bent and his feet rested on the metal armrest, revealing big holes in the soles of his shoes. Holey shoes were common during the Depression, so people often cut out cardboard soles and placed them inside their shoes.

Below and to the side of the sleeping figure, Willoughby wrote, "10 degrees below," and the caption read, "Park Bench Walker."[45]

Another Prewar Winter and Spring

One morning, Ern woke Charlie up after they both had slept in, missing breakfast. Long gone were Charlie's lectures about how farm boys get up early. Ern's bad habits had been rubbing off on Charlie, but so, too, had Ern's inspiration to strive for better things.

As they dressed for class, Ern asked, "Charlie, do you remember the Brethren national peace director, Dan West? He spoke at Etown chapel last year."

"Oh, yes, very inspiring," Ern said as he pulled on his trousers, "I decided to learn about some of Dan West's other work, and he introduced me to work camps in the United States.

"At a work camp people pay five dollars a week for the opportunity to help the underprivileged in slums, run-down coal mine towns, migrant camps, etc. Even though I benefit from FDR's programs here at the college, I feel distrustful of government programs and believe that volunteer, church-run programs are more authentic."

Ern explained the previous summer he had taken a suitcase and cot onto a Greyhound bus and headed for Scranton, Pennsylvania, where he joined other young people in building a playground for children of unemployed coal miners. They stayed on a hillside in an old house with an outdoor john and spent time in Quaker-style meditation. Their motto was, "Work is love made visible," by Kahlil Gibran, the Arab philosopher.

Charlie combed his hair. "What made it worthwhile to you, Ern?"

Ern replied he took a field trip into a coal mine and visited some social agencies in Scranton, hoping their actions might spur government action on the children's behalf.[46]

"Sounds like a way to make a difference in this world full of war." Charlie tied his shoes.

"That was why I spent sixteen days in the South with Willoughby over summer vacation. Now, Charlie, the reason I'm bringing this up is that I found out about a work camp in Moxee, Washington, near Yakima, working with children and digging privies for farmworkers. Do you think you'd be interested in going with me this summer?" Ern finished tying his shoes and slicked down his hair.

"Yes, I believe I would, Ern. Let me think about it." And the two snatched up their books, opened the door and headed out.

———

For the second year in a row, Charlie belonged to "The Candles," an elite group of male students at Elizabethtown, admitted on the basis of scholarship, leadership, and service to the college. They had to be upperclassmen—no freshmen. Its original function was a social club but later another purpose was added: to clarify student opinion through regular discussion of current campus problems. That part of it Charlie relished.

The student body considered the Candles' annual dinner in the spring to be the crowning event of the year. Past members would be joining them for an evening of nostalgia and remembrance of friendships.

"Who are you going to take to the dinner, Ern?" Charlie asked.

"I plan to take Marian, what about you?"

"I'm not really dating anyone right now. I guess I'll just wing it."

While college students planned dinners on their pristine campuses, Germany continued to advance, crushing everything in its path. How quickly it all happened that spring of 1940. While Nazis rounded up Jews to send to concentration camps, Finland, Norway, Denmark and the Netherlands all succumbed to the German assault. When German airborne units (or paratroopers) attacked Belgium, France divided its forces by sending strong reinforcements north to help hold the Belgians. But when the Germans unleashed a surprise attack on France from the east, no resistance could be drummed up against the onslaught. With no reserves to hold the Belgian center, Belgium caved, and Nazis advanced across France towards Paris.

Charlie read the news with horror, seeing lights of democracy snuffed out one by one. Hating the war, the suffering, the cost of man's inhumanity to man, he dreaded more war. He also feared a pending US military draft.

But this was all very far away from the green, country town in Pennsylvania, and it was time for The Candles' annual dinner.

Ern seated Marian at the table where candles burned softly. He had bought her a sweet-smelling corsage for less than a dollar. After a short prayer, the conversation rose and fell with talk about war in Europe, spring activities, baseball season, and the latest dress styles.

Charlie looked across the table and noticed Ern and Marian eating, or at least Ern was eating and Marian stared at her plate. She then said something to Ern, who picked up his plate and held it out to her. Marian gathered up her piece of meat and plopped it on Ern's plate. Ern seemed delighted to have an extra piece of meat and dug in with gusto.

Marian cleaned her fork with a napkin and ate her vegetables, but then again was staring at the mashed potatoes and gravy on her plate. Ern, chewing on a big piece of meat, looked over at Marian and saw her scrape the gravy off the mashed potatoes. She carefully made a pile of gravy on one side of her plate with her spoon, and used her fork to eat the white potatoes.

Ern's eyes bugged out and he shook his head slightly.[47]

Amused, Charlie admired Marian's spunk even more, despite her quirks. She was really very cute and had a mischievous quality about her which made her light-blue eyes sparkle. All the guys in the Peace Team liked and respected her. He had not paid much attention to Marian until Ern expressed an interest in her. Now he looked with new eyes at this interesting young lady.

After the night was over, the glow of candles disappeared, and war appeared in the headlines. The French suffered loss and humiliation during the Germans' march to Paris, and on June 14, the Nazis entered their capital city. By June 22, German terms to the French government had been accepted. Charlie felt an ominous, black cloud heading toward him and his peaceful life on campus.

———————

Charlie and Ern sat in their room at the end of their junior year, looking over the new yearbook. Ern leafed forward to the picture and write-up of Charles Walker of Gap.

"Who wrote this nonsense about you?" Ern laughed and read out loud, "'a monger of legerdemain, ecmnesia and decrepit jocosity.' Charlie, it'll be 'get out the dictionary' for most people to be able to translate this into a 'magician and jokester.'"

"Yes, Willoughby wrote it. I thought he was pretty clever."

"But he called you a 'zoilian harlequin from Hiatus who has verbigeratedly avalanched a plethora of encominum on his costard with his encephalic disturbances.'"[48] Who would know, other than members of E-A to the Fifth, what that means?"

"Maybe Willoughby thought it would be a good idea for some students to drag out the dictionary for a change. How would you translate it?"

Ern studied the words for a moment and then declared, "A lazy clown from Gap, who has gained high praise for his show of braininess. And the rest, 'Intumescent with intellect, this pasquinading panacea has branded himself a droll par excellence, an iconoclast of the first magnitude and an all-round machinator non pareiled.'[49] Hmm, I would say it's up to a certain amount of interpretation, but in my view it says, 'bubbling with intellect, this lampooning cure-all has branded himself a humorist without rival, a man who fiercely attacks the errors of tradition, and an unrivaled schemer.'"

"Not entirely flattering, but not bad at all," Charlie chuckled. "I was much less verbose in describing him."

"Yes, Charlie, I see you said he was 'Dear Editor, the Bill Quixote, who has drawn fire from many angles for his attacks on the problems in the recreation facilities, lack of daily newspapers in the library, and freedom of the press.'[50] At least you wrote in English," and they both laughed.

"Look at what Willoughby wrote about you, Ern."

Ern read aloud, "'Prophet, ascetic, humorist, furious and assiduous workman, technical artist, master of some, servant of all—Ern has come down out of the York County hills to be the sleepless conscience of our class. Work camps, slums, sharecroppers, co-ops—little has escaped his keen observations. Success? President of Elizabethtown College at 50, Brethren moderator at 51, excommunicated at 52, millionaire at 53.'"

Ern shook his head and put the book down. The first part about his ascetic personality was accurate, but he thought Willoughby was way off on his predictions. Later, this writing was seen as an uncanny vision into the future of young Lefever.[51]

Ern handed his yearbook to Charlie and went off on other business. When he returned, a note on Charlie's picture directed him to a long letter in the back of Ern's yearbook:

> To the other denizen of a haunted room—
>
> Ern, at times you scale the heights and then plumb the depths. You introduced me to a new philosophy through Dan West, but you also degraded me into vile habits of conduct—not getting up for breakfast, etc....
>
> I am torn between two idealists—an emperor who says, 'Get to the top and crush anyone who gets in your path,' while the other says pleading from the depths of the Holy of Holies, "Help the needy."
>
> In all respect to one who has the potentialities of becoming a leader in nonviolent approaches to a society crying with need, to one who has made me to become a lowly vassal,
>
> My fullest support and moral backing.
>
> Walker.[52]

Work Camping, Another Summer Off

The Grapes of Wrath by John Steinbeck, published in 1939, exposed the ghastly plight of American farmers from the "dust bowl," a large section of the southwestern Great Plains plagued by severe dust storms in the 1930s. Four-hundred thousand fled their farms, heading west to look for work as migrant laborers. Charlie and Ern read the popular book, and it whetted their appetites to see for themselves the life of migrant workers.

During summer break in 1940, Charlie again went to work as a stock boy at Sears, Roebuck and Company in Chicago from May 26 until August, when he would head for the work camp in Washington State.

Ern met Charlie in Chicago, and they hitchhiked to the Brethren work camp half way across the country. Having hitchhiked to Florida eight months before, Charlie was familiar with delays and uncontrollable weather associated with such long treks.

The two had little trouble getting across Iowa and Nebraska, but Wyoming proved to be a test of patience. Waiting for a ride in Laramie on US 30, Charlie and Ern stood for seventeen hours. They bought a couple of five-cent hamburgers for a meal. Once, a car passed with a Pennsylvania license plate, and they shouted, "We're from Pennsylvania, too!" But the car sped on. Ern suggested they try the railroad, and Charlie readily agreed. Anything to get on the move again.

"Let's find an empty boxcar," Ern suggested, and they hopped onto the first likely car. The possibility of discovering people inside did not worry the two, because these were depression-bred hoboes—men displaced from their jobs and looking for work in the West.

It was night, and men's faces could only be seen when the train passed towns, and streetlights shone momentarily through the boxcar's open doors. Two steam locomotives dragged the heavy train up the slopes of the Rocky Mountains, while the young students talked with strangers in the boxcar. Each person had his story to share: One was just out of college looking for crops to pick; another was an orphan nobody wanted. A short-order cook and a bricklayer had just been let go from their jobs. All were hoping for a better future.

As Charlie and Ern finally moved into a quiet corner of the boxcar for some shut-eye, they felt an affinity with these men, who were part of a growing fraternity of American citizens reaching out for a new life in the fields and towns of the West. Ern turned to Charlie and whispered, "Perhaps my true calling is to make articulate the heartbeat of the masses."[52] Charlie wondered about his own future. He hoped the work camp at Moxee would give him a clue as to where his life would lead.

They reached Idaho by morning and climbed off the train in Pocatello. When they looked at each other, Charlie exclaimed, "Ern, your face is black!"

"You're covered with soot, too!" Ern giggled. Though tired and hungry, they decided to first remedy the hobo look. Walking to a gas station, they found an attendant with a kindly face and asked him if they could use the men's room to wash up. It felt good just to get somewhat clean again.

"Good luck!" the attendant called to them, as they headed back out to Route 30. It took two more days to arrive at Yakima.

Each paying their five dollars per week for the experience, Charlie and Ern spent three weeks in Moxee, Washington, taking care of undernourished children of migrant workers in the hop fields. Many children were sick with dysentery or sleeping sickness. When the two friends' time was not taken up with children, they dug pits for toilets to help improve sanitation.

When work camp ended, Ern spent an extra few weeks with the director and his wife driving through Oregon and California and then to Chicago over Route 66. They dropped him off at Bethany Biblical Seminary in Chicago, where he decided to take a year off for "voluntary service."[53]

Willoughby, too, had decided to take off at least one semester from Elizabethtown. Charlie wanted to stay in Washington another year or so and remained at the work camp with some Brethren when Ern left. When his mother heard of it, she put her foot down. Charles would return to college and that was that! Letters and phone calls flew back and forth with pleading and ultimatums. Charlie wanted to do something for mankind, but Mina had worked too hard to get Charlie into college for her to let him throw it away!

In the meantime, the Germans had opened the Battle of Britain in August and kept up night raids for the following two years. The Nazis worked hard to cut off shipping and supplies to Great Britain, while Fascist Italy, which had entered the war in June, attacked British interests in Africa, such as the Suez Canal.

Seniors at Last

School began in early September 1940 without Charlie, Willoughby and Ern. Herb Lefever had graduated and moved to Penn State to get his master's degree. The remaining members of the E-A to the Fifth Club, plus Marian and Fridy, noticed the campus felt decidedly different without them.

A few weeks late, Charlie showed up at campus, ready to take on his classes and catch up. The administration had let him come back, perhaps because he was an excellent student and had contributed a great deal to campus life. He returned from Washington late Saturday night September 22.

A wave of excitement pulsed through the Etown student body after Walker returned. "Walker's back!" Marian first heard it as a rumor. Then one of her friends turned to her as she walked to Monday's classes and bubbled, "Did you hear? Walker's back!"

"Walker's back?" Marian thrilled at the news and could not wait to welcome him. Her joy clued her in to her strong feelings for this remarkable young man. When she saw him on campus, she threw herself into his arms and hugged him tight.

They talked long and earnestly, and he explained his mother understood not at all his wish to stay and help the needy in the West. He had come home mainly because she told him in no uncertain terms how hard it had been to persuade his father to allow him to attend college at all. She reminded him he had been awarded a full *academic scholarship*, but *she* had scraped up room and board money with a loan from his uncle. Whatever the reason, Marian was glad he was back where he belonged.

The student newspaper, edited by Lowell Ridenbaugh in Willoughby's absence, had mirrored the campus buzz about the marked absence of the three. One article reported Charlie's summer in Chicago, followed by his trip to Washington.

> THEN THERE IS THE WANDERJAHR OF WALKER. The saga takes root May 26 when a Westward Ho splits the ether and Carlos Ambulator, E-town's paladin of pacifism, strikes out for Chicago. This Cook County terrain slips under foot after twelve hops and twenty-six hours. August arrives and is three-fourths consumed when he faces westward once more, this time the goal is Moxee, Washington, and a siesta in a work camp. Ere long, however, parental displeasure at an extended vacation started him on the road back, and the prodigal docked at 3 a.m., September 22.

At the Peace Team meeting following his return to campus, Charlie strolled into the room to cheers, followed by good-natured ribbing. "I read in *The Etownian*," one of the fellows said, "that you were trying to imitate Willoughby and Ern by taking a semester off from college. The paper called those two a 'pair of peregrinating pacifists' and 'malcontents by reason of Adolf's martial exploits throughout Europe.'"[54]

"Yes, I tried, but thought better of it." Charlie smiled.

"Willoughby is planning to take time off, and Ern hopes to divide his time between a Brethren camp for youth leaders in Michigan and a freelance peace campaign."

Charlie sighed. "Elizabethtown is where I belong."

"I heard you were hitchhiking," the ribbing continued, "via digit express. What did you think of our western US?"[55]

"Volunteering in Washington was an experience I won't ever forget," Charlie replied seriously. "No matter how difficult the Depression was for my family, it's much worse for those people and their children."

Another team member piped up. "I think your mother made you come back, Walker."

"You're right about that." Charlie laughed good-naturedly. "My mother is much of the reason I came here in the first place, and she would *not* let me leave under any circumstances!"

Marian entered the conversation. "I think you'll be glad you did, Carlos Ambulator. My parents say I must drop out after two years, because they can't afford to send both my younger sister and me to college at the same time. I was the one who got straight As, but that didn't make any difference. I'd be happy to be in your shoes."

"You can't get your degree?" Charlie asked, incredulous.

"Well, my parents' plan is that after my sister is in college two years, she must drop out and let me continue with my schooling. Then she can get her degree after I graduate."

"That's crazy," Charlie exclaimed. "I never heard of such a thing."

"I never did, either," Marian said unhappily, "until I heard it from them."

Marian abruptly changed the subject. "I understand you have a new nickname—'I forgot something, Walker.' I think that fits you. You're always forgetting something. I think you'd leave your head some place if it weren't screwed on." Her comments brought chuckles from the group.

"Sometimes I wonder if you even have any screws up there," Marian added in fun. "I heard the day you returned, you put in your appearance at 'Dreamy's Dive,' left shortly after, and in five minutes, returned, saying, 'Did any of you fellows see my coat?'"[56] Curtis Day became one of Charlie's roommates his friends called 'Dreamy Day' for day dream.

Everyone laughed. Then Charlie couldn't resist a turnabout, teasing

81

Marian with a quip he had read in *The Etownian*, "They say new freshmen must be vegetarians because they no longer 'mete' out justice."[57]

Again, the laughter was good natured, with Marian chuckling too. A sophomore now, she had noticed the lack of power a freshman feels after having been a mighty high school senior.

Then they turned to the urgent topic at hand, the first peacetime military draft in American history.

"I read in the newspapers while hitchhiking home," Charlie related, "that Congress approved it by one vote and President Roosevelt signed the bill September sixteenth, the day after my twentieth birthday."

"Yeah, some birthday present," one of the fellows said. "We'll have to sort out how we feel and, as members of the Etown Peace Team, how we'll deal with conscription when we turn twenty-one."

"Except Walker here, he's already made it clear he's opposed to the draft," another member said. 'Will you be protesting compulsory military conscription, Walker?"

"Yes, I will," Charlie declared.

Romance in the Air

Marian sat next to Harry Horning in the Social Room. She and Harry had been seeing each other. Marian no longer dated Ern and was only friends with the members of the Peace Team. Charlie came in and walked past them. Suddenly on impulse, he walked back, tapped Horning on the shoulder to sit next to Marian. "I'm horning in!" he announced and squeezed in next to a surprised Marian. Her first reaction was that Charlie was being rather rude, but then realized he did it cleverly and was showing marked interest in her. He flashed his sudden smile at Marian, and she melted as they shared in delighted laughter.

"Walker! When's the next Peace Team meeting?" Marian hailed Charlie, a few steps ahead.

"Tomorrow night." Charlie looked over his shoulder, then fell back and moved in step with Marian.

Slender and sporting a flattering red sweater over her calf-length plaid wool skirt, she wore saddle shoes, as did all the girls. Charlie enjoyed Marian's company, and she delighted in finally receiving attention from the man she had always put highest on her list.

Willoughby had returned in the fall in time to join Charlie, Fridy, Ridenbaugh, Disney and Ross Coulson in the school play, *You Can't Take it With You*. "I suppose with Willoughby back," she ventured, "you'll be trapping muskrats again at Lake Placida?"

"Oh, yes. You enjoyed the result, which was the trip to Penn State last year, didn't you?"

"Yes, I did, and learned a lot. A woman named Ruth Edwards, head of the Student Christian Association at Penn State, came by as we were unpacking and said to us girls, 'Don't do too much at once! Don't become a tired liberal!' For some reason I've remembered that since."

"'Don't become a tired liberal.' That's good advice. Liberals tend to get wrapped up in too many causes and extend themselves too far."

Charlie had heard Marian roomed with Charlotte Markey and asked if they were getting along.

"We get along famously. We're in the top floor in Alpha Hall, so there's plenty of room. You're rooming with Willoughby?"

"Yes, after we both came back late, it worked out quite well. Hey, I heard a rumor that someone stole your clothes as a Halloween prank."

"Gosh, Walker, I was just washing my laundry. Some students even send their dirty laundry home in a suitcase by parcel post, and their parents mail it back all clean and folded! When I wanted to go home recently, Mom scolded me, saying I should find things to do here on weekends. They have a point, but there are no parties, no social dancing.

"Well, anyway, I'd washed out my clothes in a tub in the basement of the girls dorm and hung them on a line that I thought I saw one of the cooks use. But mysteriously, the clothes disappeared. Next thing I knew, the dean of women called me in to her office. She held up my underwear asking if they belonged to me! I guess there's a rule against hanging personal laundry."

"That must have been embarrassing!" Charlie chuckled. With a grin, he put his arm around her shoulders and started telling her about how he had to wash the family laundry at the farm house in Gap.

The sun shone with clarity that warm, November day, as the quiet freeze of winter slowly approached. Charlie also felt warmth from Marian. The blue of the sky matched the blue of her eyes, and the stirring of the leaves in the air echoed something in his chest—strange feelings and thoughts.

Above them, tall fir trees watched the two innocents walking happily. Then, as a sudden breeze blew the tree tops back and forth, they began to look like chatty, old ladies, nodding to each other in wordless gossip that Charlie and Marian deeply enjoyed each other's company.

Sometimes, Charlie waited at the dining hall entrance to meet Marian before supper. They did not eat together often because of assigned seating, which was intended to help students mingle. Also, Marian served and cleared tables to pay for tuition, so she usually did not sit down when other students ate. Occasionally, they planned a few minutes before the meal together.

Charlie and Marian were now dating. After a men's basketball game in which he had played, Charlie walked Marian back to her dorm at Alpha Hall. Classrooms and administrative offices graced the first and second floors, but some dormitory rooms for women existed on the top floor.

The girls had an earlier curfew, while the boys did not, in the belief that if women were controlled the men would behave. A double standard, yes, but it was accepted and went unchallenged.

"Now that we're on a first-name basis," Marian said, "how about if I call you Charlie instead of Walker?"

"My nickname here is Dixie, after the Yankees baseball player, Dixie Walker." Charlie suggested.

"I don't think Dixie is proper for a man. To me it sounds like a girl's name, so I'd rather stick with Charlie." He reluctantly agreed.

"Charlie, I have another suggestion. Since we can't sit together while you're playing basketball, how about if we attend the girls' basketball games together?"

Charlie thought it was a great idea. Dating was very limited at Etown, and there was little to do but attend events together.

Charlie met Marian's parents on his final Christmas break from Elizabethtown College. Raymond and Elsie Groff, impressed with the young man from Gap, thought him a nice, handsome fellow. When he said he could play piano, they asked him to entertain them with a song. When he asked, "Where's the piano?" they said it was next door! So they all trooped over to the home of Raymond's sister, Mim, and Charlie wowed them with his singing and playing.

84

"Such talent!" they exclaimed. "And he's graduating soon from college."

Living in a depression where three million Americans remained out of work, Charlie considered himself fortunate he could attend college. Christmas break had come and gone. The year was 1941 and Charlie played on a great basketball team, the Blue and Gray Phantoms, sometimes called the Gray Ghosts, led by Coach Ira Herr.[58]

Marian continued to watch Charlie play at the home games. She also loved to listen to him tickle the ivories in the social room at Alpha Hall. One evening Charlie drew out a kitchen timer, set it for one minute, and placed it on the piano to see if he could play the "Minute Waltz" in just that—one minute. Over and over he worked at it, until persistence won that night. He did it! Marian and their friends cheered.

Charlie and Willoughby helped revive the debating team after two years of dormancy. Willoughby chose to be on the affirmative team, while Charlie joined the negative team.[59]

Willoughby and Walker also found themselves facing friendly competition at ping-pong. By the time the newly-formed YWCA-sponsored ping-pong tournament rolled around, they were both finalists: Charlie prevailed in Class A (the skilled players) while Willoughby came in second place in Class B (average players.)

Fridy looked for Charlie to congratulate him on his championship in ping-pong. He found him and Marian together. "Well, Dixie, you did it!" Fridy shook Charlie's hand. "When I won the ping-pong championship last year, I thought I'd be able to keep it, but I underestimated you, or I overestimated myself. Anyway, I'm glad you came out on top."[60]

"Thank you, Fridy. We've both come a long way since our freshman year."

Charlie and Willoughby served on the program committee for their final Candles dinner at the end of March.[61] Charlie could not help remembering Ern had taken Marian to this dinner the year before. Last year Charlie had sat across from the two of them; this year Marian sat beside him. Charlie, now used to Marian's vegetarianism, did not flinch or bat an eye when she again scraped gravy off her mashed potatoes.

The leadership initiated new members into the group, after which some alumni members entertained the group with a spirited debate on the topic, "Resolved that the broom is a more important household article than the dishrag."[62] Marian thought Charlie laughed louder and longer than anyone else in the audience. It was an explosive laugh. At first, she did not know how to react, as his eyebrows lifted along with his whole face in a huge grin. But that night she recognized his boundless appreciation for clever humor.

While they ate, Charlie said quietly to Marian, "I've decided that I'm going to work like I've never worked before, and I'm going to try for a one hundred percentile in my plane geometry class."

"Why?" Marian asked politely.

"Just to prove to myself I can do it. I'm going to ace every test, every homework assignment. And because geometry is just about the hardest class I know of, I decided to pick that."

"My goodness, you're quite a student, Charlie. So ambitious."

"What do you consider your hardest subject, Marian?

"French. I hate French. I like the sciences more. My physics teacher had us take a standardized test, and I scored above the ninetieth percentile in the whole country. He thought that was wonderful and kept bragging about me! Everybody talks about how you're so smart and how you were valedictorian of your class, but I was valedictorian of my class, too."

"Really? Congratulations, Marian! What school?"

"East Lampeter. I was the only student in my class to go to college that year. I wanted to attend school at Dickinson, because we're Methodists and it's a Methodist college. But the President of Elizabethtown came to my house recruiting me, I guess because I was valedictorian. President Schlosser made my parents an offer they couldn't refuse."

"The president didn't come to my house, that I know of," Charlie mused. "I took a test, and on that basis, I got the scholarship. Are you glad now that you came?"

"Oh, yes, but in the beginning I wasn't sure at all. My parents drove me up to see the school, and I saw a couple of women teachers in long dresses and white caps and thought, 'Oh, no, they're sending me to a convent!'" Charlie and Marian laughed.

After they had eaten dessert, Marian looked up at him with her blue eyes and mentioned how difficult it was to stick with her diet.

"I guess it's not easy being a vegetarian," Charlie noted.

"No, it's not. One time recently, I was going through the lunch line. As I moved along, a lady behind the counter handed me a ham sandwich on a plate. I said I did not want the ham, and she seemed upset and angry that I was being 'picky.' So, she took the ham out of it and handed the sandwich back to me! After the ham had sat in the salad dressing and all, I did NOT want that thing! I guess I got mad back at her and said, 'If someone fixed you a mouse sandwich and you said you didn't want the mouse, and they grabbed it by its tail and pulled it out and handed the plate back to you, would you want to eat that sandwich?'"[63]

Charlie howled with delight. "What happened next?"

"The lady quickly fixed me a salad dressing sandwich and handed it to me, and as I passed on, she said to the serving person next to her, 'Did you hear what that girl said to me?' And others whispered it, too. I was bad, Charlie, I was so bad!" Marian chuckled, her mischievous eyes sparkling.

"Oh, no, Marian, you were good. You were so good!" And they laughed together till their sides hurt.

Spring, Baseball, and Graduation

Etown students prepared for final exams, while Charlie and other seniors looked forward to graduation. Spring had sprung and life was full of hope.

"How did you do in plane geometry?" Marian asked Charlie as they headed to class. "Did you get that one hundred you were aiming for?

"Well, no," Charlie answered. "I got one wrong on a test. It looks like I'm going to get a ninety-nine."

"Too bad, I hoped you'd do it."

"Even so, I'm glad I did as well as I did."

"I am, too. It's quite an accomplishment. Have you ordered your cap and gown?"

"Yes, and I'm going to graduate, but it looks like I'll have to finish up some work in summer school, mainly because I came to school a month late."

"Am I invited to your graduation, Charlie?"

"Of course, I wouldn't have it any other way. I'd love to have you there. My family's coming and I'd like you to sit with them."

The Southernaires, a popular Southern Gospel singing group, were scheduled to sing at Etown, but since their group consisted entirely of African Americans, no hotels or motels in Elizabethtown would take them in. The students, looking forward to the concert and dismayed by this turn of events, asked what could be done. So the administration and faculty put them all up in their homes. Problems also came up when racially integrated sports teams could not find accommodations either. Often volunteers within the college community would give the young men rooms for the night.

A very good year in baseball ensued, as seniors, including Charlie, demonstrated leadership for the Blue and Gray Phantoms. The Ghosts' baseball team in May mowed down their opponents in fairly close games. *The Etownian* had this to say about three of them: "Elizabethtown College came into Juniata stadium breathing revenge with every breath, and later walked out on the long end of a 5–2 count in a well-played ball game." [64] Then, at Moravian, "Elizabethtown College staged a belated rally to nip the home nine by the score of 7–6. Trailing by three runs going into the first of the ninth, the Lancastrians tied the game up on five clean blows and then went on to score the winning run in the initial half of the tenth.... Walker personally sent Elizabethtown ahead in the fourth as he homered with the sacks empty." [65] Then, a home game with Penn Military College topped all excitement. "In a thrilling extra-inning ball game, Elizabethtown College fought back on two occasions to down P.M.C., 4–3. After playing ten scoreless innings, the rivals each counted twice in the eleventh and finished up in the twelfth, as the local team outscored the invaders!" [66]

Little did Charlie know that a minor-league talent scout was watching and left the games impressed with one Charles Walker.

Spring events at the close of the school year kept everyone busy. Charlie played Beethoven's *Moonlight Sonata* at the annual piano and voice musical recital. [67] Willoughby and Charlie were in charge of invitations to the informal senior/faculty get-together, where seniors entertained their teachers with a picnic. [68] Charlie accepted his senior athletic letters at a local restaurant banquet and attended a campfire service for student volunteers, in which Willoughby gave a challenging talk under the stars.[69]

Mid-May, Charlie asked Marian to go with him to the Joint "Y" Doggie Roast. The group left in pickup trucks and rode to Chiques Rock[70] on the Susquehanna River south of Elizabethtown. Singing in antiphonal fashion, they hiked around the rock. Charlie put his arm around Marian as the group stopped to watch a fantastic sunset. Marian brought a baking potato wrapped in foil to roast among the coals, while Charlie and the others roasted hot dogs.

"I'm looking forward to the Annual Spring Outing at Mount Gretna this Saturday," Marian gushed as she put margarine on her potato. "I just loved the one they had last year. It's a wonderful thing they do for us, a day off during exams, so students can spend a day hiking and playing outdoor games at a local state park! The college even supplies a picnic lunch."

"Yes, Etown does wonderful things for its students," Charlie agreed as he bit into his hot dog. He made certain to sit close to her again, around the campfire, as a speaker instructed them on "Getting the Most out of Life." They were sad when it was time to head back.[71]

Marian asked as they rode together on sweet-smelling hay, "Charlie, isn't the moon beautiful tonight?" Charlie did not answer with words, but with a passionate kiss. He was most assuredly falling in love.

Graduation day arrived: May 26, 1941. Marian sat proudly with Joe and Mina Walker and his brothers Herb and Bill in the Elizabethtown auditorium/gymnasium at ten o'clock in the morning. She watched Charlie take his seat with the forty-two graduates, following a dignified processional to "A Mighty Fortress is Our God."

After the invocation, a song and some speakers, Charlie stood up. He had explained to Marian the program said he was to play Handel's "Largo," but he knew Beethoven's *Moonlight Sonata* perfectly and he did not think he had perfected the "Largo." Always the perfectionist! She shivered with excitement when Charlie went to the grand piano, and, with a flourish, pushed his black gown aside. He sat on the shiny piano bench. Carefully and purposefully, he raised his hands and played *Moonlight Sonata*[72] from memory, as always. He performed perfectly, with feeling, the music rising and ebbing to its holy and prayerful conclusion. The audience applauded loudly with Marian applauding the loudest and longest.

She noted among the graduates Charlie's friends—Bill Willoughby,

Wilmer Fridinger, Ross Coulson, Lowell Ridenbaugh and Stan Disney—along with her friend and roommate, Charlotte Markey.[73]

Dean A.C. Baugher presented the candidates for graduation; then President Ralph W. Schlosser conferred the degrees. The speaker, Dr. William Pearson of Hahnemann Medical College, warned the young people against falling into the trap many college graduates did, of expecting maximum pay for taking the least amount of responsibility, while doing as little work as they could. He said each of them should strive for three things: a healthy body, a trained mind and ideals inculcated by their alma mater. His parting thoughts were, "Look up, not down; look forward, not in; lend a hand."[74]

After a men's quartet sang "Pilgrim's Chorus," a benediction was given, and Etown sent its graduates out into the world.

Charlie had done it! He had graduated from college and was ready to grasp the future with both hands. It was his to mold as he chose. Elizabethtown College had helped him blend his peculiar background with world perspectives, and he was poised to shape exciting times ahead.

Chapter 3

Conscience During the War Years, 1940–1945

War … is the final flowering of many types of conflict, the open sore symptomatic of a diseased and weakened social organism, the overt manifestation of the conflicts underlying our institutions and imbedded in our attitudes at all times.

–Charles C. Walker, "Pacifism Confronts a World at War," pamphlet self-published June 3, 1943

As World War II continued overseas, the Axis ravaged nation after nation. But signs of hope appeared for the Allies in Africa, as the British destroyed more German supply ships. On May 5, 1941, Ethiopian Emperor Haile Selassie victoriously returned to Addis Ababa.

Hope was lean elsewhere, though, as Germans advanced in April through Yugoslavia to the Greek coast with an entirely airborne campaign, captured the island of Crete and held the majority of bases that controlled the Mediterranean. In June Germany invaded Russia and in August began the siege of Leningrad. The Battle of Britain continued fiercely.

Fellowship of Reconciliation Conference in Ohio

Fresh out of college, Charlie Walker faced a life-altering decision, and he felt determined to make the right one.

It was early September 1941 in Lancaster County, and Charlie dodged Amish buggies as he chugged along in the family's old, gray Plymouth on his way from Gap-in-the-Hills. The air felt pleasantly warm, the trees along the road shimmered in bright greens and the sky blazed as blue as Marian's eyes. He hoped she was off work. After he had graduated from Elizabethtown, she had left school and found employment, so her sister Mary could go to college.

As Charlie pulled up to the small, brown house on Strasburg Pike, Marian ran out onto the porch and down the steps, her dark curls flying. He hopped out, and as he gave her a hug, his own excitement grew. He planned an important trip, and he hoped she would go with him.

They walked to the side of the house to watch the stunning, roaring waterfall, which dominated the backyard. A tiny patch of lawn separated the brown house from a downward, steep bank of gray rocks with an awesome view of the waterfall. Upstream, Mill Creek meandered idyllically between farm fields before it hit the falls. Then it became a cascade fifty feet across, before it plunged twenty feet into a pool of froth and gradually returned to a swirling, eddying body of water. It gurgled under the Strasburg Road Bridge, down to the old mill race and past the family's mill where Marian's father, Raymond Groff, had worked as a young man.[1] Then it calmed and became a lazy creek, flowing toward the Conestoga River.

Charlie and Marian relaxed on lawn chairs watching the bucolic scene. Across the creek stood the picturesque brown stone mansion where Marian's grandfather, Isaac Brenneman Groff, had lived and where Marian was born. The imposing structure held sweet memories for her.[2] She told Charlie that when the Depression hit, her parents moved from Raymond's father's house to a much smaller house directly across the street next to the mill. Later they moved back across the road to the home where they now sat.

"Did you ever feel you were deprived because of moving to a much smaller house?" Charlie asked Marian.

"Why, no, I was too little for it to matter at all. I still went over to Grandfather's; we called him I. B. and played in the hay mow in the barn and enjoyed swimming in the creek, along with canoeing and ice skating. The mill was in operation then. Aunt Mim and her husband, Homer, moved in with I. B. because my grandmother, Lizzie, had died and he needed a housekeeper. But they left after his death and now live next door to us on the other side of the waterfall.

"Because of the Depression we girls had to work hard in Dad's garden, but the major reason we came through hard times was Mother's job teaching in a one-room school. Early in the 1920s the town asked her to teach, but she turned them down at first, saying she had two little girls and could not leave them. So a concerned parent managed to find a housekeeper/babysitter for her. Things were different back then. Later, I entered school at six, and my sister went to school early at age five."

They sat in silence for a moment, enjoying the peaceful roar of the waterfall and the whirl of the water far below. The smell of moss, spume and fresh-cut grass was mesmerizing. But Charlie became impatient to get going.

"Marian, there's a conference this weekend in Sandusky, Ohio, held by the Fellowship of Reconciliation, and I really want to go. I've decided to take the family car if you go with me, but if you don't, I'll hitchhike. My mom's all right with whatever I decide."

"Oh, that's the F-O-R you've talked about? That peace organization you were interested in?"

"Yes, the one Ern told me about."

"That sounds exciting, but do you think your mother's old coupe could get us there and back?"

"Yes. See if your parents will let you go."

Marian found it fairly easy to convince Elsie and Raymond Groff to let her go for the weekend. It was a last-minute plan, but they trusted her and Charlie and knew they both were strongly interested in the subject of peace. His biggest obstacle was having little money for gas, one of the reasons for hitchhiking if she could not go along. It was Thursday afternoon. They scrounged a little money and food and started driving west. Through the Allegheny Mountains they used the Pennsylvania Turnpike, which opened from Carlisle to Irwin the year before. Both having driver's licenses, they took turns driving all night. The conference was to start Friday afternoon.

Along the way, Charlie explained that the Fellowship of Reconciliation, a pacifist organization founded at the outset of World War I, was a Christian protest against war. He told her two men, an English Quaker and the pacifist chaplain to the German Kaiser, shook hands on a railway platform in Cologne, Germany, on August 13, 1914, the day before their countries declared war on each other. In 1915, the American FOR came into being.

"They work to prevent conflicts and lay foundations for peace based on justice and brotherhood rather than retaliation and revenge," Charlie explained. "They also aid conscientious objectors and work for racial harmony."[3]

Charlie explained to Marian that he was impressed with the conference message and encouraged her to read a copy he had brought along. "The

FOR sees war as meaning that children of the same Father God engage in wholesale violation of the most sacred moral laws, resulting in mass suicide. The FOR encourages its members, if it is their spiritual leading, to refuse to register for military conscription."

Marian saw Charlie was tired, and as he was notorious for falling asleep at the wheel she decided to play devil's advocate. "Don't you think the FOR might be accused of being unpatriotic for encouraging noncooperation with the law?" she asked.

"Well, the FOR disavows any sabotage or interference with war measures by our government and abhors totalitarianism in all its forms— Nazi, Fascist, Communist."

Marian continued reading the message and found the answer to her question. "Here, Charlie, they declare they are not doing this in a spirit of frivolous or deliberate defiance of government. They say, 'We have in the past tried to be law-abiding and conscientious citizens,' and say they are 'determined to continue that way in every situation except where obedience to man-made law seems to clearly violate conscience and the command of God.'"[4]

Charlie gave his attention to passing a slow car on the road, and then continued. "As I said, it recognizes that conscience is an individual matter and not just because you're a member of a sect. The three traditional peace churches are setting up *and financing* Civilian Public Service (CPS) Camps to give all sincere objectors of any denomination meaningful work, so even Methodists like me can be exempt."[5]

Marian nodded thoughtfully and looked out the window at the peaceful Ohio hills. Charlie asked, "Marian, what would you think if I became a conscientious objector? It may come to that."

Her answer was quick and definitive. "Remember how we discussed in our college Peace Team what Thoreau said in Walden Pond? Mother always taught it. I was raised Methodist, too, and many leading Methodists are against war."

Charlie's smile died as the car started jerking and slowing down. "Uh, Oh!" Charlie pulled off the road. They both got out and looked under the hood.

"Where are we?" asked Marian anxiously.

"Not too far from Sandusky, somewhere west of Cleveland. But it might as well be the middle of nowhere." Not handy with anything mechanical, Charlie felt embarrassed and helpless.

"How are we going to get out of this fix?" he complained to Marian. "We're stranded in the middle of nowhere, and I can't afford expensive repairs at some costly shop."

"How could we get to a repair shop, anyway?" Marian lamented.

But, then, a truck slowed down and pulled up behind them. The two looked cautiously up at the big rig. If he offered them a lift, how safe would it be, especially for Marian? Could they leave their car on the side of the road? Could he leave her there, while he went for help?

The driver got out and came over to the car. He looked at the engine.

"Do you have a nail file?" he asked Marian.

"Sure do!" She rifled through her purse and offered him one. He filed something down and that did the trick. Marian smiled, relieved. They would be okay after all!

Charlie no longer felt helpless and could take charge again. They both thanked the trucker profusely. In short order, they were on their way.

Charlie again became again a little too quiet, so Marian, to keep him alert, started up the conversation again. "I was wondering, Charlie, don't you think you might be considered anti-God to oppose the war? Church people could call into question your commitment to fight the evils in the world."

"That's a good point, Marian, but I read an article by A. J. Muste in the FOR magazine, *Fellowship*, called 'The Religious Basis of Pacifism.' He made some very good points, saying pacifism is Christianity rightly understood. Also, that love is the one means of salvation for the individual and society. He believed Jesus lived out this truth to the uttermost, and that fact makes him the revealer of God. God's method and weapon is the cross, not the sword."

Marian thought a minute and decided she agreed. "If you look at the New Testament, Jesus resisted the way of the sword over and over again."

"Yes, he did. Muste pointed out that religious pacifism is an inner experience, an inner attitude and way of life, not merely a tool or device." Marian felt impressed by the young idealist sitting next to her—and his hero.

"I'm looking forward to meeting Mr. Muste."

Abraham Johannes Muste was born overseas in Holland and raised in Grand Rapids, Michigan, an area of the country settled primarily by Dutch.

He graduated from Hope College near there in 1905, and in 1909 graduated from a seminary of the Dutch Reformed Church. He was ordained soon after, but later resigned his ordination because he wouldn't abandon his religious pacifist views. Muste became a labor leader, directing numerous nonviolent strikes and campaigns in the 1920s and 30s.

Charlie said, "People often mis-characterize Muste because he was briefly a member of the Communist party. But he quit after he realized Communists readily resort to violence. Muste believes violence is self-defeating, because it destroys the ends we try to achieve. Now he believes only the dynamic of religion will let us stop wars and build a better world."[6]

Having arrived in Sandusky, Charlie pulled the little two-person coupe into the Methodist Conference Center on beautiful Lake Erie and breathed a sigh of relief that they had arrived safely—actually on time!

The conference began Friday afternoon, September 5, 1941 with speakers and discussion leaders such as Muriel Lester, Norman Whitney, James Farmer, Roy McCorkel, Kenneth Boulding, Richard Gregg, and Douglas Steere. Evening speakers were Norman Thomas on the "State of the Nation" and E. Stanley Jones on the "State of the Church."

Marian and Charlie happily discovered Ern Lefever had arrived. He heard they were coming and had seen to Marian's lodging, finding her a room by herself at the conference center, which she warmly appreciated. Charlie, grateful to get a full night's sleep, looked forward to a full day Saturday.

That morning at the business meeting, they first saw FOR officials A. J. Muste, John Nevin Sayre and John Swomley. Late afternoon was free time, so Marian and Charlie walked along the beach and compared workshops.

"Richard Gregg, who led my workshop, wrote a book called *The Power of Nonviolence*. He also wrote this pamphlet, 'Non-Violent Resistance.' I'd like to read you some passages from it," Charlie said.

As Marian looked out over the expanse of water, she heard birds calling and waves lapping softly onto the sand. The young man next to her was tall, lean, tanned and handsome. In his crisp white shirt, tan slacks and white shoes, he was as fit as a top athlete. Charlie held the pamphlet in one hand and read aloud as they walked.

"'The faith of the nonviolent resister, that all people have in them some potentiality for good, need not be a blind faith. It is the assumption on the basis of sound psychological and historical evidence, that every person has in him at least some tiny spark or potentiality of goodness, even though it may be confused and encrusted over by habitual pride, prejudice, hardness, crudeness, callousness, cruelty or criminality.' For instance, he says, 'You cannot make a bud develop on a tree by striking it with an axe or hammer…. Nothing will do but soft, warm air, moisture, and sunshine repeated for many days.'" He looked up at Marian whose hair blew softly in the Lake Erie breeze. "This is what Jesus meant by forgiveness, to say gently, 'Despite the harm that you have done to me, we are brothers, we are members of the human family.'"[7]

Charlie stopped to look at a sand castle left by some child and stared out at the horizon. He thought how forces like these gentle, lapping waves can slowly change the shape of great beaches, and if he chose the path he was now considering, he'd have to be as patient and persistent as the oceans. Glancing at Marian he sighed and said, "It's like my old grandmother said, 'You can't fix a watch with a crowbar.'" They both laughed and headed back for supper.

During the conference they were treated to the exceptional tenor voice of Bayard Rustin, a young black man recently hired by the FOR.

Charlie wanted to hear Muste speak Sunday morning, so they waited until after his speech before they undertook the long trip home. Muste was dynamic, highly intelligent, humble and a great speaker, so they were glad they had stayed.

On the way back to Lancaster, Charlie told Marian he agreed with the conference's religious pacifists that no real good could be expected from a peace where Stalin's dictatorship in Russia had an equal role to Great Britain and the United States.

Marian added, "And it's troubling when they say our leaders don't see peace ahead, only more war."

"Well, I'm beginning to feel only nonviolence will free us from the cycle of war. I found a pamphlet at the conference by John Nevin Sayre, Muste's cochairman at the FOR, and it says nonviolence calls *not* for passiveness but nonviolent coercion to *resist* aggressors, after appeals to public opinion and attempts at negotiation do not work."

"Like Gandhi in India?"

"Yes. Sayre points out that even Jesus, mocked, beaten and crowned with thorns, later rose to power in men's hearts as our very best example of nonviolent resistance. He goes on to say the very highest type of pacifism depends on the pressure of moral force, that the most powerful recourse against evil is appealing to conscience through suffering of the just for the unjust. What do you think about that, Marian? That enemies should be loved and converted?"[8]

"You mean like Abraham Lincoln saying he 'eliminated' his enemies by turning them into friends?"

"Precisely!"

They rounded a bend and happened upon a spectacular Pennsylvania mountain view, majestic and summer green. Charlie wondered how much more gorgeous this scene would look in a month or so with foliage of red, orange and yellow. His life felt as exciting as the coming of his favorite season, when the landscape is a giant kaleidoscope of glorious colors. The car tooled down into the valley and started chugging up the next mountain.

"Marian, we don't have much cash for gas. I'm worried we may not get home."

"How about we coast down the hills to save on gas." So they did.

"Charlie, what is Gandhi's philosophy, and why's it so important to you?"

"Gandhi believes in something he calls *Satyagraha*, which is soul-force, truth-force or love-force. This is an intensely religious and moral force that can be harnessed by moral people who believe in the power of God and of love to change people. That's why it works! Let me tell you a story."

Marian loved stories. She settled back in her seat.

"Gandhi led the Indian people on nonviolent campaigns, to abolish not only British rule of India but also the brutal Indian caste system. This system kept the untouchables enslaved and they had every reason to hate their tormentors, but Gandhi taught that nonviolence also extends to your thoughts. The idea is to not embarrass your opponents or wish evil of them, but to win them over by the power of truth and love. One example is the story of Vykom in 1924.

"A section of the Vykom Road was completely off limits to untouchables because it went past a Brahman temple. It was believed that for a priest merely to look at an untouchable would make him unclean. So the untouchables had to take different routes, while others could use the road in complete freedom. Protesters with some untouchables in their group tried to walk on the road. Brahmans, however, beat the reformers, who offered no outward resistance."

"None? Not even in self-defense?"

"No, they took the suffering voluntarily. Really. Many were arrested and sentenced to jail, some up to a year. Then the government stepped in and ordered an end to the beatings, but told the police to forbid any demonstrators to pass on the road. So, police lined up and cordoned off the road. The people vowed to resist and formed several lines of protesters in the road, determined to stay there until they were allowed through. They organized themselves into shifts of six hours at a time and built a little hut nearby.

"Days and weeks went by and then months and the rainy season kicked in. The road filled with muddy water, but the people stood firm, mentally embracing their adversaries with love. The rain poured, and the people stood up to their shoulders in water but would not give up. Shifts were shortened to three hours. The soldiers brought in small boats and climbed into them to keep up the cordon. Once a boat started to sink, and the protesters righted the boat and helped the soldiers get back in."

"They did that?"

"Yes, this love-force was so powerful that after a year and a half the Brahmans said they could hold out no longer against the prayers made to them and were ready to let the untouchables pass through."[9]

"That's wonderful, Charlie!"

"And it was God, not violence that won the battle. It was this power of love, force and truth all wrapped into one. Gandhi's *Satyagraha*."

Later in the day Marian and Charlie headed out of the mountains, and the terrain flattened out once they passed Harrisburg. Charlie felt better on level ground. He spent the last money they had on gas and added a few silent prayers.

Charlie told Marian he had found a job for the coming fall season teaching high school near Elizabethtown in Mount Joy. He looked forward to coaching basketball and baseball. Then he remembered....

"Oh, Marian! I was approached this summer by a scout for the Harrisburg Senators, a farm team for the Philadelphia Phillies, and they asked me to try out for the team!"

"Really? For what position?"

"Catcher." Charlie smiled broadly. "They sent scouts to our games at Elizabethtown, and liked what they saw."

"My gosh, Charlie, what did you tell them?"

"It was a real hard decision, but I told them not right now, maybe later. I can always try another time. At this point, I'm worried about the war and whether I'll be in a CPS camp or in prison. I believe I'll be some kind of conscientious objector. It just seemed better to hold off and wait and see."

"Hmm, I'm excited you may have a chance at a big-league baseball career, but you have to do what you feel is right."

"I'm pleased they asked me, Marian, but I just don't think baseball is to be my life's work. It's very tempting to do something for myself and maybe make a lot of money. But something deep in my being says I must serve humanity."[10]

"Charlie, you have to do what you feel is right."

Charlie's burden lifted, as he heard Marian's reassuring words. His family would probably accept talk of conscientious objection, but many neighbors would not.

It was dark now as they reached the west edge of Lancaster city, whereas Marian lived on the east edge. The little old gray coupe suddenly coughed, chugged and started sputtering. It was out of gas! "Uh-oh, Hang on!" Charlie shouted and managed to pull the car to the side of the road. They sat for a moment, catching their breath. The two rejoiced that they were not hurt, and he had not smashed his mother's Plymouth. Talking over options, they found they had a nickel between them.

"One nickel," Marian laughed. It paid for a call home from a public phone, and Marian was relieved to get a hold of her dad. He said he'd come right over and help them get home.[11]

Grading Papers and Berkshire Mills

Deep into the red-gold of the fall season, Marian babysat at the large stone house where she had played as a child. A young couple with children lived there now, and the little ones slept in bed. Marian had just settled down in an overstuffed chair with a book. A knock on the door startled her, and she sat up, wondering who it could be. Dashing to the door and peeking out its window, she saw Charlie on the doorstep.

"Hi!" Charlie smiled as she opened the door. He lifted up a stack of papers she could have sworn was a foot high. "I stopped in at your parents' and they said you were over here. I need help grading these papers."

Marian was a bit taken aback, but Charlie was unpredictable as well as interesting. He explained the papers were from five of his high school classes and needed to be returned to the pupils tomorrow.

She agreed to assist and led him to the dining table. They spread out the piles and he gave her the key to one test. It went faster with two people working, and smiles and laughter made time fly. Marian was glad for the company, so she never asked him how he had gotten so far behind.

Marian located a snack for them, and, between bites, Charlie told of a *Fellowship* magazine article about a strike at Berkshire Knitting Mills in nearby Reading, Pennsylvania, where a new technique, nonviolent resistance, had been used in 1936.

A. J. Muste and some Quakers from Philadelphia Yearly Meeting had convinced workers at the mills to try it. They outlined a program to keep nothing secret, telling press, police, the secretary of labor, and many others where and when they planned to prevent replacement workers, sometimes called scabs, from entering the plant. Sixty workers volunteered for a daily program of training and discipline before the demonstration.

On the appointed day the one lone sign read, This Demonstration Demands Absolute Silence From Every Picket. When the first busload of replacement workers arrived and tried to pass through the gate, they were met with a human carpet of demonstrators, whom police promptly arrested. More demonstrators from behind immediately took their places, and fifty-eight had been arrested in one hour.

"When they realized arrests were not working," Charlie continued, "the police exploded tear gas and gas bombs on either side of the human carpet. The demonstrators cried tears from the fumes, struggled for air and coughed until they were exhausted, but not one of them got up or fled the scene. Only a few strikebreakers walked over the bodies, and the rest left in shock at what they'd seen.[12] Marian, this convinced people that nonviolence can work."

"You have to wonder," Marian said.

After Charlie packed up his papers, all corrected and organized, he thanked Marian profusely and left, promising to see her soon.[13]

US Enters the War

Marian and her parents ate Sunday dinner at Aunt Mim's house next door on December 7, 1941. Sister Mary now lived at college.

"Dad," Marian teased. "I forget, what college did you graduate from?"

"PBC, Pennsylvania Business College."

"Oh, I thought PBC stood for Poor Boys College," Marian's eyes twinkled with a standing joke, but Raymond was not pleased. He had *not* been poor. Abruptly, he decided to go home and tend to an errand.

He had been gone quite a while, when he all of a sudden hurried back in.

"The Japanese have bombed Pearl Harbor in Hawaii! I heard it on the radio!" They all sat dumbfounded. Marian's thoughts quickly went to Charlie. How upset he must be!

At Pearl Harbor, nineteen US Navy ships were sunk or disabled, 120 planes were destroyed on the ground, and over 2,400 people lost their lives. In addition, similar attacks had been made at bases in Guam, British Hong Kong, the Malay Peninsula, Philippines and Midway. Charlie was indeed upset. The next day the US Congress declared war on Japan. Three days later, when Germany declared war on the United States, the US government reciprocated with its own war declaration. So, despite isolationists' and peacemakers' best efforts, the nation was pitched into a deadly struggle.[14]

Over Christmas, Charlie took Marian to meet his mother and brother at Gap. Herb was now sixteen. Brother Billy, eleven, spent the holidays with Aunt Mae and her family in Cochranville. The Pennsylvania hillsides sparkled with white crystals as the little coupe rolled on snow-blanketed roads to the village of Gap-in-the-Hills.

They pulled into the driveway and hurried into the Henderson Place with a frigid wind at their backs. Inside, the shivering couple discovered Mina's warm smile and a crackling fire. Charlie presented his friend to his mother, tongue-in-cheek, "This is Marian. She's got everything wrong with her—she's a vegetarian, she's left handed, hates French and loves Physics!" Mina and Herb laughed. Mina was glad to find out Marian was Methodist and her mother had been a teacher, like herself.

At the dinner table, talk was of the war. Charlie said compulsory military service had been extended to two and a half years. Mina unhappily told them taxes had been doubled to pay for the huge military buildup now in full swing.

Herb, now sixteen and as handsome and winsome as his older brother, believed he, too, would soon be drafted. He made it clear, though, that he had no problem taking up arms for his country. "You have to admit, Charlie, that business and labor have quit quarreling because they are too busy expanding production. They've declared full cooperation."

"Yes, but you have to take in the whole scope of war and what it does to people. You might be interested in some correspondence I've been reading lately between Albert Einstein, the famous scientist, and Sigmund Freud, the psychologist.

"Einstein developed many important theories for science, but he was very concerned about his work being used responsibly. He wrote to Freud in 1932, 'Is there any way of delivering mankind from the menace of war?' As a scientist, he felt at a loss to see into the 'dark places of human will and feeling' and wondered if Freud might have some insight.

"Freud pointed out Bolshevists in Russia tried to wipe out human aggression by satisfying their material needs and forcing equality. But he feels that didn't succeed, because they are busy making arms and fostering hatred of outsiders. I was most impressed when Freud announced he and Einstein were both pacifists, finding war 'utterly intolerable.' Einstein hoped perhaps two factors—man's cultural development and a well-founded dread of the form future wars will take—might put an end to war."[15]

"I can't argue with that, Charlie," Herb declared, "but still, we can't sit around urging the Nazis to divert their aggressive tendencies into something better."

"We could suggest all those Aryans do some gospel singing and hand-clapping at our Negro churches," Charlie teased.

"Or how about training in ballet instead of firearms." Herb laughed. They loved to dig at each other's differences in views.

Charlie and Marian made small talk awhile with Mina and Herb and then left.

"I like your mother, Charlie, but she seemed a little reserved toward me," Marian said.

"Don't worry, that'll change. She's just partial to all her boys and a little protective. She'll like you." He put his arm around her as they walked out to the car.

"I hope so."

Charlie Facing the Draft

After the declaration of war, in the new year young men flocked to military recruitment offices by the thousands, determined not to wait for their draft numbers to be called. But Charlie Walker continued teaching as his thoughts coalesced.

He published a twenty-three-page pamphlet about the size of an index card, typing a few copies up himself, and calling it, "The Position of a Pacifist." This was possibly to set his thoughts for the draft board. He explained that since the pacifist is in the minority, even rare, his position is often misunderstood. Rarely do people believe he has a well-thought-out philosophy or effective strategy.

He defined a pacifist as "one who recognizes the unity of the world-wide family and wishes to explore the possibilities of love for discovering truth, dispelling antagonisms, and reconciliating (sic) people. For him the supreme and only efficient strategy is to 'overcome evil with good.'" Charlie gave Jesus' life and death as the preeminent example of this.

He also said pacifists "would act as white corpuscles in our infected society, bringing to wounded parts, health and new life." And then, in a reflection of Aldous Huxley's book, *Ends and Means*, he continued, "It is in *method* that they are distinctive.... It is a mistake to believe that if your goal is noble enough and your intentions good enough, any means available may be used to attain that goal. Means determine ends ... and peace imposed by force is not peace but suppressed conflict. The vanquished bides his time until he can get revenge. 'As ye sow, in like manner shall ye reap.' Until we begin to make our means the real solution to problems ... we can never hope to build the Kingdom of God on earth."

Then Charlie stated, "War grows out of fear, economic exploitation, race antipathies, greed, armament races, discrimination and faith in violence.... The only sound way to eliminate war, therefore, is to eliminate the basic evils of the roots of the trouble."

He continued, "'Ye shall know the truth and the truth shall make you free' was Christ's only reference to freedom. Liberty must be practiced, not denied. There is not one outstanding critic of the Bible who denies that the life and teachings of Christ were anti-war. 'Love your enemies,' 'forgive seventy times seven,' 'render to Caesar the things that are Caesar's, and to God the things that are God's,' and many others point to the way of the Cross and of Love as the Supreme way to conquer evil."

Charlie went on to say that when men in wars pray for blessings on their side and victory over their enemies, they are reducing God to a mere tribal deity, not a Father of all men. "Christ's way [is] a renunciation of violence and hatred.... 'The meek inherit the earth' in a true sense. But it must not be cringing, groveling—only fearless and dynamic humility."

Charlie registered with Selective Service at the local draft board in Lancaster on February 16 and was classified 4-E, Conscientious Objector, as a Methodist. He had no trouble convincing the draft board he was sincere. He was aided by a church pamphlet, "The Case for Methodist Conscientious Objectors," which said war was a sin, as it was an "offense not only against man but against God." It detailed offenses such as slaughter of human beings (including women and children), lying propaganda, deliberate breeding of the spirit of hate, vast destruction of property, unsettling of the economic structure, putting in place of moral law the doctrine of military necessity and "distorting the religion of Jesus into a war god."

Charlie especially underlined, "One who takes the position of a conscientious objector does so believing that he is following truth and the best light which God has given him. He believes that, in the spirit of Christ, he has seen into the character of God. He therefore hates war and rejects it."[16]

Spring came, and Charlie busied himself teaching and coaching the Mount Joy High School baseball team. A winning team. Charlie encouraged the boys to aim for the playoffs. Coach Walker called his mother one Sunday and crowed, "Mother, our team is going to the county championship!" A week later he called and told her they had won. Ecstatic, he told her the details of the victory and added, "The school board contacted me and asked me to attend one of their meetings to receive an award. They gave me twenty-five dollars!" A proud Mina reminded him she had done some teaching, too, in her early years.

Things still looked grim overseas. After crippling the US fleet at Pearl Harbor, the Japanese made quick advances in the Pacific. Charlie's brother, Herb, a Navy pilot, had been deployed to Okinawa, and Charlie sincerely hoped Herb was well.

Germans and Italians were overtaking northern Africa and had a stranglehold on Mediterranean shipping. Nazis now used flying bombs or missiles, and British bombers had started night raids in Germany, using radar and sky flares to find targets. In May of 1942 the Allies' last stronghold in the Philippines, Corregidor Island, fell to the Japanese.

But in June, having broken the Japanese secret code, US forces dealt the Japanese their first serious blow—at the battle of Midway. Now US western shores had been made safe from Japanese naval planes. In August, the Allied landing at Guadalcanal in the South Pacific began a two-year struggle to reclaim the islands of the Pacific from the Japanese. On the other side of the globe, the Battle of Stalingrad began, as Germany continued its attack on Russia.

Young Pacifist Clarifies His Views

Charlie helped his father another summer measuring fields. On August 3, he stated on a Selective Service form that he would not accept assignment to a Civilian Public Service (CPS) camp. On September 3, Charlie went to his mother with papers in hand. "I've just been ordered to report to CPS Camp Number 29 in Lyndhurst, Virginia *on September 3*. How am I supposed to get there *today*? I'm really wondering if I should have registered at all."

"Charles, I think you should go to an attorney."

So Charlie explained his position to the attorney.

———

Again, Marian waited on her porch for Charlie. It had been a year since their Sandusky trip and now the country was at war. She heard a car slowing around the curve, so figured it was the man she loved. She jumped up to look, and sure enough Charlie's car came into view and pulled into the drive. By this time Charlie was becoming serious not only about his pacifist stand, but also about Marian.

They sat by the waterfall again. Its mist cooled their skin, while they talked loudly over the churning noise. "I told them I would not go to a CPS camp, but I'm not sure that's right anymore," Charlie confided.

He brought along a paper he had written, "On Pacifism," and showed it to her. "I explain three levels of pacifism. The first is the level of means and methods, or tactics for dealing with tension and conflict." He read, "Stated negatively, pacifism imposes limits beyond which ethical standards cannot be compromised…. Stated affirmatively, 'Love conquers all,' for it is the ultimate reality."

"Hmm. That sounds good, Charlie." She liked sitting close to him, talking of things about which he was passionate.

He looked at her. "Many nonpacifists go along with us on the primacy of love in all areas except the use of force." Then he described force as like a splint on a broken arm. "Applied either too tight or too loose, the splint will hinder more than help the healing process."

"I like that. An arm splint as a use of force, demonstrating it's only good or bad depending on how it's used."

Then Charlie described how the second level is a commitment to policy. "A pacifist policy is not to be thought of as an uncompromising commitment to ideal solutions. Every problem has its loose ends, its ambiguities, its inheritance of good and evil intermixed. As we cannot rely on tactics, neither can we rely on ideals." He continued, "Pacifism is the middle ground which begins with basic commitment but is still adaptable within limits."

"What's the third level on your list?"

"It's that pacifism is a spiritual discipline. Not so much with outer struggles, as in the first two, but what happens inwardly as we confront Him whose name is Love. You see, Marian, most of us live in a tepid middle world where good and evil either mean little to us, or aren't matters of great soul searching. But as we actively seek the good, the deadly power of evil, within as well as without, is more clearly revealed to us."

As they sat silently, sweet birds called in the trees.

He read again, "Our first response in the presence of God is repentance—for our addictions to pride and greed and prestige, and the subtle 'violence' we employ to hold on to them."

"Have you been finding things in yourself you would think of as evil, Charlie?"

"Oh, yes, I have my temptations, but as I say in the final paragraph, 'Our response finally is grateful service to all God has created.... We are members of one another, both in our goodness and our guilt. Life is a seamless garment which, if weak or torn at any point, is affected in its entirety. Thus, I find it impossible to abstract pacifism out of the total claims under which I try to live.'"[17]

"How would that translate into raising children, Charlie? How do you raise children properly if you're a pacifist?"

"The Quakers have always fostered nonviolent ways of raising children, and I think it would be an interesting challenge, don't you?"

"Well, I think six would be a nice number of children. What do you think of applying your ideals to them?"

"Six kids?!"

"Yes, Charlie, six sounds good to me."

"Holy cow! Six little pacifists?" And he burst into contagious laughter while they contemplated the future by the waterfall on Mill Creek.

Ends and Means

Early September found Charlie and Mina sitting on the screened porch at the Henderson Place, as people liked to do during hot weather in order to enjoy the fresh air. They watched traffic go by the William Penn Rock—Model Ts, carriages, coupes, Amish and Mennonite buggies and people on foot.

Mina told him Gap was excited about the war, despite the large number of Mennonite conscientious objectors in the area. With great patriotic spirit, crowds had lined up at the railroad tracks across the street from their houses, to wave at troops on the trains passing by.

"Well, I'm obviously not going to be on one of those trains," Charlie mused.

"Your brother Herb has already gone."

"I've become more convinced of the C.O. position the more I study pacifism," Charlie said. "Mother, I'd like to know if I could list you on Selective Service forms as 'the person as always knowing my whereabouts' in case I should refuse to go to CPS camp."

"Certainly, Charles."

"Right now, of course, I'm still teaching at Mount Joy, and my employer is the Mount Joy School District, but I'll let you know if anything changes."

"All right, I can do that. But are you doing all right? How is Marian taking all this?"

"She's fine with it, for which I'm very grateful."

"Your Father's not pleased, but that can't be helped."

Charlie turned to her with his quick grin. "Mother, I love Aldous Huxley's *Ends and Means*, written back in '37, during the decade of a great peace movement."[18] Their conversation halted as a train heading to Philadelphia came through town with its shrill whistle and metallic clash of wheels on rails.

"Charles, what did Huxley mean by 'ends and means'?"

"Well, he said the ends cannot justify the means, because the means you employ determine the *nature* of the ends you produce."[19]

They talked about the usual family topics and then Charlie departed, promising to keep her abreast of any news of his situation.

On September 13, Charles Coates Walker of Gap was reported delinquent for failure to report September 3 to CPS Camp No. 29. The FBI was notified. Charlie expected the authorities to find him any time. He never dodged the draft, always letting them know where to locate him. He felt at peace with his decision.

On September 14, 1942, Assistant US Attorney Edward A. Kallick authorized prosecution and charged Charlie with willfully failing and refusing to comply with an order of Local Draft Board No. 4 in Lancaster. That same day, a warrant was issued for Charlie, so authorities located him and took him calmly before a magistrate, US Commissioner Norman Griffin. At that time records described him as twenty-two years old, five feet nine inches, 137 pounds with brown hair, blue eyes and average build. They released him with an order to report to Civilian Public Service camp at Lyndhurst, Virginia, by September 19.

As Charlie's mind whirled with decisions to be made, he realized he wanted to get married and needed to have some income to support his new bride. In prison he would have no income, whereas CPS campers received a small amount of pay. So he decided to report to CPS Camp. Before he left, he gave Marian a beautiful silver basketball he had won at Elizabethtown. He was very proud of that prize. Now Marian knew she was engaged.

However, they kept it a secret.

On September 26, since Charlie had arrived at CPS Camp No. 29, the complaint against him was dismissed. The FBI ordered a file on Charlie on October 31, 1942, while he was in CPS Camp. It reflected basic details but since charges had been dropped, the case was closed.[20]

CPS Camp

Civilian Public Service Camps turned out to be a disappointment to many. After entertaining high hopes that they would be doing "work of national importance," conscientious objectors discovered it was not the case. Charlie performed inconsequential chores, such as clearing brush and planting trees. They would be told to move something one day, and the next day be told to move it all back. He had pride, however, in the fact that he helped build the Blue Ridge Parkway.

Stephen Cary, a Quaker who later became Charlie's friend, was in CPS four years, some of the time as a camp director, and described mistakes the leaders of the CPS Camp program made. They assumed that all C.O.s would be reasonably homogeneous—like the young Quakers, Mennonites and Brethren they had known in First Day School and Sunday School. Cary described CPS as "'a zoo,' with humanists, atheists, fundamentalists, evangelicals—even a fascist who didn't want to fight the Nazis."[21]

"Secondly, there was an assumption … that since we were all earnest young men, we would be prepared to work for nothing…. Regular servicemen who went to war were paid good wages, but the C.O.s received perhaps two dollars and fifty cents a month."[22]

Marian visited Charlie in Virginia several times. He had arranged for her to ride with relatives of one of his friends at the camp. On one of those weekend visits they were married in a simple ceremony at the CPS camp in Lyndhurst, Virginia. He was twenty-two and she twenty-one. Samuel Harley, a Brethren minister and head of the camp, performed the ceremony with his wife a witness. The starry-eyed couple wore their Sunday best—no tux or fancy gown, no best man, bridesmaids or pictures. She did not have a wedding ring, as Charlie was not big on jewelry. Weddings of this type, extremely small and private, were common at that time. With a war going on, a big wedding would have been unseemly, and to invite family would be a waste of gasoline, which was rationed. The lovers honeymooned in a nearby city for the weekend and very reluctantly parted ways when Charlie returned to camp, while she rode back to Lancaster.[23]

Another time Marian visited the camp, a few C.O. couples had walked into town to do a little shopping, and upon their evening return were accosted by some local men. From bushes in the dark, the men threw rocks at the young couples' legs and feet, yelling and calling them "conchies," a derogatory nickname for conscientious objectors. The C.O. group ran and no one had been hurt, but Marian felt her first taste of personal discrimination. "They actually threw rocks at us!" she exclaimed, her dignity ruffled.[24]

Beginning of the Civil Rights Movement

Charlie kept in contact with the Fellowship of Reconciliation and was on its mailing list, as it gave him needed encouragement while struggling with conditions at the camp. In February 1942, Charlie picked up his mail and found that month's issue of *Fellowship* included an article titled "The Race Logic of Pacifism" by a young black man, James Farmer. Working in Chicago, Farmer was new Race Relations Secretary of the FOR. Charlie read Farmer's article eagerly.

Farmer explained how current war media pushing "preservation of the

American Way of Life" and "national unity" had intensified racism and white dominance. "The past three years have witnessed an obvious rise in discrimination against minority races, accelerated by fear and hysteria, which are the inescapable bedfellows of war." He said Negroes had been awakening to an increasing interest in democracy and the American Way. They felt righteous indignation at mistreatment in Army camps, exclusion from the Navy, and discrimination in industry.

Farmer said it was time for racial brotherhood in America to come into being through urgently needed strategies such as had been used in the labor movement. He added this national campaign would seek to abolish discrimination, not make it more bearable.[25]

This was James Farmer's famous Brotherhood Mobilization Plan, a forerunner of the civil rights movement.

Charlie was impressed but did not know he and Farmer would become great friends one day.

Charlie kept in touch with his old roommate, Ern Lefever, who expressed concern about racial discrimination. Ern had returned to Elizabethtown and graduated in 1942. He later wrote about this period of his life:

> I enrolled in [the Church of the Brethren's Bethany Biblical Seminary in Chicago], September, 1942, nine months after Pearl Harbor. Pacifists couldn't do anything to keep America out of war, but we could do something about racial equality. I wrote, "Every tenth man in America is in chains. The tears of his oppression have watered our soil for more than three hundred years. The American Negro is still crying for equality and brotherhood."[26]
>
> Jim Farmer had done a brochure on Japanese-Americans, and I became intensely interested in that issue, too. In March 1942, I helped secure the release of the first Japanese-Americans from Manzanar Internment Camp in California.[27]

Announcing the News

It was near Christmas and Charlie had weekend leave from CPS Camp to go home. He intensely wanted to see Marian again. She had kept their marriage secret because she wanted to tell her parents with Charlie present.

It was cold and wintery when he drove to her parents' house and parked outside. The dark night concealed his arrival, so he sat in the car a few minutes, anxious at how they would take the news. Carefully trekking out back through deep snow, he looked up and saw Marian through the kitchen window. Intent on washing dishes, she had missed his approach.

A slight tap-tap on the window startled her and she looked sharply into the dark. Immediately, Charlie's inquiring face appeared on the other side of the glass. With great presence of mind, she mouthed, "Go to the back door," and reached for the hand towel. Quickly drying her soapy hands, she dashed to the door and invited Charlie in.

Taking him by the hand, she led him in to the living room where Raymond Groff was reading and Elsie sewing. With a joyous smile, Marian firmly announced, "Meet your new son-in-law!"

Momentary shock was replaced with laughter, congratulations and hand shaking. Marian knew they liked Charlie and would most likely approve. And they did. It was a lovely, happy time, as Marian described the details of their wedding and brief honeymoon. Her parents were gracious and pleased for her, as they discussed with Charlie the plans he had for their future. The couple could not live together yet, as CPS camps only housed men, but Marian could continue to visit him.

Charlie worked hard at camp so he could get an outside job. He applied for a parole position[28] at a mental hospital, and on December 28 transferred to Springfield State Hospital, as part of Camp No. 47 in Sykesville, Maryland. With so many men having been drafted, a severe shortage of health workers had caused a dire situation in all hospitals. The overworked staff happily welcomed conscientious objectors and their families at the mental health facility. Marian would be able to join her new husband in Maryland.

Charlie later wrote a poem, "Saga of a C.O." The first four verses read:

'Twas the third day of September
In the year of '42
When Uncle Samuel sent me
That fatal billet-doux.

Said He, "Down in Virginny
There's a mountain road to grade.
I cordially invite you
To this anti-war crusade."

Two months of zero weather
Were quite enough for me.
Thought I: "I'll marry Marian,
She'll make it hot for me."

We both went to the loony bin
The proper place for me:
To stay in CPS camp
Was crazy as could be.[29]

Sykesville, Maryland, 1943

A large institution, Springfield State Hospital, was bustling, busy and full of patients. It struggled to get and keep good employees, since higher-paying defense industries could siphon off more reliable help. Marian came to believe many were either unreliable or did not seem to care about the patients, whereas conscientious objectors became known for truly caring about the patients. Their commitment helped psychiatrists and nurses make patients' lives better.

"I'm so glad we'll get a room and our meals as well," Marian said as they settled in to his new job at the hospital.

"And I'll have a monthly stipend, so we won't be completely penniless," Charlie added. "It looks like I'll be an orderly, and you can work if you want to, but you don't have to."

"I want to work, Charlie. I couldn't stand sitting around doing nothing."

So Charlie emptied urinals and bedpans and moved patients around, while Marian gave baths, delivered meals and attempted recreational activities with patients. The couple worked from 7 a.m. to 7 p.m. with one hour off in the afternoon.[30]

One evening after a hard day, Charlie told Marian, "There's only one registered nurse at this hospital and she's director of the nurses. One doctor comes in once or twice a week to do operations. I hear the director is trying to decide whether or not to assist the doctor in the operating room, which takes her valuable time, or to train the C.O.'s wives to hand doctors the scalpels. How do you feel about that? Do you faint at the sight of blood?"

"Oh, I can stand to look at blood. I just don't want to eat it."

"Ha, ha. That's my vegetarian," Charlie chuckled.

"Most people here are nice," she murmured. "They say we are a cut above the help they usually get, but some of them are not welcoming. Recently I tried to join a gal in the dining room who works on my floor. She was sitting with a woman who wasn't one of the C.O. wives. This woman had just been served her meal, but when she saw me try to sit down she threw her plate down on the table and left!"

"That's too bad, Marian. I wish they understood our position better, instead of believing we're cowards. I'll keep typing up and handing out my treatises on what we stand for and why we're here."

"Thank you, Charlie! Oh, that reminds me, I heard today that you were coming down the hallway trundling your beloved, borrowed typewriter on its little table with wheels, when the typewriter fell off and broke!"

"You're right. Now I've got to fix it."

Marian found some Scotch tape and worked miracles on the hapless typewriter. That evening he again typed up what she jokingly called his "propaganda." After that, the staff took to calling him "Scotch Tape Charlie."

The head nurse *did* train CPS wives in operating room procedures, so Marian became involved in the O.R. and enjoyed the work. The wives did very well, the hospital was pleased and Marian and Charlie enjoyed the camaraderie among the CPS campers there. Marian netted seventy-five dollars a month for her work, while Charlie only received fifteen. But that went a long way in the 1940s.[31]

Elsewhere as the Allies gained ground, February 2, 1943 marked the surrender of the German army in Stalingrad, Russia, and the Nazis retreated toward Berlin.

In March 1943 one evening after a long day, Charlie had been pondering the plight of the mentally ill. He said to Marian at dinner, "Theoretical psychiatry is a study of types, but practical psychiatry is a study of individuals. Each one of these lunatics is a personality in his own right, interesting to anyone taking the trouble to investigate and observe."

"You've been investigating and observing, Charlie?"

"For instance, there's Jones, a short, blonde, curly-headed fellow who takes a lot of lickings in a day's time. Says he married Greta Garbo, and at various times, went with every movie star in the books. His two pet phrases are, 'You better behave now' and 'I'm no maniac.' Has various compulsions, like crawling under chairs. 'Where is Deanna Durbin? Where is Ginger Rogers?'"

Marian laughed, leaning back and rocking in her chair.

"Then there's Younger," Charlie continued, smiling. "Just a little squirt but he talks big. He is The Lord Himself, plus several other celestial personages. Since he created the universe, he can't see why he can't have all the desserts he wants."

"I can't even have all the dessert I want," Marian quipped.

"Then, there's Old Man Koontz, Another Lord. A most unsightly creature to be that Important Functionary. 'Oh, my God and forever more. Come on and come on oh, Toby, throw down another bale of hay. Oh, Lord, but I can't do that. And forever and ever, Amen.' He shrieks at the top of his voice the whole time we try to spoon-feed him."

On a roll now and pleased with himself that he was amusing his wife so, Charlie added, "We mustn't forget Mr. Rau, who really thinks old man Koontz is the Deity. He will never eat a meal till he first goes over to where 'The Lord' is mumbling some hocus-pocus plus some profanity, kneels down devoutly, and asks if he may have some food. Of course Koontz doesn't even know he's there. If he happens to say 'yes' during a fifteen-minute period of raving, Rau is satisfied, goes back and gobbles down the victuals."

Marian's eyes sparkled. "Charlie, you rascal! You've observed many Lordly characters, haven't you?"

"Yes, religious fanaticism is quite in evidence here."

After they both had a good laugh, Charlie became more serious. "All crazy people aren't so dumb, and not even so crazy. To understand all is to forgive all. Mercy is wider than justice. How much are we to blame for creating the impossible society that has really put two strikes on these people before they start? Seven out of thirteen hospital beds throughout the nation are occupied by mental patients. Even before the war, mental disorders were decidedly on the increase. Do you know, many of these patients talk like diplomats?"[32]

Even though Charlie found himself extremely frustrated with his role in the CPS system, he had pride in the fact that CPS men who had worked in mental hospitals became key in major mental health reforms after the war. As Steve Cary said, "The greatest contribution we made in that era was in the whole field of mental health. We revolutionized mental health care in this country. The basic organizations, which today are the watchdogs and the arbiters of health conditions, were founded by C.O. s in that era."[33]

One day Charlie received a letter in the mail from an Elizabethtown College classmate, Lowell Ridenbaugh, typed on US Army stationery.

Ridenbaugh congratulated Charlie upon having been "firmly yoked" (married) since he had last seen him. Charlie's friend now worked Fort Meade in X-ray. "How's married life agreeing with you?" he inquired. "From the outside looking in it's very appealing to me. But then again, all the love in the world won't stop a bullet inscribed with the letters L.R."[34]

Charlie had long discussions with Marian, worried that he had made the wrong choice by entering the CPS system in the first place. "Marian, even though the law recognizes that conscience exists, it still holds itself up as supreme; that no power is higher than the state. We CPS men are conscripts—so we must do some work for the State, if only to demonstrate the supremacy of the State. Since conscription is a central part of the war machinery, so as long as I stay here, I'm cooperating with the war machine. Looking at it a different way, if war is truly the only way we can defend our cherished values, and still men have to be conscripted to do it, then we are denying that men are capable of being members of a responsible democracy. The alternative is that otherwise, men cannot be persuaded to fight wars."[35]

"That's a good point, Charlie. In a democracy it should be voluntary."

"Even though this law was enacted through legitimate channels of government, to disobey it openly and willingly accept the penalties, doesn't seem to me to be anarchy. Former Chief Justice Hughes wasn't accused of anarchy when he declared from the bench of the Supreme Court, 'In the forum of conscience, duty to a moral power higher than the state has always been maintained.'"

"Yes, I've always thought of conscience as being a 'command of the highest order.'"

"I was encouraged that CPS might be able to achieve prestige and a reputation for unselfish service, something like what the Quakers have earned.... But unfortunately that hasn't been the case."[36] Charlie had hoped he'd be doing work similar to the reconstruction overseas American Friends Service Committee had done after World War I.

In an order to directors and assignees in CPS Camps dated March 31, 1943, the director of Selective Service, Major General Lewis Hershey, stated, "You are informed that assignees in Civilian Public Service Camps are at all times under the supervision and control of the Selective Service System until discharged therefrom, and their actions are subject to the control of the Headquarters." Hershey further forbade CPS men to attend an upcoming FOR Conference in Chicago.[37]

Charlie discovered that in 1789, when James Madison introduced in the House of Representatives his proposals for a Federal Bill of Rights, he declared, "The right of the people to keep and bear arms shall not be infringed ... but no person religiously scrupulous of bearing arms shall be compelled to render military service in person." The last clause survived two later committee drafts and was debated by Congress, but finally deleted.[38]

Charlie finally wrote a letter April 16 to a Selective Service official, saying he could not continue in CPS. Shortly after that, Marian made him aware that he was soon to be a father. This made him ecstatically happy, and he decided not to leave at that time.

———————

Back in Pennsylvania in Gap, Charlie's father Joe Walker sat in the barber's chair waiting for a shave, his face covered with hot towels. As he relaxed and started to fall asleep, he heard some men enter the shop. "Did you hear about that draft dodger, Joe Walker's boy?" one said.

Joe jerked awake.

"Yeah, I heard about that draft dodger, Charlie Walker. Isn't that terrible? He's staying at home preaching against the war while our boys are over fighting it. I just don't appreciate people who do that."

The barber came over and started to remove the towels. Joe sat up in his seat, a fearsome expression on his face. In surprise, the men who had been talking about Charlie stopped midsentence and stared. Wondering what he would do, the two men watched Joseph Walker get up from the chair, toss off the towels and slowly rise to his feet. The air became static with suspense.

But Joe's scowling expression changed to one of defeat. His shoulders drooped, and in shame and embarrassment, he slunk out of the barbershop and drove home.[39]

Pacifism Confronts a World at War

June 3, 1943, Charlie self-published a pamphlet called *Pacifism Confronts a World at War*. With a table of contents and selected headings, it was a well-thought-out, passionate treatise.

Charlie wrote of the brotherhood of man and the unity of the human family. He said war and peace are not entities in themselves; rather they are the by-products of society's habits. "War ... is the final flowering of many types of conflict, the open sore symptomatic of a diseased and weakened social organism, the overt manifestation of the conflicts underlying our institutions and imbedded in our attitudes at all times."

After talking of political and economic crises, he spoke of a psychological crisis. "Man has achieved unprecedented control over his environment, but in control over himself he has not progressed. Really, the more he advanced in material gain, the harder it became to keep an equally distinct grasp on his purposes and values. Further engrossment led him to believe that the material was all there was to life. The 'debunking' of religion was symptomatic of that outlook." Charlie wrote of a "disbalanced" advance in physics and *means* without a corresponding advance in psychology and *ends* toward which to direct those powers, so much so that man "has come to believe himself an absolute individual wandering in a meaningless universe with no sanction for morality or conduct."

Charlie did not believe that Darwin's view of life as a blind struggle against nature could explain all the facts. He argued, "Nor is man a fighting animal in the sense we usually hear it. If that were true, why conscription?"

Charlie proposed a plan that would come to fruition later in his life in two peace organizations he helped to found.[40] "Military authorities say it takes four years to make a good seasoned soldier. It will take no less time to train an effective non-violent resister ... to acquire power over ourselves equal to the power we have over our environment.... Then we must aim at group training in the technique of civil disobedience or non-violent noncooperation and combating injustice. As an alternative to a 'world peace force'... we would train a mobile force of the best-disciplined pacifists ... to operate where conflicts or friction exist, to act as a reconciler between the two factions, and to prevent the violence from achieving sufficient intensity to lead to open war."[41]

He wrote, "The comment of the Emperor Diocletian, as he watched a Christian conscientious objector being torn by lions in a Roman arena, has often faced the pacifist in various forms: [Diocletian said,] 'That youth refused the military path because his superstition commanded its followers to bind themselves not to resist evil. These pitiful wretches enjoy the peace and splendor of Rome, but will not lift a finger to protect or to extend either.' The empire of Diocletian crumbled, but the world has never been able to get its eyes off the man who set forth that 'superstition.'"

Charlie told of modern times when people fought nonviolently. "It is told that when the Germans invaded Poland, they tore down from the public square a picture of [US President Woodrow] Wilson. During the night it was replaced, and in the morning torn down again. For days this took place, since all these years the Polish people had saved these pictures. This incident symbolizes the hope that people have in the political and moral leadership of America."

Charlie continued, "To wait to witness for truth till the majority agrees with you is poverty of thought and morality.... Even in the midst of war we must not hesitate to point out an alternative, a better way. A whole new civilization must be built before we can banish war.... This will take a long time—centuries.... We must begin now to create the patterns, the techniques, and the spiritual stuff out of which peace can be built and earned and won.

"Pacifism confronts a world at war with a choice.... Our choice will determine whether we shall be only a pawn in the horrible game of chance which Mars plays on the board of the world, or whether we shall be masters of our future."[42]

New Baby, New Challenges

Charlie wanted Marian to remain at the hospital with him until his child was born. However, Springfield would not allow pregnant women to work at the facility because of potential injury from mental patients. So Marian moved to Baltimore where she found an apartment and worked at a W.T. Grant Co. variety store. Then Charlie's FOR connections hooked her up with Emily Simon, who worked for the Baltimore FOR and had set up the Baltimore Peace Center. Emily found Marian a live-in job taking care of two ladies who were bedridden, Margaret Wooden and her Aunt Annie. They lived near Reisterstown, Maryland, northwest of Baltimore.

When Marian went into labor in June, the husband of one of the ladies took Marian to the hospital and called Charlie at Springfield Hospital. Winifred Alice Walker was born at Johns Hopkins University Hospital in Baltimore. Charlie arrived the next day to see his new daughter. After that, he raced back and sent out letters to all the family. Marian and daughter had come through a breech birth fine, and the baby was beautiful. Charlie suggested the name Winifred, meaning "friend of peace," and Alice was a family name of Marian's. After two weeks in the hospital, a normal stay at that time, mother and daughter came home to Reisterstown. Marian now had to take care of "Winnie" as well as the two ladies.

In the mail came various presents of money in lieu of a baby shower. One evening, Marian made supper, while a visiting Charlie held the baby and sang to her. "Charlie, I've been thinking of buying new clothes for Winnie. Where is the money we got for her?"

"Oh, I bought a mimeograph machine with it," Charlie said absently, as he made the baby smile.

"What! A mimeograph machine? Well, I never!"

Marian's indignation did not faze Charlie, who went right on bouncing Winifred on his knee and cooing. The blonde, curly-headed baby giggled and seemed happy enough in the clothes she was wearing.[43]

Excited about being a new father, Charlie nevertheless became restless about his situation and more convinced he should leave CPS. If he did, he would not be a draft dodger, he explained to Marian. Draft dodgers hide from the law and evade arrest. He would tell the authorities about his stand and where he would be. He knew this would likely result in prison time, but he felt ready.[44]

Marian nursed the baby in a rocking chair, while they discussed the future and his disillusionment with the Selective Service System. "Marian, the cause of the Kingdom of God cannot be served by conscription. CPS is an attempt to create a limited freedom in a context of slavery. I do not favor a benevolent dictatorship even with a preacher at the head."

"You believe the plan never matched the reality?" Marian asked.

"Yes, the plan was to give us work that demonstrates the principle of the Second Mile, or voluntary suffering. We aren't suffering much, unless you consider that we're not paid. Now, working without pay is something I'm willing to do, but others feel forced to do it."

"You feel unless it's voluntary, it's not really service?"

"Right, it isn't. The ends we seek will be corrupted by our faulty means."

"Do you feel they're hiding you C.O.s away from public notice?"

"They're definitely keeping us out of circulation. And in most cases, the work doesn't take much courage, so we are kept on the defensive, justifying our 'privileged' position. Since the public doesn't realize this, they believe we have it easy. In effect, CPS is a sugar-coated internment camp. Let the government call it what it really is, a prison."[45]

"So you feel you might as well be in a real prison?"

"That's where it looks like I'm headed. It's a very big decision, Marian., But one thing that makes it easier is knowing you have a good situation, cooking and cleaning for these ladies. Many CPS husbands have to worry about not being able to provide for their wives."

Marian thought about how she was enjoying life, hectic as it was with a new baby and taking care of two disabled, elderly women. She was thankful, since many women throughout the world faced greater struggles than she.

"When do you think you'll leave CPS, Charlie?"

"I have a plan...."

On September 23, 1943, Charlie left CPS Camp No. 47 with two days' vacation plus two days' leave. He headed to Chicago for the forbidden FOR Conference September 25 and 26. Then he refused to return to CPS and moved to Baltimore to be near Marian. He started working at the Baltimore FOR, while he waited for the wheels of justice to catch up with him. He gave his address as the FOR at the Baltimore Peace Center and Emily Simon as the contact.[46]

On October 6 he wrote and mimeographed a statement, "On Leaving CPS," in which he detailed his basic reasons and added, "There are those who say that refusal to cooperate with CPS is not demonstrating the meaning of reconciliation. True, we can keep on amiable terms with someone by not mentioning our differences or by glossing over them, but that is not reconciliation. No lasting reconciliation can be built on anything except the truth. The process begins when the cards are on the table and all sham has been cast aside."

To the charge that in prison he would be doing "no good," he countered, "No doubt Jesus could have done 'some good' by avoiding the Cross and living till he was sixty-five or so, healing and helping people. Yet, did he not release the most powerful force in the world, the power of sacrificial love to overcome injustice and transform evil?"

That month special agents from the Federal Bureau of Investigation contacted him, and he accompanied them to their Baltimore Field Office where, on October 26, he gave the FBI the following statement, "This step has been willfully taken in full knowledge of possible consequences."

Charlie emphasized that the FOR conference had in no way influenced his decision to leave CPS, nor had any member of the FOR. Their doing so could be considered seditious. He told agents his statement "On Leaving CPS," for circulation among friends and acquaintances was not intended to incite any organized movement among Civilian Public Service enrollees to leave camp and that it had not had that effect. He insisted it was merely for the purpose of outlining to his friends why he had taken the step of leaving CPS. He said the decision was wholly his own and had been long considered.[47]

Charlie sent his statement to four CPS people and twelve to fifteen friends outside CPS. "We must not hesitate to cry out against injustice," he urged. "This must be done in clear conscience and without fear." He asked the FBI to consider the law in England, where all those unable to accept conscription receive absolute exemption from the law and are assigned to work of genuine need, such as with juvenile delinquents. "I would register for such an act," he declared.

The facts were to be presented in November to the United States Grand Jury for the District of Maryland.[48]

———————

"My relatives are coming!" Marian rushed into the apartment with a letter. "They don't think you should go to prison. They're coming down to talk you out of it."

"I wish them luck." Charlie grinned.

They came to the Wooden house in a black car from Lancaster. Marian's mother, Elsie, and her mother's sisters—Aunt Mary and Aunt Grace—and her mother's mother, Grandma Shank.[49] They wore their gray hair in buns at the backs of their heads, dresses that went to midcalf, and glasses for failing eyes. They sat around with cups of tea and talked with Marian and her husband. Mary and Elsie were upset Charlie was going to prison. It was a trauma to the family, they believed, for him to leave his wife to fend for herself.

"Are you upset that he'll be away from the baby?" Marian asked.

"No, it's just not the thing to do," Aunt Mary answered.

"It's a waste of time," Grandma added.

Their objections didn't hold much water for the young couple, but Charlie and Marian were polite and courteous. Charlie earnestly explained his position.

Then the ladies looked around at each other, as if to ask what the verdict was.

Aunt Grace spoke up in her inimitable bossy tone, "Now, I don't want to hear any more said about Charlie Walker. He doesn't drink, he doesn't swear and he doesn't smoke!"

And that was that.[50]

"Charlie, let me go with you to court!" Marian pleaded.

"No, this is something I need to do by myself."

"I promise I won't cry or embarrass you."

"It's not that. I just want to focus on the trial and not worry about anything else."

"Stubborn man!"[51]

On November 12, Charlie appeared in US District Court and pled guilty. He read a statement to the court defending his position. "I believe in the dignity and value of human personality; I believe in civil and religious liberty. 'Our fathers chained in prisons dark, were still in heart and conscience free.'[52] They not only enjoyed freedom; they earned it." And quoting Thoreau, "Under a government that imprisons any unjustly, the true place for a just man is also a prison."[53] Afterwards Charlie was sentenced to four years in prison, which is what he expected.

On November 17, 1943, Charles Coates Walker was delivered to the Federal Penitentiary in Petersburg, Virginia after a brief stay in the Baltimore jail.

On December 12, a letter was placed in Charlie's FBI file regarding "sedition." An investigation of this letter and situation was requested, but nothing further came of it.

Charlie wrote another verse to his poem about this era of his life:

If I'm to be a jailbird,

I prefer to take mine straight.

"Four Years," intoned His Highness,

"Till you can graduate."[54]

FOR and Beginnings of CORE

From September to mid-November 1943 while at the Fellowship of Reconciliation with Emily Simon, Charlie had access to information sent to FOR offices. He read about a new organization that FOR staffer James Farmer had formed in Chicago in June 1942, the Committee of Racial Equality. It was called CORE, because they believed they were attacking the problem of racial inequality at the core.

Earlier, in 1941, a group of six Christian pacifists with a high opinion of the direct-action techniques of union sit-down strikers,[55] all members of the FOR and many of them divinity students at the University of Chicago, had formed a Fellowship of Reconciliation Peace Team. Four of them, eventually founders of CORE, found themselves in the vanguard of the United States' changing mood toward racism. They were James Farmer, George Houser, Bernice Fisher, and Homer Jack.

Since they were experiencing little success in the peace field with a war going on, these young people received permission from national FOR to tentatively carry out a plan to try out aggressive Gandhian tactics in the field of race relations. Muste liked the plan and sent it to national council. James Farmer advocated making nonviolence and legal action "twin weapons." George Houser, a white cofounder of the group, advocated that discrimination "must be challenged directly without violence or hatred, but without compromise."[56]

In April 1942, CORE decided to challenge a skating rink open to "whites only," in defiance of state laws barring segregation. It named itself White City Roller Rink. First, a group of twelve whites went in with no trouble. This group put on their skates near the door to help the second group gain admittance. When a group of about the same size made up of both black and white persons attempted admittance, they were refused— told that White City was a private club which required membership cards. As planned, the first group inside pointed out they had gained admittance to the rink without membership cards. This defeated the owner's argument, and CORE took him and some employees to court. But Farmer astonished them, after having them arrested, by bailing them all out as a gesture of goodwill![57]

In the spring of 1942, Farmer, Houser, Fisher and Jack attended an FOR National Council meeting in Columbus, Ohio, to see if FOR wanted to take on CORE as its own national organization. It would use Gandhian principles of love and nonviolence and be based on Farmer's Brotherhood Mobilization Plan. Farmer wanted to include nonpacifists in an autonomous group that would use FOR cells as nuclei, and he expected it to be a mass movement within a decade. But CORE ran into FOR ideological arguments.

Farmer's account of the meeting in his autobiography went, "The debate went on for two hours until a woman blurted out, 'But James, your program causes conflict. We don't want conflict. We want peace and tranquility.' I could be silent no longer. I rose in indignation and quoted a modern theologian, Gregory Vlastos: 'He who preaches love in a society based upon injustice can purchase immunity from conflict only at the price of hypocrisy!....' A. J., sitting alone in the back of the room, arched his brows sharply and a smile slowly materialized under them.[58]

The FOR council decided not to *sponsor* CORE at that meeting, but did *endorse* it, authorizing Farmer on FOR time to make the Committee into an organization in Chicago based on his vision. FOR would decide later where they would go with it. In June, they chose the name Committee of Racial Equality and performed the first successful sit-ins at Chicago's Jack Spratt's Restaurant. The fall of 1942 saw FOR creating a Department of Race Relations under the direction of James Farmer and Bayard Rustin, Rustin working out of New York and Farmer out of Chicago.[59]

Charlie shared with Marian his findings. "This group of FOR people who started CORE is doing here in America what Gandhi is doing in India. Real direct-action projects based on nonviolence! Pacifists cannot stop this war but can work on injustice at home. They are eager to apply nonviolence to the whole race problem. And Bayard Rustin, remember that young Negro we met in Sandusky, Ohio? He's started weekend institutes on race relations and nonviolence."[60]

"Yes, I remember Bayard. It seems like the FOR is on the right track."

"It's something I'd love to be a part of, even if my situation is not conducive to it now."

Charlie later wrote, "It was in the staff of the Fellowship of Reconciliation ... that decisions were made which set the future course of nonviolent action to the field of racial justice.... It soon became clear that the FOR could not carry on this task alone. There were few Negroes who would take such a radical position, and some of them had little interest in a religious organization. Furthermore, there was a very small minority of religious pacifists who were constrained to involve themselves in this kind of activity. A new organization was formed in 1942 called the Committee of Racial Equality ... with a strategic commitment to nonviolent methods and discipline."[61]

The FOR sadly missed its chance. Later, when FOR would have happily taken it on, CORE wanted to keep its independence. In June 1943 about a year later, an official founding conference in Chicago formed a national organization, changing its name as it grew to Congress of Racial Equality. Although the leaders were pacifists, it was not a pacifist organization, but one based on commitment to nonviolence. A pacifist will not use violence at any time. However, a person committed to nonviolence will not resort to violence in any demonstration, but may defend himself and others in a personal situation. Nonviolence appealed to a much wider segment of Americans.

In the long run, CORE achieved much more fame and success than FOR, but FOR worked in tandem with CORE over a decade giving them vital funds, office space, supplies and technical support they could not have done without.[62] It was during the second half of the time frame when FOR gave CORE vital support, that Charlie headed up the Philadelphia FOR and its Middle Atlantic Region as Executive Secretary (1948 through the mid-1950s), working with Jim Farmer, his FOR counterpart in Chicago.

Prison Life

Charlie entered the penitentiary at Petersburg, Virginia, on November 17, 1943. Many people, when they hear the clang of a jail cell, are filled with remorse, but not so Charlie Walker.

"When I finally heard that jail door clang, it was a relief!" Charlie wrote later. "For months I had been debating with myself whether to become a non-cooperator, weighing conflicting and equally passionate arguments of valued friends…. Richard Gregg, author of *The Power of Nonviolence*, had told me in a crucial talk with him about it: 'Never, never get discouraged—and you will be mightily tempted. You will be doing one of the most valuable things in the world: getting people to think about important questions. Many will misunderstand, and you'll want to explain. But your actions will do the talking more than any of your best words.' Many a day and night those words rescued me from despondency."

Charlie described life in prison. "A major factor in doing time is simply temperament. It's tougher for some than others. I was discouraged at how many men could fit into a routine of eating, working, relaxing, fooling around, sleeping—especially sleeping—day or night, even with noise around. Some were restless, talkative, troubled and troublesome. That was true for the C.O.s as well as others. Finally, I realized that each copes in his own way."

126

How did Charlie cope?

A key word about prison is *resourcefulness*. One's imagination is either dulled or it becomes hyperactive. All those plans and plots to do this or that! It's a fine edge to travel. Without it, the depths beckon.

As a prisoner, I learned most vividly what Reinhold Niebuhr later put into epigram: "The difference between a little injustice, and a little more injustice, is tremendous." It's overwhelmingly true for all those who live, "on the margin," where life is dominated by the so-called "little things." A little more food, a little better food, the right medicine, or a guard a little less abusive today, a letter in the mail, sun not quite so hot, or frozen ground yielding today to the pick and crowbar.[63]

───────

Charlie's experience in prison changed him forever in that he developed a heart to improve the lot of prisoners and the conditions in which they existed. He said later: "There is an almost unbridgeable chasm psychologically between those who have been in prison and those who have not. Part of the reason is ... the fact of imprisonment itself and what this basic fact does to the attitude of the prisoner. It is not uncommon that on the way to prison, the convicted person is provided a meal from which his custodial guard pockets part of the allotment. This is an inauspicious beginning for his 'rehabilitation.'"[64]

Charlie quickly made friends, writing a booklet of limericks, "Cryme in Rhyme," with poems about his C.O. friends. The following poems are quoted in part. One was Ken Cuthbertson from Philadelphia, who clashed with the warden as many of them did, who appears to have been named Dave Nicholson (Dave and Nick in the poems). The limerick about Ken was titled, "When Ken was in the Can":

There was a young fellow from Philly:
In soc. he is really a ditty.
Though he pled with the judge,
The old boy wouldn't budge:
"You are going to jail, willy-nilly."

Now, Ken had some trouble with Dave;
He rather believed him a knave.
They would start in to chat;
At the drop of a hat,
One would bluster, the other would rave.

Another good friend was Doug Collins. His poem, "The Handsome Hero of Hatboro:"

> There was a young man they call Doug,
> Who was bit by a pacifist bug.
> For taking the pains
> Of using his brains,
> They gave him three years in the jug.

Bill Holderith's poem was entitled, "Genie's Little Genius," after his wife, Eugenia, or Genie:

> There was a young C.O. from Union,
> Said the neighbors, "The man's off his onion!
> His doctrine's heretic;
> On the body politic
> This fellow is simply a bunion."

> Now, Willie was loathe from the first
> To work, let old Nick do his worst.
> In a cell solitaire
> He sang songs proletaire,
> While Nicholson threatened and cursed.

> I doubt if Nick covets reunion
> With that little blonde fella from Union.
> When all is fini,
> It is likely that he
> Agrees with the neighbors' opinion!

And his best friend in the slammer, John Griffith, with the poem titled "#11998—Not Wanted!" The first stanza went:

> A Methodist fellow named Griff
> Had a date with the local sheriff.
> When Justice got whizzin',
> They clapped him in prison.
> Said he with a shrug, "What's the diff?"

"Griff" told Charlie the first jail where he was placed after being arrested, a county jail, had foot-long rats in it with no fear of humans. His supper consisted of seven slices of bread with a cup of stale syrup which he could not stomach. No mattress was provided for the cold steel bed he slept on, but, even so, bedbugs in the cracks ate his flesh till he was desperate. This jail had been condemned at the time. After he was transferred to a better jail, his father, a Methodist minister, bailed him out with $16,000, using funds provided by two courageous families from his church. They had put up their own homes to provide security for the bond. That was big money in 1942.

His father had pressed him to register to avoid prison, but he had refused. To add insult to injury, as soon as he had been arrested, the family of the girl he had planned to marry insisted she break it off. Because he could not persuade his son to register for the draft, the board of his father's church turned on him, told lies about him, and worked to have him ousted.

Charlie and John had a great time discussing anything and everything, even to the point of rousing the ire of the guards. One day as he and John worked on the farm crew, each used a five-gallon bucket full of fertilizer he scattered by hand in a long row across the field. The men normally talked freely with each other as they performed this task. The only taboo—criticizing the prison administration. But profanity and lewd jokes were certainly standard. John and Charlie found themselves in the middle of the line one day having an animated conversation, when the guard suddenly stopped the line, came over and, with profanity, told John to get himself over to the far end of the line.

"Why are you asking me to move?" John asked.

"I'm tired of hearing about poets, authors and all that g-d d--n draft-dodging crap."

John stood up straight. "I'm sorry, but I don't feel our conversation warrants that kind of behavior on your part, and I will not move to the end of the line."

The guard ordered them to finish the broadcasting, and when they reached the end of the field, the guard took John to the main office and charged him with insubordination. John spent about two weeks in the "hole"—solitary confinement—literally on bread and water. He later told Charlie he had been in a cell in the basement with no windows and no furniture. Food was passed through a small hole. No toilet existed, only a small round hole in the floor, a cold-water faucet and one small light bulb in a ten-foot ceiling. At night, he was given a filthy, urine-stinking mattress along with a dirty army blanket. His clothing consisted of a coverall and socks, no shoes. His daily food allotment was two slices of white bread only. Starvation rations. No reading material permitted, either.

"I know Gandhi instructed his followers to be model prisoners as part of their pacifist witness," John said, "but after this experience, I decided I could no longer function under the supervision of guards who were intent on humiliating me. My father visited me a few days after my time in the hole. He was angry and wanted to complain to the prison officials for my ghost-like appearance. But I told him I wanted to fight my own battle."

He nevertheless, worked to have John's situation improved by complaining to prison officials that the punishment for talking to another C.O. about pacifism was too severe. Because of these complaints and subsequent investigations, food allotments in solitary improved to a 1,500-calorie daily diet with vegetables and meat added.

John's father was transferred to a much smaller pastorate. Sadly, in May 1944 the Methodist Church rescinded its long-standing statement against war and its equally strong support of conscientious objection.[65]

"Hey, Dixie! How was the baseball game today?" The prisoners called Charlie Dixie, from his college nickname. John Griffith had hailed him one evening as they met to do some push-ups and chin-ups on a pole located on a large sign. There was no gym. Competing to see who could do the most was not only fun, it helped earn the respect and cool the tempers of inmates who loved to hate "draft dodgers."

"We won the game," Charlie grinned, knowing he still wielded the college talent that almost landed him a career in baseball.

"You're playing for the prison teams has developed admiration among the men around here. I, however, spend most of my time reading. By the way, how's Marian faring?"

"Good. Marian always sticks up for me and my C.O. stance. I'm lucky, because she believes any decisions I make should be based on my conscience, not her welfare. She says she knew going into the marriage that it was 'always part of the package.'"

"I admire that, Dixie. She's a spunky gal."[66]

"Yes, she is! That's my Marian!" Then they each challenged the other to twenty chin-ups and one hundred push-ups.

Charlie and John worked on the farm gang, which one day had the assignment of clearing land and cutting brush and trees to enlarge the cultivated land for the prison farm. It became dark for the time of day, and Charlie pointed to the sky, where a major storm developed in the distance.

"That's heading right toward us," Charlie warned the guard, named Williams. The rest of the men spoke in alarmed tones of impending rain, but Williams ignored them and insisted they continue to work. Finally, a torrent broke on the vulnerable men in the field, at which time Williams finally let them climb onto the back of a flat-bed truck.

"Why didn't that idiot just let us get out of the storm when we had the chance?" Charlie raved, as they endured a drenching, lightning-popping ride back to the prison barn. "Williams, of course, gets to drive back in an enclosed cab!"

"Charlie, you sure have a low level of tolerance for stupidity, don't you?" John chuckled. But Charlie didn't laugh.

That evening, John and Charlie played checkers in their "free time." Charlie was winning as he usually did, and took great pleasure in doing so.

"Charlie, your competitive streak has helped me improve my game considerably."

"You know, at least life here is predictable. At the CPS unit I was working at last year, as I took a schizophrenic patient for a walk, out of nowhere he knocked me down with a punch to the mouth. When I asked why he'd hit me, he said, 'No one calls me an S.O.B. and gets away with it!' Perhaps life is safer with hardened criminals than with mental patients." They both laughed.[67]

Griffith later went on a work strike, protesting the guards' treatment of the prisoners and protesting a prison project which made cargo nets for the Navy. John was transferred to the federal penitentiary in Ashland, Kentucky, where he continued on work strike.

The second stanza of Charlie's poem about Griff:

If they put me on work I dislike,
I'll simply go out on a strike.
Thus put on the spot,
Dave is sure to get hot,
So, off to Kentucky I'll hike.

When John Griffith arrived at the prison in Kentucky, he found Bayard Rustin, assigned to that prison for conscientious objection, languishing in solitary for some infraction of prison rules. John wrote later, "I was released 'unconditionally' from Ashland six months before I would have completed my thirty month sentence. Unconditionally means just that, no papers, no draft card, no promises, a free man. The guard who tried his best to intimidate me into signing 'conditional release papers' told me when he delivered me to the train with a ticket to South Carolina: 'Griffith, I hope I never see you again.'

"Later, after release from prison, I was arrested while hitchhiking for not having a draft card. I was held for several hours while the officers called Washington to find out what to do with me. That ended up with an officer taking me back to the highway and letting me continue my journey. That incident convinced me that someone in the Federal system didn't want me back in prison."[68]

Charlie did not exaggerate in his last stanza about Griffith:

No doubt it is hard to believe-O,
Six months ere his time came to leave-O,
So sore did he vex them,
Said they, "Gad, we'll fix him!"
So Long John was given the heave-O![69]

Charlie heard of other C.O. s in prison elsewhere taking part in strikes. For instance, at Danbury and Lewisburg prisons, C.O. s insisted that officials in the dining rooms allow blacks and whites to sit at an interracial table. The wardens refused, so strikers dug in their heels and hoped for a change of heart—or at least mind.[70]

Stoner's Restaurant Sit in

Ern Lefever corresponded with Charlie in prison, writing about what he was doing the previous year. "I drew up a manifesto on race, and came out in favor of getting rid of discrimination in the armed forces."[71]

Ern had been in Chicago at Bethany when CORE had its first national conference in June 1943. He had been one of the excited official founders of CORE at its three-day conference and thrilled to be part of its first official sit-in at Stoner's Restaurant, which took place on the second day of the conference.[72] "On June 6," he later wrote, "I was an eager participant in one of the first nonviolent civil rights demonstrations in the country.

> About forty people gathered on a Saturday afternoon at 3:00 p.m. for a first briefing. Then at 4:15 p.m., I joined them for a second meeting at a Negro church where they organized our approach by forming seven small groups, five all white and two mixed. Our target was Stoner's Restaurant, the only eating place in the Loop that refused to serve Negroes. I was excited, feeling I was on the "cutting edge of change."
> The strategy was planned and detailed in a mimeographed handout by a local planning committee. Our tactics were very clever and effective. Dressed for a "first-class" restaurant and observing good manners, we [groups of whites] entered at eight-minute intervals starting at 4:30 p.m. We were to try to sit in the front of the restaurant and avoid booths which could obstruct our view. We would attempt to spread out and cover as large an area as possible by 5:15 p.m., at which time the first interracial group would enter. The second would enter if there were any problem with the first mixed group. A signal would be given for us

to call attention to the groups not being served, if that turned out to be the case.

Our witness was peaceful, and we broke no law, and we acted only after a year of friendly but fruitless persuasion, including talks with Mr. Stoner and his Methodist pastor. We were determined we were going to be ladies and gentlemen. We were not going to talk loudly. We would not make any noise. We would not obstruct the sidewalks. The five white groups were seated immediately. The mixed groups stood waiting for more than an hour. We were all going to sit there until we all were served. Stoner was called to the restaurant. He never spent Saturdays there. In frustration he called the police. They came and promptly left saying, "We see no disturbance."

Eventually everyone was seated, but the blacks were served only empty grapefruit shells. All of us refused to eat until everyone was properly served. It was a genuine, Gandhian, peaceful demonstration. We sat in there for two hours, and finally we were all served! We broke into singing a Negro spiritual, and other patrons who had waited at their tables to see what the outcome would be, also joined in! And that was the end of that. It was a great feeling of exhilaration. I'm still proud that I was a member of that small advance party of victories to come.[73]

I would have loved being there, Charlie thought.

Ern added, "I joined CORE shortly after it was founded, here in Chicago, June 15, right after the Stoner Restaurant action. I am a part-time staffer for the FOR, working weekends in Indiana, while Farmer, Houser and Rustin are full time. The chief of these young staffers is John Swomley, and A. J. Muste is the father of us all, and I admire him greatly."[74]

Charlie kept reading of horrific things happening overseas in the war; nevertheless, the tide had turned. In April 1944 Mussolini's opposition captured him in Italy and executed him. On May 2 the German commander in chief for Italy surrendered, and the Italian campaign was over.

Charlie, severely limited in his correspondence, asked Marian to write to A. J. Muste, who was not on the prison's list of ten approved people. In April 1944 Marian received a letter from Muste saying, "I think it is safe to say that although the Historic Peace Churches may go on with the present CPS pattern, etc., for the duration of the war (if it does not last too long), they are most unlikely ever again to adopt a similar pattern in which the churches and pacifist organizations get tied up in the actual administration of conscription."[75]

Marian visited Charlie in prison every so often, bringing Charlie's mother, Mina, and Baby Winnie with her on the long train and bus ride from Baltimore. Because of gas rationing, travelers packed public transportation.

The prison was cold and gray. To visit loved ones, prisoners sat at cubby-holes fixed with grates to separate them from the public. Guards watched closely to see that no one passed anything—suspicious or not—in or out.

When she finally got to talk to Charlie she told him rather breathlessly, "To get to the prison we had to go through an army base, where they were shooting bullets! Scared the heck out of me!"

"Look at Winifred! She's growing so fast! You ladies are a sight for sore eyes! I'm so glad for the package you sent, but they took out some of the candy you sent me."

Mina filled Charlie in on the doings of his brothers and other family news. Her usual cheerful self, she told funny stories of the people in Gap and his friends from college. She also explained people's difficulties coping with rationing and higher taxes.

Marian had been feeding Winnie juice from a bottle to keep her quiet and at the same time listening to Mina, when all of a sudden they heard coughing. Winnie promptly threw up onto Marian's lap, which created a mess and a bit of chaos while the two women cleaned up.

Then Marian remembered something. "Charlie, I asked Muste about the books you requested, and I understand you're only allowed to have books sent to you if they are mailed from the publishers themselves. That's true of candy, too. It has to come from the manufacturer. I guess that's to prevent people smuggling weapons in, or something like that, but I think it's silly. They certainly don't have to worry about you pacifists on that. Oh, well, Muste sends his greetings to you and any other of his friends at Petersburg."[76]

"That's good of him. It's so nice to hear about folks on the outside." Charlie could not stop grinning.

Marian grinned back. "On May third, I inquired of the National Religious Service Board, like you asked, about what kind of work you might do if you got the parole you applied for.[77]

"Then a lady from the NRSB wrote back saying there are no restrictions on job, salary or location. You said you expect to get IV-F and she said under that classification you will either go to CPS or to detached service, which would likely be a mental hospital."

"We can hope for the best," Charlie smiled encouragingly. "Thank you for all you're doing for me." He looked longingly at Winnie. Growing up so fast. Eleven months old. Walking already! "Out of the ten people I chose to write to me, the more famous ones write the least. You're my best correspondent."

Her eyes shone with tears while she smiled for a moment. Then, remembering where they were, she sat up straight. "How are you doing here, Charlie? Okay?"

"Yes, better than okay. I'm working in the prison library where I get to read most of the time. And the prison baseball team is great! They appreciate having a good pitcher. I was mainly a catcher in college, but here I get to pitch. The food is good and federal prisons are mostly clean, as opposed to the dirty, vermin-infested county and city jails I encountered in Baltimore."

Charlie was suddenly thoughtful. "You know, Marian, the key to prison life is understanding behavior in extreme situations."

"Hmm, I guess you've seen a lot of extremes here."

"Yes and because the behaviors are extreme, it has enormous potential for good and evil. But the good doesn't come from the system; it comes from struggle, and from grace."[78] Staring into her lovely blue eyes he unconsciously reached for her hand, but was stopped by the grate.

When time was up they parted with longing, but with a feeling that life was all right, for the moment. Charlie felt better in his soul than he had in a long time.

Alexian Brothers Hospital

During World War II, over 70,000 Americans were conscientious objectors—25,000 filled noncombatant roles in the military, 27,000 failed their physical exam and were exempted, and 12,000 were assigned to CPS camps for alternative service. About 6,000 rejected the system altogether and ended up in prison. Walkouts from CPS, leading to imprisonment, began in 1942 and gathered momentum until the war's end.[79]

June 6, 1944 was D-Day in France, when Allied forces landed in Normandy, gave the Germans their first defeat in Western Europe, a crucial turning point, and waged an offensive war. On August 25, Paris was liberated, and a few days later so were Brussels and Antwerp.

After eight months at Petersburg, Charlie received his request for parole from prison, but did not get his first choice to work in a mental hospital. In August 1944 he was assigned parole to a general hospital, the

Alexian Brothers Hospital in Elizabeth, New Jersey, across the Hudson River from New York City. He would again be an orderly.

The next stanza in Charlie's "Saga of a C.O." read:

In eight months' time I climbed up
From prisoner's rank to admiral's
In charge of all the vessels—
The bedpans and the urinals.[80]

Now Charlie now could live with Marian and Winnie. "Charlie, I'm so relieved to be with you, again." Marian smiled broadly as they moved into the third floor of a decent apartment house in Elizabeth. "This is so roomy, and we even have two bedrooms!" The lady across the hall became a good friend and even babysat Winnie sometimes.

After a few months, just when Marian and baby were getting used to a routine, Charlie's father became too ill to work. Mina certainly would not take him in, and he was too feeble to live alone.

"Could we keep him for a while?" Charlie asked Marian.

"What's wrong with him that he cannot work anymore?"

"Hardening of the arteries, general failing of the systems and aging difficulties."

"I think we can. I'm staying at home anyway with Winnie. I can take care of one more. The Wooden ladies gave me experience with this kind of thing."

Joe Walker moved in. Marian was surprised he looked much the same as she remembered him—Lincoln-esque, only grayer. He only ate corn flakes but enjoyed going with her to an occasional movie.

Charlie's youngest brother, Bill, called and asked how their father's care and funeral expenses were to be paid for. Charlie answered that Joe had turned over all his finances to Charlie, so he'd be cared for and his expenses paid.

Joe soon became bedridden, and Marian nursed him attentively. He gave Marian the only thing of value he owned, an ancient property deed signed by William Penn, Quaker founder of Pennsylvania. It is believed to be the deed to the Penn Tract the Walker family had lived on for generations.[81]

"This is for you," he said, "for taking care of me."

Joseph Lewis Walker died of heart problems at the age of 69. He was buried near Gap at the Homeville Friends Meeting cemetery with his two children who had died young. Many years later Mina, who had never divorced him, was buried there, too.[82]

A Discipline for Peacemakers

In December, US Forces, although trapped in snow-filled Ardennes forests in France, the Battle of the Bulge, managed to hold, and with the help of US air power, crushed the final major German counter-offensive of the war. British and US armies crossed the Rhine River and advanced into Germany from the West, while Russian troops continued their dash to Berlin from the East.

In January 1945, Charlie wrote a paper, "A Discipline for Peacemakers," a well-thought-out treatise:

> It is not so discouraging to see how the evil prosper as it is to see how the good fail. Jesus is scarcely more popular today than he was with the Jews in his own day, if you measure popularity not by the nice things people say about him but the number of people who follow in his way. If Jesus would come preaching today, some of the churches would throw him out; others would say it is impossible to carry out his recipe under the present circumstances.
>
> The real difficulty in taking him seriously, I believe, isn't such problems as the virgin birth, the divine inspiration of the Bible, or miracles. The real trouble is this: is it possible for men to carry out what he taught, and if they did, could they be practical and—if I may be trite—realistic?
>
> Too often the church has been saying something like this: "Don't drink, don't gamble, don't commit adultery, don't steal illegally, and don't be dishonest (except in legitimate business deals)." But when it comes to such business issues as international relations, doing justice to the Negro, feeding the starving children of Europe, power politics and imperialism—well, that's different. You've got to be practical....
>
> Jesus taught simple truths: that the human family is one, that men should treat each other as brothers, that God is their Father. Not all Gentiles, or all Methodists, or all white men, but all men whatever the pigment of their skin, the language they speak, or the kinkiness of their hair. Despite all the sectarianism, few deny this is what he taught. But in a world of violence and aggression, exploitation, the Gestapo—can a person still remain loving, long-suffering, compassionate, forgiving? Can one afford not to?
>
> Whatever else Jesus was, he wasn't cruel. He didn't demand we make bricks without straw. Nor was he enunciating beautiful ideals of conduct to look at afar off but never attain.... Others dismiss his teaching as an opiate for the people, a drug to turn their attention away from the squalor and misery of their unhappy existence, a promise of "pie in the sky" instead of daily bread....

It seems to me Jesus told us, as accurately as would he a chemical formula, a way of living that can overcome the world, even a world of totalitarians. The reason there is so little evidence for believing this was stated by G.K. Chesterton; "Christianity has not been tried and found wanting, it has been found difficult and not tried." Again, we ask, why is it that the good so often fail, and in the year of our Lord 1945, the ideals of the Master still seem so pointless and futile and agonizingly unreal?

The peacemaker must do more than veto, however courageously. He must demonstrate convincingly that there is a power as real, as active, and as potent as weapons of destruction. For want of a better term, we call it spiritual power. That power lies at the heart of the universe. It remains for us to stop hindering it working within our lives. To become channels and instruments of that power for the healing of nations. But that won't just happen. It will require work, patience, faith, discipline.

We should like to be calm in crises, brave in danger, unaffected by insult, undisturbed by loss, indifferent to pain. Sometimes we wish we could be perfectly generous and truthful. We know that our health, our sleep, our reputation, our influence would improve if we were to make all our actions intentional and devoted.

None of us would expect someone to play the Moonlight Sonata without training and practice. Countless hours of training, detailed study, and persistence are required before the pianist can show others what Beethoven meant and felt in the Moonlight Sonata. Likewise, we should scarcely expect an untrained athlete to win the mile, an untrained surgeon to save a life, an undisciplined army to win a battle. Why should we expect undisciplined peacemakers to do much toward creating a peaceful world? Why should we expect undisciplined good to triumph over disciplined evil?

The aim of training is not to be mean to one's self nor to become a smoothly-running machine in which the springs of life have been dried up; its aim is to release energy. We want to learn how to carry out our intentions, and improve this situation where our acting badly makes a mockery of our excellent motives....

Is it possible—and are we willing—to be charged up with ... [a] dynamic will to fight the injustice, the entrenched evil, the strongholds of hate and bigotry and greed and pride that lie between us and a world of peace and freedom?

Peacemaking like charity, begins at home. For men who know no peace within will never build peace without.... Here are some suggestions I have found helpful, though they are greatly condensed. This is a sketchy and by no means perfect discipline, but I must hold to it except for a better one. [The following twelve points are edited by the author.]

1) **Be reconciled to one's biological heritage**. An unshapely nose, poor hearing, an ungainly figure have ruined many a life. Yet many handsome people have ugly personalities. Thus, accepting one's

biological bequest is a prime responsibility to maintain good health.

2) **Not a cringing but a proper humility**. The Beatitudes (which are really a summary of Jesus' rules for training) begin: 'Blessed are the poor in spirit.' Humility is the beginning of wisdom. One must indeed lose his life to find it.

3) **Voluntary simplicity**. Expensive clothes or furnishings set up barriers, and create envy and contention. We must practice brotherhood in economics, too. Muriel Lester goes so far as to say: "If I have more than I need while others are in want, I am stealing."

4) **Work with the disinherited**. This helps demonstrate one's sincerity and feeling of unity with the victims of injustice.

5) **Have respect for personality**. A person should be treated as a human being with an individual personality. Every life is of infinite worth, so this respect for personality will know no barriers.

6) **Control and outgrow fears**. Fear of the dark belongs to childhood; fear of losing standing to adolescence; fear of losing property to adulthood. Fear of ridicule and death to all stages. But it is profoundly true that perfect love casteth out all fear.

7. **The discipline of controlling anger**. This is exceedingly important and the distinctive mark of a Christian. It is a choice spirit that "delights to endure all things ... to outlive all wrath and contention, to weary out all exaltation and cruelty." As a mother bears the trouble and mischief of children because she is looking beyond their present acts to their future possibilities, so should we look at every person we meet; not so much for what they are, as for what they may become.

8) **Insisting on the truth as a habit**. The habit of truthfulness is one of the soundest roads to self-respect. Let us love the Lord our God with all our mind.

9) **Learning for a lifetime**. A book a week for twenty years is only a thousand books; there are millions of useful books. There are enough lies floating around already without our adding to them because of our own ignorance and misinformation.

10) **Maintain self-respect**. Money, social standing and education—these are not the standards we value as peacemakers. Our aim is to obey the laws of life. Without getting arrogant about it, we can realize we have our unique contribution to make, nor need we be ashamed to make it.

11) **Keep group loyalties expanding**. The practice of constantly reaching across barriers of color and nation helps tear down discrimination and exclusion; it strengthens our feeling of community with those who we are continually asked to despise or ignore.

12) **Maintain poise through daily worship**. To keep ourselves sensitive requires the daily exposure of our inmost selves to the Will of God. Complacency, fatigue, sloth, rationalization—all these prey on our faith and energy, like a grey cloud over the freshness of our vitality. "Blessed are the pure in heart, for they shall see God." We should try to balance imports and exports: opening ourselves to the power that is

ours if we obey the laws of life, and then expending it in service for those in need.

Each person must work out his own rules for training. The vision we have seen is the Kingdom of God on earth. It will come only when people no longer say, "I am a Christian," but, "I am a Christian, therefore—..." Such people, of course, will not be immune from suffering. But though they sow in tears, they will reap in joy. And millions of others, whose names will never be known, may better be able to turn their footsteps into the ways of peace, stumbling blindly through the shell-holes of the spirit, for their having shown them how.[83]

Final Years of World War II

In February 1945, an aging President Roosevelt made the trip to Yalta for a conference with Churchill and Stalin. By that time, Hitler's empire approached its doom. Paris and Rome had been freed, and the Allied armies had reached the German border. The Big Three heads of state in Yalta went over the problems of (1) the occupation and control of Germany, (2) the situations of liberated countries, (3) Soviet participation in the coming war with Japan, and (4) the establishment of a permanent organization for peace. Charlie was overjoyed at the proposals for a United Nations. Roosevelt addressed Congress March 1 and said, "We are not making the mistake of waiting until the end of the war to set up the machinery of peace."

Peace!

But the war was not over yet.

The Allies continued to close in on Berlin. On April 25, US and Soviet troops met on the banks of the Elbe, and in the same month Berlin fell. The United States continued to take island after island in the Pacific and in April the fighting reached Okinawa. Charlie's thoughts and prayers often went to his brother, Herb, in Okinawa. Roosevelt died suddenly in April, and Vice President Harry Truman succeeded him in carrying on the war. The Allies prepared to attack the Japanese Islands. They warned Japan it must give up the fight or face an unpleasant invasion of her home islands.

"Charlie, I have good news!" Marian and Charlie walked back from a movie, having left Winnie with a babysitter. "You are about to be a father again."

"That's wonderful! When?" He took her hand and squeezed it.

"November."

"Now, with two children, we'll need more room. Where we're staying is really too expensive for what I make. Do you want a girl or a boy this time?" Charlie put his arm around his wife.

"I think a boy would be nice. We're on our way to our six children, Charlie," she teased.

"If he's half as beautiful as Winifred, I'll be happy." He beamed.

"You're going to be changing a lot of diapers."

"You're right, Marian, but I've always declared I wanted to be an *agent of change!*" They moved to an apartment closer to the hospital, and Charlie saved money by walking to work.

The Allies continued to close in on Berlin, and in April the German capital fell to Soviet troops. The United States continued to take island after island in the Pacific. Hitler committed suicide, and on May 7, 1945, Hitler's successor commanded the German soldiers to lay down their arms. The next day in France, German delegates signed papers of unconditional surrender at General Dwight Eisenhower's headquarters in Reims.

In three and one-half years, from Pearl Harbor to V-J Day, the United States paid out nearly $300 billion on war. American deaths were almost 400,000, and if one adds the missing and wounded, the count surpasses one million. The twelve million men in the armed services during the war were seventy percent of the able-bodied men in the United States between eighteen and thirty-eight years old. On the positive side, the United States did not have to fight on her own soil.

America came out in good shape economically and made ready to convert war factories into civilian production and find jobs for returning soldiers. Europe was in need of aid in many devastated areas. Additionally, the United States needed to be ready to help settle European squabbles and point the way for restoring and keeping the peace.

Charlie had joined FOR earlier in the year and had been in touch with FOR leadership. George Houser, one of the founders of CORE, now worked at the Cleveland FOR. In addition to working for FOR, he had been chosen to fill the unsalaried, part-time position of executive secretary for CORE. Bayard Rustin was still in jail as a C.O., and Jim Farmer had resigned his job with FOR to become CORE's national chairman. Jim now lived in New York near the Walkers in Elizabeth, New Jersey. In October FOR formed a new Middle Atlantic Region based at its Philadelphia branch.

November arrived, and so did the new baby, Larry Charles Walker.

Marian preferred to give birth at a different hospital from the one where Charlie worked, so when she called Charlie at 5:15 that morning, saying it was "the real thing," he dashed home and called a taxi for them. "We were at the hospital by 7 o'clock," he reported in a letter to relatives and friends.

> The original plan was that I help Marian while away the time, but the nurse put her foot—size 8—down on the idea. I went back to the hospital, slept an hour, got a friend to waken me (our alarm clock is hors de combat since Winifred gave it a workout), and went to visit Marian at 10 o'clock. She seemed plucky enough. Left about 11:15 a.m., promising to come back "tonite."
>
> When I woke up, it was just about six o'clock in the evening. Gad, the population of Elizabeth could have doubled in that time! Rushing downstairs, I phoned and asked if there was anything new in the "Walker case." (I've been told I'm a case, at least.) The man said "Yes, she delivered."... No, they hadn't weighed the baby yet. Everything was OK.
>
> They said about four o'clock, the labor pains got down to serious business, and she was taken into the delivery room. Larry was born at 4:31 p.m., with the aid of a couple whiffs of ether. At seven, when I got there, Marian was restless, complaining of pains in her back and tummy. It is claimed there are more pains with the second baby. I comforted and cajoled, finally got her to relax a little. They were going to give her something to make her sleep, and I imagine the pains will have left to a great extent by this morning.
>
> I rushed home, mimeographed the announcements and was two hours late for work. Larry looks something like Winifred, but mostly like other babies. He cried a little, was behaving admirably. Old Man Walker[84]

When Marian saw Charlie's mimeographed letter she was not particularly pleased. "Why did you write such a crazy letter? Some people might think it's funny, but my folks would not appreciate the flippant tone. And I didn't take any ether!"

"Okay, I was just having a little fun and am so excited about the birth of our son!"

"You're just a little enthusiastic, aren't you?" She gave the infant to his father to hold and love.

"I want to thank you, Marian, for all you've done in these two and a half years." He smiled and rocked little Larry. "I feel I owe you a debt not just for two beautiful children, but also for supporting me in all the ups and downs I've gone through. If not for you, life would have been much harder."

"Why, thank you Charlie." Marian was truly touched.

Photographs

Joseph and Mina Coates Walker,
Charlie's parents as newlyweds

Charlie Walker, 2 ½ years old

Top (from left): Mai Coates Albright, Molly Kreider Coates (Grammy), Mildred
Coates Zimmerman, Joseph Walker, Rhea Albright. Bottom: Robert L. Coates (16,
Mina's brother), Charlie Walker (7) kneeling, Pearl Albright, Mina Coates Walker
holding Herb (2), at Walker farm

Little Marian Groff with mother, Elsie Groff, holding baby Mary

Marian Groff, high school photo East Lampeter, PA

Charlie high school photo, Salisbury High School, age 15, 1935

Walker brothers, Herb and Charlie in back, Bill in front

Charlie at bat for the Elizabethtown College Ghosts

Charlie, Elizabethtown College student

Charlie's Junior Class yearbook photo at Elizabethtown College, 1940

Marian's Freshman Class yearbook photo at Elizabethtown College, 1940

Elizabethtown Candles Club: Back row far left, Charlie Walker, Ern Lefever second from right; Front row far right, Bill Willoughby

Elizabethtown basketball team; Charlie in third row far right; Coach Ira Herr to his right; Curtis Day, bottom row extreme left

Charlie at CPS Camp, on left

Charlie and Marian, newlyweds, Virginia, 1942

Henderson Place in Gap, PA, Walker family residence

Newly married Marian and Charlie at Henderson Place

Joseph Walker with Bill, and Herb in uniform, 1943

Charlie and Marian with baby Winnie, 1943

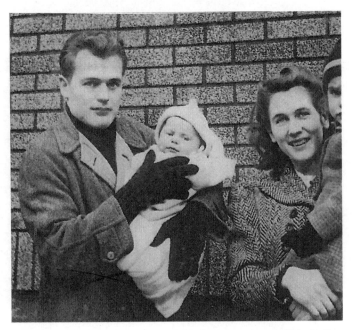

Charlie and Marian with Winnie and baby Larry (in middle), 1945

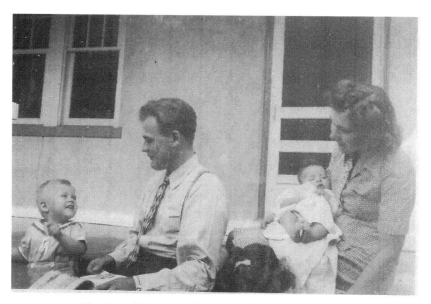

Charlie and Marian with Larry and baby Brenda, 1947

(From left) Brenda, Winnie and Larry Walker, 1948

(From left) Brenda, Allan and Winnie Walker, 1950

Baby Valerie, 1951

Valerie, baby Gloria, Brenda, 1954

Bill Walker, college graduation photo, 1948

Marian's parents Raymond and Elsie Groff, with Marian's sister, Mary, at her
college graduation

Walker, Coolidge and Dixon families, at work session of United Pacifists of West
Chester (PA) and Vicinity, 1948

Charlie Walker, late 40s or early 50s

Charlie playing piano, 1950s

Charlie Walker working for the Fellowship of Reconciliation, early 1950s

Lewis Walker family home, Rehobeth, at Valley Forge, since torn down

Charlie and Marian, 1950s

Larry Walker, helping at Grandma Mina Walker's gas station, mid-1950s

Charlie Walker as Mr. Average Citizen, radio show WCOJ

Working together in the FOR; Charlie Walker and Bayard Rustin in middle row, Charlie second from left (middle of picture), Bayard fourth from left. Clarence Pickett of the AFSC is in the bottom row, closest to the railing

Group photo of FOR staff, Rev. James Lawson and Charlie Walker in back row

Charlie Walker and A. J. Muste

Concord Friends Meeting, Concordville, PA

Chapter 4

Postwar Years, 1946-1948

It is my task ... to demonstrate convincingly, in life and actions, that [the] power of the spirit is real, that it is an alternative to violence, that it can work for the healing of nations.

–Charles C. Walker "Captive of the Spirit," article in *Motive* magazine,
January 1946

The Atlantic Charter in 1941 defined the United Nations as the kind of peace for which the Allies would strive. January 1, 1942 marked the signing of the Declaration of the United Nations by delegates from twenty-six countries, a pledge of partnership against vicious forces working to overpower the world. Unlike its desertion of the League of Nations twenty-five years prior, the US Senate approved overwhelmingly its pledge to support the United Nations in 1943. It then ratified the U.N. Charter in July of 1945. Not a world government, but a voluntary organization of independent countries jealous of their sovereign powers. Charlie Walker had pushed for this step and it brought him great hope.[1]

Captive of the Spirit

"Marian, come see my article in *Motive* magazine!" He hurried into the apartment to show his wife the article in the January issue of the Methodist youth magazine. "It's titled, 'Captive of the Spirit.' See, here it is!"

Marian put down her broom and grabbed the magazine. "And they printed your college picture with it. It's wonderful!"

He looked over her shoulder at the article and pointed to the text. "See, it starts with a quote from Plato: 'He who sees a vision of a better world becomes at that moment a citizen of that world.'

"Then, I wrote that the new universe then becomes the frame of reference against which all values are tested and a new dimension added to one's existence. It says, 'To the person who has not yet beheld this better world, the conduct of one who has, seems very puzzling at times.'"

He smiled as they sat down together. "How about reading the rest to me?"

She happily obliged in her clear, feminine voice. "'At a time when the relentless tide of totalitarianism threatens to engulf the whole world, *individuals* appear to be nothing. These vast forces seem impersonal and unfeeling. What folly it is, what madness to struggle against fate or inexorable trends or the wave of the future.

"'The Second World War (or rather, round two of the Twentieth Century War) has accelerated immensely the descent of civilization into … every conceivable savagery into which men are driven.… Now the United States and Russia are lining up for the *Battle of the Champs*. To mention in the same breath the relevance of love or brotherhood brings anything from a snort of derision to a wistful smile.'… "I think," Marian interrupted her reading, "I might have experienced more snorts than smiles."

Charlie glanced up. "You experienced them because of me." He grasped her hand, then let go.

She took the magazine in two hands and continued. "'However, is this the whole story? Men have almost universally believed that they were meant to be heirs to a better world. The stubborn optimism of the common man, in face of unremitting exploitation and suffering, is nothing short of remarkable.

"'Some force that is not violence … must transform our lives.… Atomic energy is not the only basic force in the universe. Behind the fuss and fanfare, the wars and rumors of wars, something incredibly real and active works silently, indefatigably. For those who have met its conditions, it is more than a belief; it is an experience. May it not be that this force, creeping in through the crannies of the world like so many soft rootlets, is the only power that can call us back from the abyss?'"

"That's the power of love, isn't it?" Marian added thoughtfully.

Charlie nodded. "Yes, it's the power of the love of God working in our lives."

She resumed reading. "'It is my task … to demonstrate convincingly, in life and actions, that this power of the spirit is real, that it is an alternative to violence, that it can work for the healing of nations.… *If one desires to paint a red picture, he must reject the green.* The pacifist says no to war because he has said yes to something else.'"

Marian paused to reflect. "I like that, Charlie. It's a more positive way to put it. You say no to one thing, because you have said yes to something greater."

"'To excuse the ineffectiveness of pacifists as peacemakers, we usually plead misunderstanding, or a prejudicial press, or the selfish desires of others to place security above all else. We are never given a chance to put our policies into practice. But there is one little acre where the field is wide open, and that is *ourselves*....'

"'Earlier I had worked in a mental hospital. Experiences with mental patients and with prisoners did not weaken my beliefs a mite. Those who respond ungratefully to love will react even more malevolently to violence. Only love holds the possibility of redemption.'

"I agree with that, Charlie, from my experiences with mental patients."

He smiled at her. "Yes, you've worked with them, too."

She continued reading. "'With the need so desperate, and the time so short, any selfishness, any sidetracking on our part which hinders the working of love in our lives is almost criminal. This, henceforth, is my dedication: *to live by virtue of that spirit that taketh away the occasion for war.* Nothing less is worth the effort. Nothing less can meet our needs.'"[2]

"Charlie, what's that reference to 'the spirit and how it relates to war'?"

"I was quoting the founder of Quakerism, George Fox, who said, when he was asked to explain his unwillingness to join the army, 'I told them ... that I lived in the virtue of that life and power that taketh away the occasion of all wars.'"[3]

"Going back to your Quaker roots, Charlie?"

"Yes, and it's an exciting adventure."

Ern Lefever had also published an article in *Motive*, featuring his work with the YMCA. His message:

> Although bread is absolutely essential in bringing order out of the chaos called Europe, there is something equally fundamental which Christian youth must share—*and that is faith.* As I traveled through Germany, Belgium, Denmark, Sweden, and Norway, I found the people enslaved by a fear of another and more horrible war.
>
> To these disillusioned masses of Europe, American Christianity must bring faith and courage.... And perhaps by blending our optimism and their pessimism, we can emerge with a Christian realism strong enough to command the loyalty of those groping for light. This means that Christian youth must come to Europe ... to enter into their sufferings, and to bring faith for a better tomorrow. *We need new missionaries for a new age—we need the best America can offer—we need Christian*

youth ribbed with steel.[4]

Graduate Studies, CORE'S difficulties

On August 2, Charlie received a letter from the National Service Board for Religious Objectors saying, in part, "We received your letter regarding a change in your present parole assignment. We shall be glad to present your case to the Department of Justice in the next few days.... As you point out in your letter, you are a father of two children and this would make you eligible for parole without restrictions."[5]

One afternoon, as Charlie emerged from sleep needed from working night shift, his children greeted him with shrieks of joy. It was playtime with Daddy! He threw Winnie into the air and caught her. As he bounced her on one knee and Larry on the other, Marian handed him a letter from New York University. He set the children down and tore open the letter, "Maybe I've been accepted for graduate studies!" Charlie had felt the need to better himself with a master's or doctorate degree. With a postgraduate degree, he believed he would be more valuable to the Peace Movement.

He *had* been accepted at NYU and began classes in sociology, taking the train across the Hudson and grabbing the subway to the city campus. With his usual straight As, Charlie and his work were well received. One professor, so impressed with Charlie, paid him to grade examinations and term papers.[6]

"Guess what, Marian, Bayard Rustin is out of prison, too, and in New York!" Charlie took off his coat and hat, shivering from the cold outside.

"Really!" With a baby on one hip Marian walked over and kissed him.

"Yes. Not only that, but George Houser, one of the founders of CORE, has moved here to join Rustin to become co-secretary of the FOR's Racial and Industrial Department. Part of his move was due to Houser's frustrations with CORE."

"It's too bad CORE's having problems."

The previous fall, after a year of inactivity, an African American schoolteacher, Gerald Bullock, had tried to get the Chicago CORE going again with less strict rules. But the Trotskyites Socialist Workers Party had taken over the group and chose to use almost no discipline in their demonstrations. The new group referred to their protests as joint CORE/Socialist Worker Party, or SWP projects. From Cleveland, Houser had warned Bullock that the SWP had no commitment to nonviolence since Trotskyites had subverted other organizations to put forth their own agendas.

Charlie continued, "In August the Chicago CORE meetings argued 'violence versus nonviolence,' with many of the five hundred dues-paying members scoffing at nonviolence. Even the newsletters, edited by a Trotskyite, advocated retaliatory violence and urged people to attend SWP rallies in lieu of canceled CORE meetings."

"Wasn't George able to do anything about that?" asked Marian.

"He wrote some letters as CORE executive secretary, but his hands were tied because local groups are very strong and independent. It made him realize, too, how weak the national office really is. Local chapters don't want to finance paid national staff or a national program, and this upset him. He wrote recently, 'There is practically no contact between the groups except as an occasional bulletin sent to chapter officers from the volunteer secretary.... Practically no financial support comes to the national office from the local groups. Last year this amounted to $113.'"[7]

"Only $113? That's nothing! No wonder he gave up."

"But he is nearby now, and the New York FOR will gain from his presence."

One day, Charlie took care of the children while Marian shopped. When she returned home and set the bag of groceries on the kitchen table, Charlie called out to her, "We have a visitor!" It was John Griffith, Charlie's friend from Petersburg prison, visiting from the Midwest.

"Pleased to meet you, Marian, and your two darling children," John said. "I finally get to meet the lady who was so supportive of Charlie in prison. I hear you're moving again, just as I managed to get here to see you!"

"Yes, Charlie will start a new job in Columbus, Ohio, with Ken Cuthbertson, one of the founders of CORE." She turned to Charlie, smiling. "Ken's from Petersburg, too."

"Yes, but I don't remember him," John commented. They sat down as Marian put on the tea kettle.

Charlie told John, "I had asked Ken to recommend me for a job as director of the American Friends Service Committee office in Columbus and he said he would. But instead, he got the job himself. He told me he felt like a 'gold-plated heel.' But he did recommend me for College Secretary—in charge of reaching out to college students with our message of peace and social concerns, recruiting them for summer projects, encouraging them to work for Quaker ideals—and I've been hired. Let bygones be bygones."

Marian smiled and set out tea cups and sugar.

Charlie showed John the small book of limericks he had written about his C.O. friends, "Cryme in Rhyme," and they chuckled over the one about John. Charlie then showed him his "Saga of a C.O." The final stanza referred to Charlie's new job in Columbus.

> Now I'm to work in colleges;
> I should object to these:
> In war they kill you quickly,
> While there it's by degrees.[8]

Move to Columbus, Ohio

Charlie started working for AFSC in Ohio, and Marian moved with the two children from northern New Jersey back to Pennsylvania with her parents, while Charlie looked for a place for the family to live in Columbus.

One day, Charlie called Marian on the phone. "Ken Cuthbertson is a great boss here at the Service Committee. Do you remember Ken and his wife Polly, early workers in CORE? Polly is now head of the YWCA at Ohio State University, while Cecil Thomas is head of the YMCA. The Quaker meeting out here is held at the YWCA, nothing fancy, but I have become a regular attender." Polly, Ken and Cecil became friends with the Walkers in Columbus and later in Pennsylvania.

On October 19, 1946, Charlie sent Marian a jumbo-sized post card. The front pictured a black-and-white aerial photo of Ohio State University, and printed on the back: "Culturally rich with more colleges and universities than any foreign country, Ohio has 48 colleges and universities. Largest of these is Ohio State with an enrollment of more than 15,000."

Charlie wrote on it, "I must try to curb my appetite, which has grown to very alarming proportions. I didn't get to see Winifred learn to walk, nor will I get to see Larry, apparently. I didn't realize what a dandy pun that last word would be [a-parent-ly]. The pants to the green suit are going to fall apart any day now…. I have your birthday present figured out already. You have two months in which to guess it wrong…. Predict Boston wins tomorrow, the third game [in the World Series]…. This setup is costing the best years of my wife."[9]

Charlie's graduate schooling at New York University lasted only one semester, due to Charlie's day job in the Midwest, so he spent more time studying at public libraries.

Late in the evening, Charlie sat in the Columbus Public Library surrounded by books on William Penn and Quaker history. Ever since he knew he'd be working for Quakers, he'd been studying the history of the Friends. He became impressed with Friends' influence on the founding of the United States and their reputation for being ahead of their time by two hundred to three hundred years. For example, from its founding in 1647, women enjoyed equality with their men.[10]

He went home and told Marian, "Just about all the leading suffragettes were Quakers. Four of the five women who called the first US convention on women's rights in 1848 at Seneca Falls, New York, were Quakers."

"Was Lucretia Mott one of them?" Marian asked.

"Yes, and Susan B. Anthony, another leading suffragette was a Quaker."

"I think I heard the name Alice Paul somewhere."

"Yes, another Quaker, she was a younger proponent of women getting the vote."

Charlie had discovered a local osteopath, Dr. Shearer, to be in need of a live-in housekeeper. His two small boys needed care because of an absent wife. So the Walker family moved in with the good doctor, and Marian took care of all four children.

"My wife will be here by Thanksgiving," the doctor told them. But she did not arrive then. The doctor assured them, "She'll be here by Christmas," but she was not home by then, either. Next, he was hoping she'd be home by Valentine's Day.

"He's running out of holidays," Charlie joked privately. Mrs. Shearer did not return, as long as the Walkers lived there.

Charlie wrote the following letter to President Harry Truman dated "29 November 1946,"

> It is becoming more of a rarity these days to see people acting on conscience, without regard to personal consequences to themselves. Conscience is one of the motivating forces we should prize the highest, even when it is mistaken.

For you at Christmas time to grant amnesty to the conscientious objectors in prison would be more than an act of magnanimity; what they and their families have to undergo for their beliefs involves more than "justice" need exact. We might do here what has already been done in enemy countries! I earnestly urge, with others of my friends, that you do grant amnesty to these men. It would be the kind of actions that may help rub the tarnish off some of our ideals of religious liberty.

Sincerely yours, Charles Walker.[11]

On December 23, 1946, President Truman did indeed pardon 1,523 young men who had been imprisoned as conscientious objectors during World War II. By Christmas, Charlie Walker was a free man.

New Year, New Challenges

Charlie wrote Ern Lefever on February 21, 1947, "I covet the day when we can sit down and have an old-fashioned session…. About the only significant change in my physical appearance has been the beginnings of that process known as balding: it's only a mild case." He said he still felt strong in the spirit. "We know that in our own lives, those in whom this spirit shone most clearly have been the ones who moved us most.

"I recently planned some events for Muste, who did his usual top-notch job. Tomorrow [John] Swomley is coming to one of my college conferences." The AFSC welcomed appearances from FOR leaders.

Charlie shared his concerns about the current college climate with his old roommate. "College kids are apathetic and frustrated. Having been fooled so many times, they are reluctant to jump on any bandwagon, because there is always someone waiting to call, 'Sucker!' The fact that I am an ex-con doesn't phase [sic] anyone…. I have covered about twenty-five colleges so far, and am gratified with progress. Agape, Charlie."[12]

AFSC's programs to feed the hungry impressed Charlie. He learned that during the winter of 1945-46, Quakers had made appeals to the US government to create funding to feed the starving people of Europe. Quoting "If Thine Enemy Hunger, Feed Him" from Romans 12, they urged, "Fellow Americans, in our efforts to feed the hungry in war-stricken lands, let us not neglect the German children and all those who have been our enemies. They also must live if there is to be a new birth of hope and peace among the people of Europe. Not that we suggest any preference for Germans; all hungry people must be given food. But let the distribution of our help be impartial, according to need, to friend and foe alike…."[13]

The AFSC started relief work in Finland and France, with former

President Herbert Hoover, a Quaker himself, helping in relief efforts to Finland.[14] Earlier, in 1946, President Truman had appointed Hoover to visit Germany to report on the food situation. Hoover had worked with the AFSC after WWI in popular relief efforts that helped make him President in 1929. In April of 1947, upon Hoover's initiative, forty thousand tons of American food was distributed to starving folks in Germany. Charlie enjoyed working for this humanitarian organization.

One day in late February, Marian needed to run errands, so she borrowed the Service Committee car. She had been having signs that she was pregnant again, but had not yet told Charlie. Morning sickness and dizziness were becoming acute, but she did not realize how bad it really had become ... until she blacked out while driving.

When she awoke, she lay on the street with a circle of people looking down at her. "It's Maxine! I know it's Maxine!" cried a woman somewhere outside the crowd. Marian knew she *wasn't* Maxine and told a kindly person who she was and how to contact her husband at the American Friends Service Committee.

At the hospital Marian shook with fear. Her thoughts raced inside her head. When the doctor entered the room, she urgently whispered, "I'm afraid I'm pregnant. Did I lose the baby? Was it hurt?"

He examined her thoroughly, all the while her fears jumping restlessly. He finally leaned toward her and gently said, "The baby is fine! But you broke your pelvis in three places and you will be bedridden for quite a while. And you will always walk with a limp."

"Darned if I'm going to have a limp the rest of my life!" she angrily told Charlie. "I will not!!"

The two Walker children, to their great pleasure, took a "vacation" with relatives in Pennsylvania, while Dr. Shearer managed to find a young woman recently estranged from her husband to help with the household. The Walkers learned she had nursing experience, a welcome situation, as health workers had become scarce after the war. So Winnie and Larry returned to Columbus, and this young woman took care of Marian, as well as all four youngsters (Shearers and Walkers).

All went well, until the nurse decided to go back with her husband. So Marian and the children went back east to her parents' home for special care. In Lancaster, her mother Elsie helped the young mother get back on her feet. Marian spent restful days in the backyard watching the waterfall. As soon as she could walk, she concentrated on not having a limp. She walked and walked, not favoring the weak leg and purposefully moved as naturally as she could. It worked! She got over the limp and eventually walked like nothing had happened. Marian was an extraordinarily determined person!

Journey of Reconciliation

As the weather became nicer, Charlie traveled more to colleges. One afternoon when he had some free time at a university, he called Marian in Lancaster to ask how she was doing. He was overjoyed to find she no longer limped.

"How's Winifred?" he asked. He knew the children played in the meadows and enjoyed smelling Grandma Groff's famous roses.

"Oh, she likes to spend time with the Amish children across the street. They play dolls in the corn crib and she comes back with corn silk in her hair and a big smile on her face."

"Wonderful! I'm hoping you come back soon and have the baby here."

Marian assured him she planned to do just that. They talked about family news, and then Charlie told her about a new development in CORE.

"Early this year, some members who were University of Chicago students, discouraged by Communists trying to take over Chicago CORE, left to form their own campus chapter, hoping the Trotskyites would lose interest. They did and left. But, unfortunately, energy for civil rights work has also dissipated. The chapter is even looking at disaffiliation."[15]

"Oh, dear," Marian said.

"But that's the bad news," Charlie hastened to add. "The good news is that the national office has decided to do something to revive interest in national CORE with a project called 'Journey of Reconciliation.' This will be a two-week trip in April to test the South's compliance with last year's Supreme Court decision against segregation."

"Negroes shouldn't have to sit in the back of interstate buses?" Marian asked.

"Yes, but bus companies have no intention of following that ruling, so CORE plans, along with the FOR, a two-week foray into states close to the Mason-Dixon Line. Racially mixed groups will sit in the fronts of the buses to test the ruling, so it could be dangerous. But they hope to get national attention, bring in enough money to hire an executive secretary, and fire up local groups."[16]

"That sounds exciting, Charlie. And it's certainly an opportunity for them to try out a nonviolent project on a bigger scale—to show that it can work!"

"That's absolutely right."

Marian and kids returned to Columbus later in the spring of 1947 and settled in to life there. Marian especially enjoyed a breakfast group with Fran and Cecil Thomas, Polly and Ken Cuthbertson, Lorena and Bill Blackburn, and other similar-thinking couples who planned and carried out local actions. Evenings were so busy, they met in the morning, bringing the children to play together.

One day a group discussion centered on the success of the Journey of Reconciliation. Ken and Charlie told of reading a letter from CORE, saying the Journey had been successful. Participants included Bayard Rustin, George Houser and another CORE founder, Homer Jack. The interracial group of sixteen traveled two weeks through four Southern states and made twenty-six tests of train and bus policies.

Charlie added it was significant no violence had been done to them on the buses. Passengers were courteous, and the group remained disciplined in a nonviolent, goodwill attitude.[17] The worst incident took place near Chapel Hill, North Carolina, where a white Presbyterian minister drove the group to his home one evening, followed by angry whites in two taxis armed with sticks and rocks. Arriving home, he received a phone call saying, "Get those d--n n-----s out of town or we'll burn your house down!" The mixed group left right away, taking back roads to Greensboro.[18]

Ken added that twelve out of the sixteen on the Journey had been arrested, mostly blacks, for refusing to move to the back of the bus, but also whites who insisted on sitting in the back. Two of those arrested received thirty-day sentences on a North Carolina road gang.

Bayard Rustin, unwilling to give up his seat at the front of the bus, went to jail. So CORE had called for funds for his defense and the others waiting for trial. Notables such as A. Philip Randolph and a young Hollywood star, John Raitt, backed the Journey of Reconciliation."[19] Raitt was the male lead actor and singer in the movie *Annie, Get Your Gun* and Broadway stage version of *Carousel*.[20]

Another Accident Wreaks Havoc with Family Life

Anticipating the arrival of a new baby, the Walkers decided to move from Dr. Shearer's house in Columbus to an apartment on High Street, with more room. Eight months pregnant, Marian felt big and cumbersome and did not like the idea of moving—especially in the July heat. She did not foresee how very difficult this move would be.

Forbidden to lift anything heavy, Marian supervised the moving and unpacking, while Charlie moved boxes upstairs to their third-floor apartment. They had just eaten lunch at a nearby restaurant and had returned to the process of moving. The children rushed about exploring the rooms.

"Where's my purse? I can't find it!" Marian suddenly said in alarm. Afraid she had left it at the restaurant, she began to search the apartment. Winnie climbed onto the sill of a large bedroom window—opened to air out the room—with a view of the alley below. A screen remained between her and the outside. Out of the corner of her eye, Marian saw the girl jump up and down on the window sill.

"Winnie, get down from there," she barked and continued looking for her purse, assuming the four-year-old had obeyed. Blond-headed Larry, almost two, looked over at his sister, wondering why she did not obey her mother. Instead, Winnie knelt down and continued to look at the alley through the screen.

Winnie had chatted to Larry earlier about laundry she had seen clipped to clothes lines attached to pulleys across the alleys. She seemed fascinated that people in cities hung up and took down wash by pulling lines in and out of their windows, so perhaps she watched a neighbor pull in her clothes. She leaned against the screen. Suddenly, the screen gave way, and Winnie toppled out.

Marian heard a noise and turned around just in time to see Winnie fly out the window. "Oh, Mommy!" she cried, and was gone.

In horror, Marian screamed to Charlie on the steps. "Winnie fell out the window! Get to the alley!" With a shocked yell, he headed downstairs immediately. Marian snatched up Larry, held him close to her huge tummy and ran down the many steps with boxes in the way, a flight or so behind Charlie. She reached the main floor, and, rushing out the back door to the alley, saw Charlie had found the unconscious child in the alley and picked her up from the asphalt.

Desperately the family ran out to the main street, where Charlie hailed a passing car to take them to the local hospital. The bumpy, lurching ride was unbearable, with the young couple wondering if their beautiful, vivacious daughter still lived. Upon arriving they were assured that she was indeed alive.

However, the full hospital had no rooms for new patients, so they placed little Winnie in a hallway on a mattress. Soon a doctor came to examine her. Worried about internal bleeding and punctures, Charlie winced as the doctor rolled Winnie over to check the extent of her injuries. But the final diagnosis was that she only had a broken hip, crushed ribs on one side, and a bad concussion.

The couple breathed a sigh of relief. "She'll live, then! She'll be okay!" Marian felt like crying. Charlie breathed a huge sigh of relief and gave thanks to God.

Next day, the headline in the local newspaper said, "Child is Hurt in 40-Foot Fall." In the first paragraph, it read, "Winifred Walker, 4, was in critical condition in University Hospital today. She fell 40 feet from a third-story window yesterday." The article said she had been playing in a third-floor bedroom in the Walker apartment, when a screen against which she leaned gave way. "The child struck the paved alley below. She has a possible fractured skull and internal injuries." A picture of a happy, grinning, blond, curly-haired Winifred Walker had been inset into the short article.[21]

Would she ever grin like that again?

Marian liked the doctor who treated Winnie for her injuries. He did the best he could and sent her home. "Do not let her walk for six weeks," he cautioned. He asked Marian what she'd be feeding her, and when the mom listed a vegetarian diet, he heartily approved.

"How am I going to keep Winnie from walking?" Marian wondered in frustration, as she and Charlie drove the tot home. Rounding a corner, she saw a small girl riding a tricycle on the sidewalk and had an idea. "That's it!" she cried, "We'll get her a tricycle!"

Marian called Dr. Shearer and told him about the accident. "If anyone can recover from this, it'll be Winnie," he said encouragingly. Marian's Aunt Mary came out to help, bringing a tricycle on the train with her! The child rode it everywhere. She thrived on her mother's vegetarian diet, and when Winnie arrived at the hospital for her six-week checkup, the doctor was impressed with her progress. "I could tell she hadn't been walking!" he crowed.

One of the first things Charlie did after the accident was to block that bedroom window with small boards. One could still look out the partially-blocked window, but it was now safe.

After all that, Marian found her purse in the apartment.

Arrival of a New Baby

In late August, Marian prepared to give birth to their third child. At the hospital, Marian labored in the heat while Charlie paced in the waiting room. In 1947 husbands were not allowed to take part in babies' births. The staff had been alerted to the fact that since Marian's pelvis was so newly-knitted, a C-section could be necessary. Happily, this was not the case. A nurse finally gave him the wonderful news and showed him in to see his new daughter.

"Charlie," Marian intoned weakly but rather indignantly, "my doctor decided to go golfing in the afternoon, since labor was going slowly. He went off and left me! He thought he had plenty of time, but I felt really uncomfortable. He got back around supper time, just in time for the baby to be born!"

They spent some days deciding a name, and finally narrowed it down to Wendy Irene (Irene being the Greek name for peace) and Brenda Irene. Wendy meant "wanderer" and Brenda meant "firebrand," almost opposites. The couple desired contemporary names for their children, not old-fashioned ones, thus Winifred,[22] Larry, not Lawrence, and no "juniors." The couple decided to ask relatives for advice.

When Charlie called Marian's parents, Elsie Groff was definite. "Brenda is a nice name." So Brenda it was. "Fire-Brand for Peace" seemed an appropriate name for a Baby Boomer, born in the large boom of babies after the war. Many Boomers had names meaning "peace" in them. Everybody wanted peace; they merely differed in how to go about it.

One of the students Charlie had counseled, a young lady who signed her letters simply Adrienne, from Detroit, wrote September 1 about war, peace and resisting conscription. She ended with, "I hope the father survived all right and don't forget, Charlie, I expect a cigar!"[23]

By September 8, Charlie answered Adrienne's questions, saying, "Now that the baby is here and things seem to be going according to plan, it's time to catch up on correspondence…. There are many heart-breaking arguments involved in deciding about going into the Army or resisting. Can a father leave his wife and children with no support by going to jail? What if his wife does not agree with his position—as some do not—and is humiliated by being associated with both a 'slacker' and a 'jailbird'? What about the person who trained many years for his vocation and then was faced with losing it because of a prison sentence? You see, there are difficult spots all along the line....

"The defense most people put up is selected to bolster an emotional opinion. A 'fact' means something only in a certain perspective. One thing religious pacifism has done for me is to afford a tool for insight. It is a core of belief around which knowledge can be integrated, in the light of which, more facts fit into place and fall into focus.

"Be assured, Adrienne, there is no easy answer to all of these problems, [but] if evil cannot be overcome by good, it cannot be overcome at all."[24]

At Work with AFSC in Columbus, Ohio

September 29, 1947, Charlie wrote to Molly Blackburn, daughter to Bill and Lorena of the Columbus breakfast group.

> Do you happen to have a generous supply of the milk of human kindness? Can you muster up enough forgiveness to include me? This is by way of apologizing abjectly for not having written to you before.
>
> Marian tells me you gave me the tennis racquet for a birthday present. Are there any strings attached? Of course, since I have the racquet now, I'm in a better position to say and the verdict is yes: The strings are attached and doing fine, thank you. I mean thank you very much for the present and the past, too. There doesn't seem to be any way of getting out of this paragraph. THANX!
>
> Listen, kiddo, watsa matter with Brenda as a name? If you had a girl of your own, wouldn't Brenda be the first name you would think of? I am unable to read Marian's scrawl, so am unable to identify the horrible nom de plume or something that you have suggested. We ruled Mary out as a name since there were already two Mari-es in the family. Or is it Marys or Mary's, or doesn't anybody give a hoot? When your hair is turned to silver, will they call you THE OLD GRAY MARY? Then you and Whinny [a pun on Winifred's nickname, Winnie] would make a team.
>
> I'm writing a popular song called, 'Who Buried the Electric Light Bulb?' or 'Mazda's in the Cold, Cold Ground.' [Mazda made light bulbs.] Do you think it will be popular?... At least it's an outlet for my

energies. Or should I have said energy—not plural? Switching back to this electric motif, wire you so unsympathetic to the idea? This is getting crazy, in other words, a loco motif. (I get this way sometimes.) She was an engineer's daughter, but Whoo! Whoo!

After more wild joke telling, Charlie calmed down and at the end of the letter penned, "It looks, from several clues, that Brenda is going to be more like Larry than like Winnie. Either way she won't be doing bad. My best to you. Sincerely, Charlie."[25]

––––––––––––

It was fall of '47 and Charlie sorted through the daily mail. With his ready grin, Charlie showed Ken Cuthbertson a booklet about American foreign policy. "The information I requested from the State Department came today! It's about peacemaking in Europe."

"Let me know what you find out." Ken pored over his own mail.

Later Charlie shared what he had read of increasing problems overseas. "Ken, the peace treaties have made little difference on the long road to peace. It's been over two years since the end of the war, and most of the world is still in a technical state of war with Germany and Japan. Added to that, Austria and Korea although liberated, are still under military occupation."[26]

"Not much of a postwar peace," Ken commented dryly.

"No." Charlie shook his head. "We have, as former Secretary of State Burns said, 'not the best which human wit could devise, but they are the best which human wit could get the four principal Allies to agree upon.'[27] The US wants demilitarization of Germany guaranteed, but Russia won't agree."

"Russia has done nothing but stalemate, hasn't it?"

"True. Each of the four powers occupies a zone in Germany. Basic democratic freedoms have been given to Germans in the American zone, and France and England seem willing to merge zones. But the Soviet Union won't allow democracy in its zone."[28]

"It looks like," Ken groaned, "we're headed to a divided Germany."

"Yes, it does." Charlie nodded sadly and went back to reading.

Peacemakers, William Penn

In 1947 Charlie became part of Peacemakers, based in New York City. They listed him on the executive committee along with Bayard Rustin and

A. J. Muste. Their flyer, "A Declaration to the American People," urged building of world community. In part, it said, "Every individual must find for himself the power to lead the life of nonviolence and brotherhood, even if it is necessary to stand alone against great social pressure. But association with others who seek the same kind of life, is the natural expression of the spirit of brotherhood."[29]

Charlie continued to study Quaker history and discovered William Penn had been involved in a legal case which affects our rights today. Back in England, young Penn, arrested only for preaching in the street, had been charged with inciting to riot and unlawful assembly. The jury refused twice when *ordered* to return with a guilty verdict. They were punished the first time with no food or heat and the second time with prison. After being released, *the jury filed suit against the recorder and mayor.* In a historic decision ending the practice of judges bullying jurors, Penn's jury won their case in the Court of Common Pleas and set a precedent that a "judge may try to open the eyes of the jurors, but not lead them by the nose."[30]

Penn was a fantastic visionary, Charlie thought, as he read Penn's "Plan of Union of the American Colonies," a forerunner of American government. *And, he said government must have its authority from the consent of the people!*

Penn suggested a remarkable plan for a European Union, "An Essay towards the Present and Future Peace of Europe." In it, Penn said a European parliament must be formed to decide disputes and enforce their decisions, and also use a secret ballot to prevent corruption.[31] Penn wrote this more than two hundred and fifty years before the United Nations formed and about three hundred years before the European Union came about.

Thomas Jefferson admired Penn, calling him "the first, either in ancient or modern times, who has laid the foundation of government in the pure and unadulterated principles of peace, of reason, and of right."[32] Young Charlie Walker hoped his life could help transform the world, as had William Penn's.

For William Penn, Pennsylvania was a "Holy Experiment" in seeing what God could do, what love could do. And Charlie believed he, as a United States citizen, was part of this ongoing Holy Experiment.

Planning AFSC Conferences

On October 14, 1947, Charlie wrote a letter to college campus leaders inviting them to a Spiritual Life Retreat sponsored by the AFSC, saying,

"Most campuses have too many organizations. Unless your campus is an exception, a few people often shoulder much of the work. Those who wish to bring into their work a spiritual depth seldom have the time to cultivate the spiritual resources they know they lack."

At the retreat, Eugene Exman, editor of religious books at Harper & Co., would talk on "Reality of the Spiritual World," and later about "Individual and Group Discipline"; Charles Walker would hold forth on the mechanics of a peace group; and Exman was to finish up with "An Inspirational Talk."[33] Charlie became a fast and lifetime friend with Exman, who had been head of a prayer group in New York City, of which Charlie was a member when the Walkers had lived nearby in New Jersey. Charlie and Exman worked together on various projects through the years.

Charlie also planned a workshop at an Ohio Methodist Student Conference held November 14–16 at Ohio Wesleyan University. Along with Herman Will of the Midwest Office of the AFSC in Chicago, he designed sessions on rehabilitating the world's countries in postwar conditions.

His background statistics cited a world survey which concluded, "Half of the world population is constantly hungry. Two-third is constantly undernourished, eighty-one percent have a real income per bread-winner of ten dollars a week, and fifty-three percent have less than four dollars a week." Another problem for the group to address would be … that the world's population doubled from 1850 to 1940, and each century seems to add another billion people.

Housing needs were urgent, as nearly all German cities were 40–80 percent destroyed. "Fribourg has two-and-one-half persons per room and is lucky. Kassel has six persons per room, including the kitchen." Many agencies tackled these problems: Church World Service, United Jewish Appeal, the AFSC, CARE and others. Other sources of order and hope were co-ops, trade unions, and churches. Clothing drives asked additionally for soap and medicine.

And people need political security. Charlie pointed out people need to be free from fears of war, the police state and imperialism. Lastly, he felt we must "rehabilitate the rest of the world physically—but we must be rehabilitated morally if we are to achieve the confidence of the rest of the world."[34]

Nobel Peace Prize

Charlie walked on air. The Quakers, with their service organizations, the AFSC and its British counterpart, had won the Nobel Peace Prize for their stellar work in helping feed the needy on both sides of the war. He rushed home with the November 1947 issue of the *North Central Area News*, published by the AFSC in Columbus. A copy of the cable which informed AFSC Chairman and cofounder Henry Cadbury of the prestigious award followed the headline "Service Committee Shares Nobel Award."

Charlie showed Marian the newsletter, "Clarence Pickett, the executive secretary, commented that the Nobel Committee, while making the award to the two Friends' service bodies, was in reality basing it on a three-hundred-year history of dedication on the part of many Friends and like-minded persons.... He went on to say "he felt the award was a hopeful omen in that it showed the Nobel Committee's desire to focus attention on the importance of concern for human beings as such, over and above political considerations."[35]

"Charlie, does this mean you won the Nobel Prize, too?"

"Marian, the Service Committee won the prize, but I guess everyone working for it helped win that prize." They smiled at each other. "Mine was a small role, but even so, it's exciting to be part of it!"

"Charlie, look, there's an article about you, right under the article about the Peace Prize!"

The article displayed his picture as a new hire, and announced he was to run the newly-organized college section of the American Friends Service Committee in the North Central region. "The area is most fortunate in having Charles Walker in this area as college secretary," it said.[36]

Charlie wrote later about the Quakers and their "kind of work which led to the Nobel Peace Prize in 1947: 'a service from the nameless to the nameless' as it was described in the award ceremony.... Early action in these emergencies enables Friends to call attention to situations requiring immediate and urgent response. To feed and help on both sides has been something Friends are especially known for."[37]

Home for the Holidays, 1947

For the Christmas holiday the Walkers traveled home to Pennsylvania. They stayed some of the time with Charlie's mother, Mina, but more with Marian's parents, since Raymond and Elsie had extra room. The young family had no automobile, so typically took the train from Columbus to Lancaster when they went east to visit. Larry, two, and Winnie, four, especially enjoyed Christmas with their grandparents.

The holiday over, the family boarded a train called "The Spirit of Saint Louis." It took that name because of its route from Philadelphia to St. Louis, Missouri. They found train car seats that faced each other so they could watch the children better, and Marian and Charlie could finally relax after the Christmas rush. They felt relieved not to have to change trains on the way to Columbus, since they now had a four-month-old baby to carry.

"I'm so glad we packed up our presents and mailed them home." Marian leaned back and checked on sleeping little Brenda.

"Certainly presents *plus luggage* would be too much for me to carry!"

"Oh, yes, but weren't my parents thrilled to meet Brenda?"

"They certainly were. We keep adding to the beautiful babies they can coo over."

Marian and Charlie chuckled and settled down for a nap, as the comforting motion of the swaying train and the clackety-clack of wheels on rails calmed the children to sleep.

Later, as they ate a meal they had brought with them, they looked nostalgically out at the lovely Pennsylvania countryside—looming Allegheny Mountains covered with fluffy snow. It was so beautiful compared with the flat lands of Ohio. They had both grown up in the Allegheny foothills, and it was hard to call the Midwest home.

"Marian, I thought you'd be interested in a story I heard at the office." Charlie spoke out of the mesmerizing quiet.

"Umm. What is it?" she murmured.

"I heard that Henry Cadbury was chosen to represent the Quakers and receive the Nobel Peace Prize, but, typical of most Quakers, he didn't have a long-tailed coat!"

Marian sat up to listen. "So, how did they outfit him?"

"Well, it was the beginning of December, and Henry knew the AFSC warehouse contained all sorts of clothing donated for the overseas poor. So he decided to go down there and see if he could find something his size. And, what do you know! The Budapest Symphony Orchestra had been in need of formal coats and tails for a concert in London, and the Service Committee had collected formal wear for them. A coat was found out of that! He borrowed it for the award ceremony in Sweden, and when he was done returned it to the warehouse! I bet the musician who later wore it had no idea his suit coat helped accept a Nobel Prize!"

Charlie's explosive laugh filled the train car and his eyebrows jumped up and down with glee, while Marian joined him with peals of laughter. She tried to picture the "borrowed," used, long-tailed jacket from a warehouse for the poor, worn for a highly-esteemed ceremony attended by leaders in expensive attire from all over the world!

Cadbury's acceptance speech had said in part: "The common people of all nations want peace. In the presence of great, impersonal force, they feel individually helpless to promote it. You [addressing the Nobel Prize Committee] are saying to them here today that common folk—not statesmen, nor generals, nor great men of affairs, but just simple, plain men and women like the few thousand Quakers and their friends—if they devote themselves to resolute insistence on goodwill in place of force ... can do something to build a better, peaceful world."[38]

Charlie added, "I think it's important that the Nobel Peace Prize recognized not just the two Friends' organizations for their work in feeding starving children and helping Europe rebuild, but they commended the excellent work of Quakers for three hundred years."

As Charlie became more impressed with the Quakers of his ancestry during his job in Columbus, he continued to devour the writings of the Fellowship of Reconciliation (FOR). Tossed into his box of papers were A. J. Muste's notes on an FOR national conference held in 1947. Muste wrote, "First of all, the Fellowship [of Reconciliation] is not located on earth at all, but in heaven, in God. Unless its idea, its message, its dynamic, have their source there, we are another purely human and secular organization."

Charlie liked Muste's uplifting words and style. "Secondly, the Fellowship is located within the human being, each of us, in so far as it exists at all. Thence ... the need of 'cultivating the inner life.' Need of humility, detachment from self, divesting oneself of every vestige of jealousy and subtle hate for others, self-discipline, simplicity of living, truthfulness, joy radiating on others, complete love for all whom we contact."[39] The FOR's challenge to live the deep spiritual life combined with committed, energetic activism spoke to Charlie. He could not help but feel called.

Understandably, Charlie became intrigued when he received a letter dated December 22 from his friend, Herman Will, saying he planned to resign from the Chicago FOR, and the Midwest Committee needed to find another Midwest Secretary.

"You have been suggested as a person who might be interested in this type of work and qualified to undertake the responsibilities of the position," Will wrote. "The Midwest Secretary of the Fellowship of Reconciliation has responsibility for the FOR work in twelve states." The list of states spanned from Ohio to the Dakotas. If he took the position, Charlie would have considerable latitude in planning his work and travel. The letter arrived at Charlie's office after Christmas, just as he felt a financial pinch for his growing family.

He talked the matter over with his wife. "Marian, what do you think of this job? There would be a raise in salary. I would be getting from $3,000 to $3,500, depending on the size of my family."

"Well, since we have just added a new baby, more money sure would come in handy," she offered tentatively. "Twelve states, Charlie! You'd have to work twelve states. It also says here, they want someone to commit for five years, and I already find it hard to be so far from family. Chicago is even farther than Columbus." As they talked and considered and weighed the pros and cons, it became clear that they really did not want to move to Chicago at that time. So Charlie got out his typewriter, set it on the kitchen table, and began typing his reply to the Chicago FOR.

When he was only half done, he decided to spend some time with Marian, as he'd be leaving the next day to work a student conference. He would not be home for New Year's Eve, so they decided to celebrate the ending of 1947 that night. "What a year!" he exclaimed as they sat down together.

"Yes," Marian agreed, smiling, "a baby girl born safely, a bad accident overcome, the Nobel Prize."

"Not only that, but the first ever black player made it into major league baseball," Charlie crowed.

"Yes, Jackie Robinson!" Marian chimed in, "and didn't he win Rookie of the Year?"

Charlie nodded. "And that four billion dollars Congress gave out in tax relief, should help our finances.

"What's more," Marian laughed, "Princess Elizabeth of England married Duke Phillip Mountbatten. I love weddings, and royal weddings are so special."

"Gandhi's work freed India from the British this year!"

"And proved that nonviolence does work!"

Charlie continued the trend, "The Marshall Plan is providing millions for relief for foreign nations to recover from the war. But on the down side, the first US ballistic missile was fired, the Atomic Energy Commission established, and now Truman wants to fight a new war."

Startled, Marian looked questioningly at her husband. "What new war, Charlie?"

"They think it may be a Third World War."

"Another World War?"

"Well, not fought with conventional weapons, but a war based on fear of that hideous nuclear bomb. We are already facing off with Russia in an armaments build-up. An 'Arms Race' they're starting to call it. Our politics in the next decades will probably be based on fear of being able to annihilate each other."

"Another World War. That sounds ominous," Marian sipped her tea thoughtfully. "An early Happy New Year anyway, Charlie, my dear." For the rest of the evening, they forgot the world situation, toasted each other, kissed, and laughed merrily before the clock struck midnight.

1948, Death of Gandhi

It was another new year, 1948, and Charlie carried out a resolution to write his college friend Ern Lefever, who was still out of the country. "Dear Ernie: There are three more in our family that you never saw. Brenda, the latest, is about four months old. Larry looks very much like me except that he's fatter. We can't figure out whom Brenda resembles. We are very fortunate indeed with the family we now have. None of them promises to be a moron, and all look as if they will be able to hold their own."

He told the story of Winnie's fall from the third-story window adding, "She seems to have recovered fully but for a slight slackening of vitality."

Charlie explained to Ern that, though he previously had worked as College Secretary under the AFSC's Peace Section, recent reorganization had him now working under a new Student Section. "This kind of work is just about perfect for me."

"Sometimes even those who are full-time religious workers ... are startled when they come across someone who takes God seriously," he continued. "On one occasion recently, a college YMCA worker wanted something to work out very much but was expressing doubts.... I remarked that we find things happening when we are less troubled about results as such, and that after all it is not we who work [but God working in us]. The guy stopped suddenly and actually flushed. Then he said, 'Of course, my religious background and my theology say I should believe the same, but I can never say it with the same certainty that the Quakers do.'"

A hopeful note finished the letter. "A new organization is being built up among students, on the basis of an interest in the race problem, that may grow into a liberal (in the better sense of that word) student organization, offsetting the much more conservative National Student Assembly....

"I have come to believe that ... the fastest way people grow is when they are confronted with a moral issue that has a personal implication. It is true there is a collective guilt, but when it is put on that basis, the reaction seldom goes beyond a feeling of discomfiture at the moment. As Muste put it, a moral decision is always a unilateral one."

Charlie added a P.S. about the pleasure it brought him to be asked by Elizabethtown College President A.C. Baugher to speak at chapel January 10. Marian attended, saying she wouldn't miss it for the world.[40]

———

On January 30, 1948 an assassin's bullet killed Mahatma Gandhi. What a blow to Charlie and all those men of peace who looked upon him as their leader and hero! Ern Lefever wrote in a letter a piece he called his "last rhapsody on Gandhi."

> Gandhi is dead! But even as the rose is made more fragrant in the crushing, so is a great soul made eternal by crucifixion. The death of the Mahatma, like the murder of Jesus, will immortalize the values for which he lived—values cast aside by our contemporary civilization—values which nevertheless will live forever.
>
> Gandhi showed that spiritual power was greater than the sword—that love was more powerful than hate—that the small quiet voice spoke more effectively than the proud utterings of the haughty. The world mourns Gandhi. The world worships Gandhi. But when will the world follow Gandhi?[41]

Charlie avidly studied Gandhi in the years to come, and became noted for his advancement of Gandhi's teachings on nonviolence and direct action.

———

On February 3, Charlie wrote John Ewbank at the Graduate School of Chemistry at Purdue University in Lafayette, Indiana, asking him if he knew of any foreign students who might be interested in the AFSC's International Service Seminars. These projects provided foreign students the opportunity to spend eight weeks in cooperative living and studying international relations and peace. Charlie said he'd be making a trip to Purdue February 11–13.[42] This would be Charlie's first contact with Ewbank, who became a fast friend after they later both moved east.

Charlie had another short trip planned. "Marian, I'll be gone April second through the fourth for a Peacemakers' conference in Chicago. It's called 'More Disciplined and Revolutionary Pacifist Activity.' I'm to help with some of the planning of it. A. J. Muste sent out a call to all Peacemakers to come to this conference. He says now that Gandhi is gone, it's even more important than ever that his work be carried forward, especially in the United States."

Marian finished changing a diaper and washed her hands. She came out drying them with a hand towel. "How does Muste feel pacifists can be more disciplined?"

"Well, he says Gandhi's death has created a situation where the idea of nonviolence has been brought to the attention of millions who may be ready to give it further consideration."

"They're going to discuss ways to further nonviolence in the US?"

"Yes, they are now seeing it as a spiritual philosophy of life and an effective social technique. They're also going to talk about equal opportunity for all people in the US regardless of race, religion, and national origin."

"We need to get people talking about that."

"Muste also suggests discussing disarmament. He thinks military appropriations could be diverted to developing atomic energy for peaceful purposes. He especially wants to stop the use of atomic and bacterial weapons."[43]

"Bacterial weapons?" Marian was aghast. "What're those?"

"Scientists are developing and putting into refrigerators terrible diseases to wipe out whole cities, and even countries, Marian. Unbelievable, that man could come to this!"

"Man's inhumanity to man," Marian said slowly. "How could our government be doing this?"

"Bacterial weaponry is something I'm going to stop, even if it takes my whole life to do it," Charlie pledged.

"There is No Way TO Peace—Peace IS The Way." These words titled A. J. Muste's Holy Week 1948 Message. Charlie had the start of a very good Muste writings collection. Muste had written, "The Way of the Cross is still the one true Way for men and nations. There is no magic road to peace, no carefully contrived vehicle to carry us to peace, no super weapon to blast the enemies of peace from the earth. Peace, which is God's gift, is itself the road on which we must walk. It is the vehicle to carry mankind to its God-appointed goal."[44] After reading it, and saying to himself, *I've got to keep this,* Charlie tossed the message into a pile of papers, including his personal letters, which he boxed up and carted along every place they moved.

Working for Peace in Columbus

On May 11, Charlie wrote his editor friend, Eugene Exman, in charge of religious books at Harper's. Charlie felt comfortable discussing religious topics with him. "You may be troubled, as I have been as I look back," Charlie pondered, "on the number of times I raise questions about the social and the eternal. It is not, I hope, that I doubt in the slightest the reality of the spiritual life and the entirety in which the world is in God's hands. We are vice-creators, however, and therefore have a terrible power in our hands every moment. My only worry … is that I may be using this power wrongly. There are surely many ways in which I should be witnessing to the truth, and failing."

Charlie defended his preoccupation with the temporal, believing it ties in with the eternal. He used students as an example. "One of the great hopes is in the Student Christian Movement, not in the organization, but in the dedicated souls who are in it. Those who dismiss the church out of hand for its ineptitude and downright perniciousness are not aware of the many, many times young people are brought to face moral questions, face them, and struggle with them together."

Charlie told Exman he had become particularly impressed with the story of the prophet Micaiah in 1 Kings 22. The wicked King Ahab, married to the scheming Jezebel, summoned Micaiah. The messenger told the prophet to agree with what the other prophets said, and promise victory in the upcoming battle. But Micaiah vowed he would only say what God told him to, the only prophet who predicted the battle would go badly for Ahab. "Of course, Micaiah was slapped, mocked and imprisoned for telling the truth," Charlie wrote. "The king died in battle, and we can only suppose the hapless Micaiah spent his remaining days languishing in prison." Since Charlie had spent time in prison, he felt a particular affinity with that long-ago prophet.

"I wonder," Charlie asked Exman, "how soon some of us may be called upon to be Micaiah's in the very near future?"[45]

Charlie rode home from work on the trolley. Early June in Columbus, the trees greened with tiny leaves and the streets smelled of spring. Not quite as wonderful as it would be in the country back home in Lancaster County, but still full of new life and hope. He felt happy in the city—where he wanted to be. It teemed with people doing important things. People he wished to reach with his message of good news!

Wearing a sport jacket he walked to his apartment building and sprang up the dark stairs to the small, but nice, place Marian had made into a home. He greeted Marian with a big smile and a hug. He had good news for her.

"Marian, here's a letter from Eugene Exman. You remember we had lunch with him in New York City?"

"Oh, yes, what does he say?"

"He says, 'You always give me such a lift with your letters. Few people have the ability to bring themselves so easily and well through letters as you do.'"

Charlie had expressed a concern that creative work could be used wrongly, so Charlie read aloud Exman's answer to Charlie's feelings about not being perfect enough to do the work God wanted him to do, "Of course, this is a fundamental question, and we must always keep it in mind. The only help I have ever found is to know that I cannot take myself too seriously; that I must try to bring everything I do into the bifocal direction of humility and charity.... Thanks also for having me read the story of Micaiah. I hadn't known it and it's a good one."[46]

"Charlie," declared Marian, "I agree with Eugene that you don't have to worry about your motives. I know you."

Charlie planned to attend the Peacemakers' conference in Chicago the weekend of July 31–August 1, 1948. This became the actual founding of the national pacifist organization of which Charlie later became national head.

Charlie left work early and just managed to catch Marian in front of their apartment, taking the children for a walk to the local park. He offered to push a cooing Brenda in the baby carriage. Marian took Winnie and Larry's hands and they headed off. Without Charlie, she'd have insisted Winnie hold onto the carriage and also Larry's hand.

"By the way, Marian, I'm looking into a job opening in Philadelphia with the Fellowship of Reconciliation. I'll be going east in September to see about it. Don't get your hopes up yet."

But she couldn't hide her happiness. Move home! Humming and smiling, she walked with a spring in her step the whole way home.

Charlie had officially become a member of a member of the Religious Society of Friends while he and his family attended Quaker Meeting in Columbus. He felt a particular significance in making this step in his spiritual journey. Sitting in the silence of the Quaker meeting for worship, he could see in his mind—Walkers renouncing their royal titles to become humble Friends of the Truth; Walkers sailing to the New World to seek freedom for their burgeoning sect; Walkers living on the one thousand acres Lewis Walker bought from William Penn and, to building a forge in the valley, called Walker and Sons, later known as Valley Forge; Walkers giving land or money to build new Quaker Meetings; Walkers distraught that Revolutionary War soldiers stayed on their property at Valley Forge; Walkers like his parents and grandparents farming on the Penn Tract in Gap.

Now, another Walker, he would take his Quaker heritage seriously, hoping to walk in the footsteps of his ancestors and be a leader in reconciliation—reconciliation between individuals and their consciences, reconciliation between factions all over the country and the world.

Chapter 5

Working for the FOR, MLK Encounter, Late 1940s

I think Muste is right in that the single, most-important political item now is the development, nurture and organization of a non-violent revolutionary movement in this country.

–Charles Walker, letter to Charles Parmer, November 1, 1949

In October 1948, the National Council of the Fellowship of Reconciliation decided to focus upon college students because of the declining membership in that part of the population. John Swomley of the National FOR staff began working with Charlie Walker, who had had had AFSC [American Friends Service Committee] experience working with students in Ohio and western Pennsylvania. Plans were made for expansion in the mid-Atlantic region to work with other student programs and conferences. Walker, based in the Philadelphia area, worked simultaneously with various other organizations and conferences, besides FOR and AFSC. Bayard Rustin, director of the national College Section, worked closely with Walker in student conferences.
—Swarthmore College Peace Collection[1]

FOR Region Secretary in Philadelphia, 1948

The Fellowship of Reconciliation, a Christian peace organization, seizing the opportunity to bring Charlie on board in Philadelphia, planned to use him not only as part-time Executive Secretary for Philadelphia and the Middle Atlantic Region, but also as their college representative in Ohio, Pennsylvania and New Jersey. Ideal for the position, he would be especially valuable to their organization because he was already familiar with these areas.

No one was more ecstatic than Charlie. His dream job! He'd be working with A. J. Muste, Bayard Rustin, James Farmer, George Houser and other leaders in the field of war resistance and nonviolent social change. Charlie could hardly wait to get started.

Because of his family needs, he told the FOR he needed to have some assurance no later than the first of September that an FOR job would be available. Rather than lose this opportunity, the national FOR staff invited him to work for them beginning in October through the end of the year, in the hope that an arrangement of joint financing and sponsorship might be worked out between National FOR and the Philadelphia FOR branch, beginning the first of 1949.[2]

The National Office of the FOR would pay one-third to one-half of Charlie's salary of $3,000 per year, and the Philadelphia branch would pay the rest, along with furnishing the office and providing secretarial help. He'd report to the National Committee, as well as a Philadelphia Executive Committee.[3]

John Swomley, who ran the Student Program of the National FOR, wrote to a colleague regarding hiring Charlie Walker, "We feel that one of our best ways of winning people to pacifism is to go after the young people in the colleges and seminaries, where many of them are already thinking about problems relating to war and peace. I imagine that you are just as happy as we, that plans are in the offing for a joint Philadelphia-Middle Atlantic Secretary."[4]

By himself Charlie went east in September 1948, to sign on with the FOR and look for housing, staying with Marian's parents. At the end of September Charlie returned to Columbus.

Charlie anticipated Marian and the children would move east in November, and the burgeoning family would stay with his mother, who had a room available, until a residence could be found to rent. Mina had sold the house in Gap and now lived in Exton in Chester County. They were so very happy. This was the first time since the couple had been married that they could live in Pennsylvania. Marian especially wanted to go back east. She'd go anywhere Charlie did, but felt glad to go home at last.

Charlie wrote in September from Marian's parents' place in Lancaster to a friend at the Columbus YMCA saying, "It is a pleasure to write this letter. Events have conspired to enable me to work in Ohio and Pennsylvania. My work will not change radically, except that membership problems will take the place of recruiting for summer projects."

He gave a schedule for his new job, dashing from one school to the next from October 1–14, with two days at each of eight Ohio colleges or universities—Ohio State, Ohio Wesleyan, Wilmington, Wilberforce, Antioch, Oberlin, Baldwin-Wallace and Wooster. Half of them showed split days in two different colleges. Charlie explained, "The duplication in days results from the fact that I like the plan of arriving at a school in the evening, about dinner time."[5]

In a memo dated September 24 Charlie asked Swomley: "Could you send me the names of persons for contact people at University of Pennsylvania, Temple, Swarthmore, Haverford, and Ursinus? Also, West Chester and Cheyney, if you deem it worthwhile."[6]

Charlie would work for the FOR in Ohio colleges for the month of October while he still lived in Ohio. In a memo sent a few days later, on September 28, Charlie wrote to Swomley, checking plans for the start of his new job and beginning a little apologetically, "Maybe one isn't supposed to send memoranda till he is officially in an organization." But Charlie was excited about upcoming FOR conferences in Ohio. He told Swomley he had recently met his son, Jim Swomley, while still working for the AFSC, "When up at Ohio Wesleyan, I met Jim. He is president of Wesley this year." He added, "I shall probably have to make the ultimate sacrifice and not see a World Series game, even though I shall probably be on top of it."[7] Cleveland beat Boston in the 1948 World Series.

On October 1, Charlie wrote to Swomley, that he had been told a young Negro, Jim Lawson, a student at Baldwin-Wallace, had joined the FOR at the Grand Rapids conference. He also wrote, "Gene Sharp, a good pal of mine, who joined the FOR at Grand Rapids also, has been made the national secretary of the national youth group for independent political action."[8]

Charlie wrote to Swomley at 3:15 in the morning on October 9 expressing frustrations. "The check still didn't come. I am a fiscal wreck.... I'll drop a note to the finance office.... Wrote to Hank Houser, George Houser's son, at Swarthmore some time ago about a visit to Swarthmore on the 19th and 20th. So far no reply. It is virtually impossible to plan an eastern itinerary when I don't know the situation."[9]

Around that time, Charlie marked some paragraphs from the Social Creed of the Methodist Church in 1948 from the Church's Discipline, distributed by its Commission on World Peace. Section 15 particularly interested him: "The methods of Jesus," the creed continued, "and the methods of war belong to different worlds. War is a crude and primitive force. It arouses passions which in the beginning may be unselfish and generous, but in the end war betrays those who trust in it. It offers no security that its decisions will be just and righteous. It leaves arrogance in the heart of the victor and resentment in the heart of the vanquished."[10]

Swomley wrote October 18 to Charlie, "Don't let the fact of non-religious pacifists at Oberlin keep you from forming an FOR group and keeping in touch with them. Of course, if they are anti-religious that might alter things. In any event, the FOR is broadly religious and there ought to be [groups] of those who would want that approach."[11]

November 1, Charlie's last day before moving from Columbus to Pennsylvania, he penned a letter to his former high school teacher, Charles Parmer, now teaching at State College, Pennsylvania. Parmer wished to start up an International Club and had asked if his former student could give him a list of needy people in Europe. Charlie first directed him to Ernie Lefever in New Haven, Connecticut. "My former roommate in college just returned from several years of work in Germany with prisoners of war. He has a list of many needy people, if the group you mentioned is interested in helping the Germans."

Charlie also provided names of organizations sending relief to Europe. "CARE is most popular. However, it is very slow in comparison to some other groups and the overhead is a bit high, too. SAFE (Save a Friend in Europe, Inc.) is much the fastest. They have a 21-lb. package for $10.... Unlike CARE they do operate in the Russian Zone of Germany. Packages have been known to arrive 12 days from the time of ordering. CARE averages about two months.

"The AFSC can buy in bulk and save tremendously ... works on only one basis: need. They most of all reach the people who have no friends, whose political beliefs may not be the currently popular ones to have. Clothing is much needed all the time. So are books! Oh, I forgot, the FOR has a list of pacifists in Europe who need help, particularly those who resisted the Nazis throughout."

Charlie continued:

> I think Muste is right in that the single, most-important political item now is the development, nurture and organization of a nonviolent revolutionary movement in this country, the country that in so many ways holds the keys to the power relationships in the world now. The Russian people are much less free to deal with their government or the issues, to put it mildly.... The basic analysis isn't new, but is very old. The real and basic difference is [people] only talked.... Isn't it a bit utopian to expect the bosses and the politicians, as well as the militarists who readily serve both, to do the repenting and the changing of the

system? Why should we expect those who profit from the system to change it?… If *persons* don't break out of the vicious circle, then of course nothing will happen, and before long there won't even be talk![12]

Move from Columbus

The Columbus apartment, a jumble of confusion, boxes of clothes, household items and books, was prepared for the Walkers' move. Charlie had rented a haul-it-yourself truck to transport the family and their goods to Pennsylvania.

"Charlie, do we have to bring all those papers along?" Marian complained. It was hard enough getting everything squeezed into one truck, but Charlie's collection recorded not only his life and work, but also a history of pacifism.

"Yes, that's my work, Marian. I guess you married me and my irritating boxes."

"I guess I did," she looked down. She then lifted her head, smiled and ordered. "Load 'em up! I'm just happy to be going back east again!" It was not first class, but Marian would have journeyed home in a freight box if necessary.

It was fall of 1948 when the Walker family moved to Pennsylvania. A few flaming leaves clung to the trees, rustling whispers of impending winter. Having found no place to rent yet, they lived in the small room at Mina's house in Exton, about thirty miles west of Philadelphia, so Charlie's mother could drive him to and from the Exton train station. Riding the train to work in Philadelphia was fine with Charlie. He also became quite adept at using public transportation to get around the city for his job.

Upon arrival in southeastern Pennsylvania, they stored their possessions at a place called Stagecoach Farms. Charlie's mother had seen an ad in the county newspaper for a barn with room for storage, located on Tanguy Road half way between Tanguy [13] Homesteads and the town of Cheyney.[14]

Tanguy Homesteads was an experimental, intentional interracial community in Delaware County founded largely by Quakers. Community members, after utilizing temporary housing in the old Tanguy farm buildings, were expected to buy a small plot of land on the former farm and build their own homes. Although Tanguy was intriguing, the Walkers did not feel financially prepared to build, so they continued to look for a place to rent in the area.

Move to Cheyney

Charlie soon wrote Swomley, "By some good fortune, we found a five-room house [in Cheyney] near Westtown School, for only forty dollars a month. It will be necessary to take a couple of days to complete the moving."[15]

The town of Cheyney's claim to fame was a college (originally called the Institute for Colored Youth) founded in Philadelphia in 1832 on a bequest from Quaker Richard Humphreys. He believed a school should offer African Americans instruction in various branches of mechanical arts and also train them as teachers. In1902, the Institute had moved to Cheyney.

The name of the institute changed several times over the years, but it was Cheyney State Teachers College at the time they moved there. It boasted a great basketball team and a beautiful quad made up of Pennsylvania fieldstone buildings. The biggest event each year had become a May Day celebration with a parade and festivities, including English-style dancing around colorful Maypoles.

The community of Cheyney sprawled around a small cluster of homes and businesses on Station Road, the center of which was a tiny post office facing the quaint train station on the railroad line from West Chester to Philadelphia. The Walker children enjoyed the general store across the street because of the penny candy inside the welcoming, white house with its long, front porch.

The East Branch of Chester Creek wound around the college and through a large field near the railroad tracks, while old, stone bridges hunched over lazy waters. Lazy except when floods from spring and summer rains spilled into neighboring swamps and lawns.

It was time for the Walkers to move. They had saved enough to purchase a used car, which would be needed for Marian to get around with three children and a new baby who would arrive in the summer.

The elderly owner of the property, Ada George, said she'd rent to the Walkers until she retired. The small house, which had three stories, was built onto a grassy hill on an acre of land situated down a long, wooded lane. The first floor contained a kitchen and dining room large enough for a play area and a bathroom with a furnace to heat the whole house. Inside steps to the second story led to a living room, but outdoor steps also provided a second entrance to the big living room. A third floor contained two bedrooms. Marian and Charlie liked the layout and workable rent, so they moved in. Even though rented, it was their first house!

They chose this location in Cheyney, partly because of its close proximity to the railroad station, and Charlie could get to work in Philadelphia by leaving the car at the train station. Since they were a one-car family, on days when Marian needed the car, he walked to catch the train, an easy five-minute stroll in good weather. Neighbors gave him a lift, when they saw him walking. Whenever Charlie needed the car for a long work-related trip, his mother came from Exton and drove Marian to the grocery store.

Charlie Settles in at FOR

John Swomley wrote a memo in early November to Charlie, George Houser and other FOR staff working with students. Houser, a white man who while working for the FOR had been one of the original founders of CORE, now worked at the New York FOR. Bayard Rustin had been put in charge of race relations, along with student outreach. Swomley urged them all to work on race relations issues with students. Houser was to arrange a conference in Michigan, and Charlie to organize one in Ohio or Pennsylvania, wherever he thought was best. Swomley said at least fifty students should be expected to attend and hopefully a larger attendance of one hundred to two hundred.

By November 20 Charlie had settled in at the Philadelphia Fellowship of Reconciliation office and wrote to his friend, Herman Will, at the Methodist Peace Commission in Chicago. "I am now working in the Middle Atlantic Region of the FOR. Although I am no longer a Methodist, I am more or less a fellow traveler of the Methodists, if officially a Quaker." Charlie signed it "Regional Secretary."[16] This was a role he held through the 1950s.

Charlie shivered inside his heavy wool coat and swayed with the movement of the train, as it maneuvered on its tracks around curves toward Philadelphia on his morning commute. It was late December, and the lovely countryside became whiter with snow and colder by the minute. More people filled the train the closer it came to Philly. He preferred train over bus, as the train stopped and started less and was not as crowded. It was more conducive to reading, and Charlie needed to use his travel time for reading and working. So he ignored the increasing number of passengers, as he read a reprint from the October 1948 issue of *Fellowship*, the FOR's monthly magazine.

The article, "We Tried the United Front" by Dorothy Detzer, described a congress of anti-fascist peace groups she had been trying to organize in 1934. There was her group—the Women's International League for Peace and Freedom, WILPF, or more commonly "the WIL"—and two other anti-fascist organizations, one of which was the Communist Party. "It seemed to me only intelligent for the WIL to join hands with all those forces marshaled against the banded power of war and fascism," she wrote. She called for a big congress of peace delegates to be held in Madison Square Garden in New York City.

By the time the huge meeting rolled around, Detzer already felt uneasy from boisterous planning meetings, which contrasted with the complete democracy and order of the WIL. "It was somewhat disconcerting to discover," she wrote, "that the Communists imagined that if five of them yelled louder than twenty other members of a subcommittee, the noise they made constituted an affirmative vote on a given question. Or that it was perfectly ethical to postpone a vote on a motion until most of the committee members present had to leave to catch trains."

She told how the leader of the Communist delegates became firmly opposed to permitting a certain trade union from being part of the congress and started a riot with rubber truncheons, clubs and fists to prevent it. It took Detzer at least an hour to stop the melee so the meeting could continue.

Charlie looked up from his reading to see the beautiful campus of the University of Pennsylvania slide past the window, then went back to his article.

"Our experience…," Detzer concluded, "taught me that there is no basis for cooperative ventures where there is no basis of moral integrity.… Trust and good faith are the necessary underpinnings of cooperation." The WIL gave up on the attempted alliance.[17]

Charlie considered the threat from Communists to be serious, as their philosophy of "disrupt and control" worked exactly opposite the religious pacifist view. His mood remained somber as he exited the train and headed to his office building, shielding his face from the wind and biting snow.

Charlie trudged up the gray stone steps of the former Victorian home at 2006 Walnut Street. The Women's International League for Peace and Freedom owned the building, known as Jane Addams House.[18] The WIL used the first and second floors and rented out the third to the Fellowship of Reconciliation and the Central Committee for Conscientious Objectors. The CCCO was a respected organization headed by George Willoughby, who had succeeded Arlo Tatum.[19] Charlie and George often worked together on mailings and other projects and held informal discussions on topics of interest.

In the vestibule, Charlie shook off his coat and hat. Glad to be inside and out of the cold, he headed up the steps directly in front of him. Reminiscent of more opulent times, a large wooden banister, curved at the foot, followed two long flights of stairs. At the second floor, dark-brown paneled hallways led to the WIL offices. Finally, at the third floor, he entered a bright level with cheerful offices and bustling activity. Charlie's office, along with other offices on the outside wall of the building, contained large windows that spilled light through rippled-glass partitions to a large room in the middle. This central room contained the secretaries' desks and several tables. A fireplace left over from a bygone era sat unused, as the building had been "modernized" with central heat. Charlie greeted everyone and settled in to work, planning trips, conferences, speeches, correspondence and projects.

Charlie had begun to feel comfortable with his job, throwing in some of his characteristic humor. A letter to his friend at the Columbus YMCA dated December 20 began, "I trust that the State Directors of Student Religious Work still meet with some degree of regularity. I would like to throw a conference in the pot which the FOR plans to hold the weekend of February 18–20. The scene of the crime will be Oberlin College. The speaker, we hope, will be Amiya Chakravarty, former close coworker with Gandhi and secretary to Tagore [the famous Indian poet]. I hope this does not conflict with any of the conferences you esteemed gentlemen may have up your sleeves."[20]

Charlie checked over a letter he'd written to Reverend Worth of the Gap Methodist Episcopal Church saying he had been disappointed not to be able to attend the church's seventy-fifth anniversary services, as he used to be a member there and was one-time president of the Methodist Youth League. Charlie detailed his background as a conscientious objector and said he hoped to return to the church and speak. He especially wanted the chance to set forth his beliefs to those around Gap who knew him. He added, "In conjunction with my work, it would probably be a wholesome stimulus for the Methodists there to hear the pacifist case stated."[21]

He wrote notes for a memo to Swomley. "Enclosed is a tentative prospectus of the Ohio conference, as I would like to see it develop.... In the opening address, it might set a good note for the conference if Amiya Chakravarty gave examples where non-violence worked: in Calcutta, in the Hindu-Muslim riots elsewhere, in the total political context, etc. That would serve several purposes: (1) inspire confidence in the power of non-violence, (2) avoid the argumentative tone one often encounters at the beginning, and (3) show how NVDA [nonviolent direct action] is a way for meeting personal, racial and national conflict, a way to peace, freedom and justice.... It's always a difficult business to keep a sizeable bulk of the students over thru Sunday morning. Consequently, I believe it would be well to have an attractive feature, such as a discussion of political action techniques."

Charlie eagerly looked forward to starting a new year working for the Fellowship of Reconciliation.

Marian tired of living on a shoestring. "What do you mean you told the FOR we don't need a bonus? They offered a fifty-dollar Christmas bonus, and you were too humble to take it?!"

"They *did* want us to have a bonus," Charlie replied sheepishly. "And I told them I didn't see how we could take it when impoverished people all over the world need it worse than we do. But they insisted I take it. They felt I was doing a good job and wasn't getting a great salary. So, here it is."

"Well, your wife accepts it," she admonished, "even if you don't!"

"All right," he sighed.

Marian bought a sorely needed vacuum cleaner for her new home, since she had been using her grandmother's ancient one. But she was still a little sore at Charlie.[22]

1949: Rifts, Struggles, and Success

Because of his experiences overseas and studies under Reinhold Niebuhr at Yale Divinity School, Ern Lefever had moved sharply from his strictly pacifist stance. This so distressed Charlie that he sent an impassioned letter to him over Christmas break. Ern shot back, obviously hurt and angry, declaring he had not done "an ideological about-face." He dated his reply January 1, 1949.

"One wonders whether one should start the new year by answering a letter which does not deserve it.... This matter of the lesser of two evils seems to disturb you unduly, even though everyone is constantly referring to this principle in his daily moral choices. Common sense demands that we use our heads.... The perfect alternative is usually a figment of the imagination. Bismarck said: 'Politics is the art of the possible.' Perhaps moral actions must take place in the arena of the possible? Ideal and utterly unrealistic moral decisions are probably neither moral nor decisions, but a form of evasion and escape."[23]

Charlie and Ern drifted apart ideologically, but never stopped being friends.

Interest increased for the February conference in Oberlin, Ohio. On January 4 Charlie wrote to Reed Smith, "I'm delighted to hear that it is possible for us to hold a conference there, and I am going ahead with plans." He talked about numbers of rooms needed and a midsized hall to be secured.

Charlie chose his words carefully, "At the last National Council meeting, some of the staff members discussed further the business of establishing local groups. It was finally agreed that, although it is very desirable to have a group in the name of the FOR whenever possible, it is not advisable to push the issue to the point of losing local effectiveness.... In my judgment it is a sign of organization maturity to be able to work functionally with organizations who are 'going my way,' even though one does not agree with all details."[24]

Charlie perhaps thought of Ern in showing flexibility with people and groups who did not see eye-to-eye with him. To Charlie's relief, Reed allayed any such worries about the Ohio group by replying, "I thought I had mentioned that we have gone ahead and taken steps to affiliate as a regular FOR chapter.... Faculty approval is now pending. If it doesn't come through by February 18, the Y will sponsor the conference here."[25]

Charlie worked closely with the YWCA (Young Women's Christian Association) in Ohio and Pennsylvania, because of their dedication to eliminate racism.[26] Marian later helped found a local YWCA, as part of the couple's commitment to bring the races together in harmonious activities.

On January 22 Charlie reported to his boss that he had already visited thirteen colleges in the new year, 1949. He added, "FOR groups are functioning at Penn State, Susquehanna, Bryn Mawr, Ohio State and Oberlin. At Bucknell a group is forming, and at Juniata, Bluffton and Wilmington, there are peace groups where FOR people are active in leadership."

On January 31 Swomley sent a memo to Charlie indicating Bayard Rustin would be in Ohio at the end of March per requests to speak at Baldwin-Wallace and Ohio University.[27] Charlie wrote back to Swomley on January 4, saying he thought the FOR should target Lincoln University, a college with a lot of potential for reaching black students with the nonviolence message. "Bayard visited the campus once before—a couple of years ago."

The student newspaper for Susquehanna University on February 8 carried an announcement on its front page that Charles Walker would be addressing the Student Christian Association February 15 as a representative of the Philadelphia Branch of the FOR. He would be "available on campus all day Tuesday to meet with any students who desire personal interviews."[28]

The February conference in Oberlin College, Charlie's first as an FOR staffer, was a resounding success. Although Reed Smith reported the college erroneously scheduled another peace conference that weekend, Charlie decided to hold the conference anyway. Called "Training for Campus Peace Action," its purpose was "to explore ways that nonviolent tactics have won freedom, peace and justice.... The heart of the program will be the workshops, which will emphasize know-how." Fifteen faculty and administration members' names from fifteen different colleges and universities in Ohio appeared on the conference brochure as lending moral support, including President Samuel Marble of Wilmington College.

Amiya Chakravarty of India spoke on "Gandhi as Peacemaker" and "Gandhi's Message to the West." Swomley spoke on "Militarism Confronts the College Student" and "Political Action Techniques." George Houser, third speaker for the conference, listed as Racial-Industrial Secretary of the FOR and one of the leaders and organizers of the dramatic Journey of Reconciliation, would work on the side as Executive Secretary of CORE. He spoke on "Racism on the Campus" and led a socio-drama.[29]

Charlie wrote of the conference, "We had a very good Student

Conference at Oberlin recently. It led me to believe there is more student interest in problems of peace and social justice than I had earlier thought. One of the speakers at the Oberlin Conference was Chakravarty. The crowning point of the Conference for me was his Sunday morning talk, where he showed it is impossible to divorce nonviolence as the method, from the philosophy from which it flows. He illustrated it from some of the remarkable ways Gandhi worked, amid the many tensions in India. I hope that American FOR members never lose sight of the distinctly spiritual nature of the movement, and that more steps are taken to re-examine the implications."[30]

Charlie felt flattered to receive a note dated March 9 from the Michigan FOR saying they were so impressed with Charlie's plan for the Oberlin program that they patterned their conference largely from his.[31] By then, Charlie had planned his next conference, this time for Pennsylvania students.

On March 22 Charlie wrote to Swomley, "It is now definite that Bayard will be our speaker on April 21 for our quarterly meeting.... He will stop on his way home." Bayard had just been released from the road gang he had been assigned to as a result of the Journey of Reconciliation.[32]

In April Charlie wrote to Emily Longstreth, an important Philadelphia Quaker and wife of Walter Longstreth. Walter had represented John Griffith at his CO trial. "We scheduled Bayard Rustin for the quarterly meeting quite deliberately. Because of the moribund state of affairs in the FOR, we wanted to bring a speaker who would be sure to get the people out. I am sure you appreciate how difficult it is to get Philadelphians to attend meetings. We do hope to make this a big meeting; however, we hope to do it under our own sponsorship, so that we can use it as a springboard for reorganizing our outlying groups. We have engaged a central city church to accommodate a larger crowd.

"After Bayard completes his description of India and the road gang, then I am going to ask him to close with a plea for organizing something like a Gandhian movement. If people in this vicinity realize that we do have plans for a more active program, it may be an encouragement for them.... I hope you can come and that you will urge as many people as possible to come." [33]

Charlie also began a program called the Noontime Pacifist Discussion Group at a Philadelphia restaurant. The first meeting scheduled A. J. Muste as speaker with about three dozen people attending, including Roy McCorkel, Red Schaal, Jim Bristol, Walter Longstreth, Ernest Kurkjian and George Walton. The next week Rustin spoke. The venture appeared to be a success.[34]

FOR Finances

Charlie mulled over the carbon copy of a letter to him and other Philadelphia staff that day from Swomley in New York about the FOR's financial situation. "We seem to have been hit," Swomley explained … "by a combination of continued inflation … and the beginning of recession, which is worrying some heavier contributors to the FOR. As a result, although our income has been about as good as last year, we have not increased it substantially as we had hoped."

Swomley urged Charlie and others to appeal for funds for the FOR's work in every meeting he addressed. And he wanted Rustin to make a financial appeal at the end of the quarterly meeting. "I am writing you about this not only because of our need, but also because … the FOR has made a substantial investment in Bayard's trip to India and in the whole Journey of Reconciliation, including the court and other arrangements which culminated in his recent road gang experience. We thought that the Philadelphia FOR might, because of this, want to contribute in this fashion to our work." He concluded by saying he felt constantly appreciative of the good work Charlie was doing in Philadelphia.[35]

Charlie left the office worried about finances, and seated himself in the car for his drive home. A pinch in finances was never good with a baby on the way. When Charlie needed to attend a luncheon, meeting or event, give a speech, visit a college or university, drive passengers somewhere, or if his event required his taking literature or books to sell, he drove into Philadelphia. Today he had driven the car to the city.

He steered the old blue Ford home after a busy day at the office, noting the blustery April day with angry clouds galloping across a gray sky. Charlie enjoyed West Chester Pike, no matter the weather. A flock of geese rose in the sunset, calling to each other. It lifted his spirit to take in lovely surroundings and an occasional glimpse of wildlife.

Charlie turned on to the lane at his house and pulled into his parking place under the trees. He looked up to see Winnie and Brenda in little dresses, swinging on the porch railing, while Larry rode on the hill on his tricycle. With shouts of "Daddy's home!" the children ran joyfully down the hill for a big Daddy-hug. Marian, about six months pregnant, had begun to feel uncomfortable with her belly growing bigger. He met her with a kiss and, hopeful for a chance of rain, commented about the sweltering weather they had had in the neighborhood. "It's been so hot here that whenever fish go up the creek they leave a trail of dust a mile long!"[36] He burst into laughter, his eyebrows jumping up and down. Marian could not suppress her mirth, more at him than the joke.

At Work in the FOR

Charlie sent a letter dated July 7 to Bob James at the Student Christian Movement (SCM), which was part of the YMCA and YWCA program. Charlie enumerated the many services provided by the FOR. "I should imagine the main contribution we could make ... would be ... to help those student groups where there is little social vision to feel a sense of identification with the victims of injustice, and to have a passion for social justice."[37]

He suggested Bayard Rustin and George Houser could help with the *racial democracy* question, John Swomley with *militarism in education*, and A. J. Muste would be excellent at speaking in relation to *Christianity and Communism,* since Muste had once belonged to the Communist Party and was well-versed on this issue.

The following month, Bayard Rustin, Director of Race Relations, sent a copy of Charlie's SCM letter to other FOR secretaries, suggesting, "I think you will agree with me that this is a good approach, and I am sharing this letter with you in the hope that you will do something similar in regard to the SCM Secretary in your area."[38]

Bob James replied to Charlie on July 12, "It seems to me that there could be a very effective cross-correlation of interests and leadership, although we are both aware that there is still at certain points [religious] prejudice, in addition to 'ideological differences.'"[39]

On July 21, Charlie wrote to Mary Miner in Philadelphia, "At the FOR Annual Day we talked about the problem of what a pacifist would do if he were confronted by a threat of violence against his person or that of a friend or family." He listed various writings by other people about what to do nonviolently in case of an intruder. "I could also cite the long history of the Quakers in dealing with the Indians. It should be pointed out that this kind of ... incident is quite rare and that it is no wise a parallel with war, which is a mass attack against persons on an impersonal basis. Confronted as I have been in mental hospital work with violence, I have tried to act nonviolently, mostly as a test when I might have to face in public a much greater test of faith and courage—and training."[40]

That same day, Charlie wrote to a man in Downingtown, "I have for some time been interested, deeply interested, in the spiritual life, having been drawn to it first through the impact of Gerald Heard. Also in New York City I was a member of the prayer group of which Eugene Exman, of Harper and Co., is the head. Recently at Tanguy Homesteads near Cheyney, we have started two groups, one based on an hour of silence and another on a half hour."[41]

New Baby, New Challenges

Charlie sat at his office desk in Philadelphia looking over a request from the World Affairs Council of Philadelphia to join their Speakers' Bureau. The phone rang. It was Marian. "Charlie, I'm in labor. Get here as quickly as you can!"

"All right, Marian, I'll catch the first train!"

He dropped everything, left notes with his secretary, and took off. He was a little concerned, because the baby was three weeks early. Charlie had driven the car in the morning to the Cheyney train station and left it there, so was relieved he could drive the short distance home from the station. By the time he rushed in the door, Marian was packed and sitting down, waiting. She looked up, happy he had made it home in time and started to her feet. Charlie rushed to help her stand, which was accomplished, however awkwardly.

The three children played upstairs with the babysitter, who had arrived in a hurry from Tanguy.

Heading out to the car, Marian believed she was experienced at this by now, but still felt the need to hang onto Charlie's arm. She stopped and waited for a contraction to finish before clambering into the car and gingerly lowering herself onto the seat. They headed to Chester County Hospital in West Chester.

There, Charlie paced the halls, worrying and considering names. His instinct told him this would be a boy. *Marian likes the name David, but I don't. I want James, which she doesn't like. Says there are a zillion Jameses. I also like the name Michael with the nickname "Mickey." James is a solid name of Walker lineage, and I'd really like that. Jim or Jimmy Walker sounds very good. I don't know. I guess we'll see what we can agree on.*

The little boy was born at 10:30 the next morning and was five pounds even, the smallest baby of them all. Due to a change of hospital policy, Marian only had to stay in bed there a few days instead of two weeks.

Charlie rejoiced in adding another boy, making the family even with two girls and two boys. The baby was very cute, and looked a little more like Marian than the others. Sometimes Charlie thought Brenda looked more like Marian's father than like him, although people insisted she was a chip off the old block. Larry definitely resembled Charlie, while Winnie had become a clever combination of Walker and Groff.

Charlie and Marian wrestled with the choice of name at the hospital, while Marian nursed the baby. She was proud of the fact that she nursed all her babies. "Charlie," she declared in frustration. "I just don't like Mickey or James. David is such a nice, strong name."

"But David doesn't have the right associations for me," Charlie said. So they looked again through the name book and right in the A's, there was Allan. It stood out and seemed like a good compromise. Renfred was chosen for the middle name, because it meant "bringer of peace." Allan Renfred Walker it was.

They brought the new Walker home one lovely summer day in August, to the delight of the other three: Winnie, six; Larry nearing four; and Brenda almost two. They all wanted to hold him, but just Winnie was allowed, and then only when she sat down.

They all sat around the kitchen table on the lower level with the new baby. "Now, Charlie, the doctor says I must not climb any steps for two weeks. How can I get up to the living room on the second floor?"

Charlie laughed, "I guess I can push you up the hill outside. How about that?"

"Okay!"

So they left the cooing baby in Winnie's arms, went out the door and faced uphill. Charlie put his hands gently on her back.

"All right now, when I give the signal. Ready ... Set ... Go!"

He pushed, and she rushed a few feet up the grassy incline with Charlie right behind. When he again said ready, they started up once more. After reaching the top, they sat on the porch chairs bursting with laughter. They tripped inside, and Charlie glided downstairs to bring the infant up to be nursed. Later, while both mother and son napped, Charlie straightened up the house. He stayed at home a few days, but the young couple needed more help.

Relatives came to assist Marian one at a time, for a few days each. Marian's Grandmother Shank, who lived in the Lancaster area, was one of the most memorable. "Let me chop those vegetables! You don't chop them small enough!" Grandmother scolded.

"Well, I usually just chop them small enough to fit on a spoon." Marian pushed the chopping block toward the older woman with a sheepish smile. Despite the bossiness, Marian was glad to have Grandmother there. The old woman loved to take care of children and enjoyed working in Marian's garden.

Gardening was very important for Marian because of her vegetarian lifestyle. Since she had situated her garden on a hillside, by necessity she planted a series of vegetable patches in raised beds to keep the soil from eroding.

Fall of 1949 became a very busy time for Charlie. He had agreed to be part of the Speakers Bureau of the World Affairs Council. On Friday, October 21, he spoke to South Philadelphia High School for Girls for fifteen minutes on the "United Nations." He had appointments to speak at Mastbaum Vocational School on Monday, October 24, to two assemblies for a total of 1,800 students on the same topic.[42]

Concord Meeting

The James and Edwards families encouraged the Walkers to attend Quaker Meeting at nearby Concordville with them. Many Tanguy families had become members there. A lively Meeting with peace and social justice emphasis, it hosted a great children's religious education program. It was and is called Concord Monthly Meeting of the Religious Society of Friends, as it meets once a month to conduct business.

On Marian and Charlie's first visit to Concord Meeting, they drove through green, hilly country with fields on either side. Concord Meeting House was built extra large with a balcony, so it could house the Quarterly Meetings—groups of Meetings that meet four times per year. This meetinghouse had two stories, unlike many in the area. Concord Meeting was organized in 1688; six years after William Penn came to Pennsylvania.

The Walkers pulled into the driveway to see a striking, red-brick structure. The date 1728, the year it was built, loomed high above the front porch roof near the peak. The year 1788, when it was rebuilt after a fire, stood proudly etched on the other side. Charlie parked facing a long building, which Marian recognized as a stone carriage house with horse stalls. She noted square openings on the other side of each stall big enough to allow a horse in earlier centuries to peer out toward the old cemetery.

They exited the car and walked toward the stately meetinghouse with a saddle house on the other side of the driveway. As they entered the building, they noticed rows of benches arranged roughly in a circular pattern. Quakers sit quietly in group worship until the Spirit of God leads someone to speak. This is why they were nicknamed Quakers, for quaking in the presence of the Living God.

Members directed the young couple to the First Day School through another door in a dark wood panel, which in early days had separated the women's from the men's business meetings. The women's side now housed a nursery and children's classrooms. This panel could be raised, through a system of pulleys, to accommodate one big meeting. Larry, Brenda and Allan remained in the nursery, and a delighted Winnie found herself in the first grade program.

As she sat listening to the discussion of the journal of George Fox, the founder of Quakerism, Marian faintly heard childish voices singing "Jesus Loves Me." Several families at Concord had children the age of hers, and this pleased Marian—the Saverys, Palmers, Closes, Hartsoughs, as well as Jameses and Edwardses. Everyone welcomed them warmly; Marian and Charlie felt at home.

At the end of class, the children filed in and sat down with their families. After a few announcements, old hymns such as "I Would Be True," "God of Our Fathers," and "All Things Bright and Beautiful" came alive. Then the smallest ones returned to the nursery, and the remaining persons closed their eyes and settled into gathered silence. After a time, various people stood and spoke what was on their heart—a testimony of some way God had helped them that week, a story of the Spirit working somewhere in the world, a thought which came out of the speaker's relationship with Jesus, or a current event which often became a call to action from the speaker.

At noon, the Clerk of the Meeting up front shook hands with the person next to him, and everyone took the cue and shook each other's hands, greeting and talking to one another. After a short time, they headed to the children's area for punch and cookies and more fellowship. On the way home, Marian told Charlie, "The ladies were so nice. They asked me to join the Social Committee, and I told them I would."

"Quakers have a lot of committees," Charlie laughed. "That's the way they get things done in place of having a minister."

Martin Luther King, Muste, and Charlie Walker at Crozer Seminary

Charlie's first encounter with Martin Luther King came in 1949, when he helped introduce the young King to nonviolence. Charlie later described it this way: "When I worked for the FOR in Philadelphia, one year we had a push to get into seminaries getting a crack at these 'religious leaders.' As a routine thing, I scheduled A. J. Muste (leading US pacifist)[43] at Crozer Baptist Seminary in Chester [PA]. He gave a fairly good talk.... In that meeting was young Martin Luther King."[44]

The Martin Luther King official papers relate that, Charlie spoke on Gandhi and nonviolence at Crozer Theological Seminary while King was a student there at Chester.[45] William Penn first landed his ship, the *Welcome*, in 1682 in Chester, a suburb of Philadelphia.

After Charlie's talk the students at Crozer were visibly enthusiastic about stories of Gandhi's pacifist movement in India. He was so well-received, he decided to invite his boss A. J. Muste, executive director of the FOR, to speak there later in the year in November.[46]

According to Charlie Walker in a chapter he wrote for a book about Gandhi, edited by an Indian and published in India, the subject of Muste's talk was "The Implications of Nonviolence for the Christian Church."[47] Gandhi had taught that violence springs from seven root causes: wealth without work, pleasure without conscience, knowledge without character, commerce without morality, science without humanity, worship without sacrifice, and politics without principles.[48] Gandhi believed nonviolence is the law of love, of using good to overcome evil, not evil to overcome evil. Gandhi's whole movement was a discipline based on using God's love to overcome oppression by turning one's adversaries into friends. This law is also a Christian belief.

Charlie was pleased with Muste's speech. As confirmed by a Muste biographer, JoAnn Ooiman [*Abraham Went Out*] and a memo to Bayard Rustin located in the Swarthmore Peace Collection, Charlie wrote, "At Crozer he got a fairly good reception, marred by the chilly attitude of the acting president and the worst outburst of invective I have ever heard leveled at a person in public."[49] [50]

That last referred to a young veteran under strain from his war experience, who flew out of his seat and shouted at Muste. In that meeting was a young Martin Luther King. This meeting Charlie vividly remembered over the years.[51][52] He later wrote a King biographer to correct the version of the event recorded in the writer's book. "I was the organizer, as a FOR staff member then, and recall the occasion clearly. The part I note in particular is [your] description of a 'heated argument' between Muste and King, from which one could conclude Muste wasn't particularly persuasive. It didn't happen.[53]

"The explosive event … came when a former young veteran, said later to have been under emotional strain from his war experience (he did, after all, come to a meeting where a pacifist was speaking) blew up. He jumped up and shouted (yes, shouted) something like this (not quoting exactly, of course): 'What right do you have to assume what soldiers think in battle? When have you ever faced war?' He said a little more, then stalked out. A. J. called out to him: 'Wait a minute brother! Come on back and let's talk about this.' He didn't return then, and I'm unsure about whether he returned when the meeting adjourned, and if he did, it wasn't to talk to Muste." Elsewhere, Charlie wrote that after the veteran's departure, the room was quiet for a time. And since no one was speaking, an older man started in on a religious message not related to the meeting at all: turned out to be the janitor waiting for the meeting to be over! This roiled the waters some more.[54]

Charlie told the biographer, "If Martin said anything, or asked a question, I cannot recall, but don't remember that he did. But then, I didn't think of him in particular, not knowing him then (that came later)."[55]

King, in his second year of seminary, excelled as an outstanding student who would in his third year become the first black student body president. His parents in Georgia had sent him for an education in the North, before he found his calling in the South.

Martin Luther King later wrote in his book *Stride Toward Freedom*, the story of his life leading up to the Montgomery Bus Boycott, "During my stay at Crozer, I was … exposed for the first time to the pacifist position in a lecture by Dr. A. J. Muste. I was deeply moved by Dr. Muste's talk, but far from convinced of the practicability of his position…. Then one Sunday afternoon I traveled to Philadelphia to hear a sermon by Dr. Mordecai Johnson, President of Howard University.[56] He was there to preach for the

Fellowship House of Philadelphia. Dr. Johnson had just returned from a trip to India, and, to my great interest, he spoke of the life and teachings of Mahatma Gandhi. His message was so profound and electrifying that I left the meeting and bought a half-dozen books on Gandhi's life and works."[57]

Charlie took pride in the fact that he had originated, facilitated and attended this historic event. Charlie wrote, "He was somewhat impressed, but not convinced. That came later. It was such a memorable meeting that it stood out more than usual."[58] [59]

Nat Hentoff included this story in the Muste biography *Peace Agitator* in 1963: "Martin Luther King says that his own ideas have been considerably influenced by Muste. King is a member of the Fellowship of Reconciliation. Before he came to know and work with Muste in that context, however, King, as a student at Crozer Theological Seminary in Pennsylvania, had heard Muste lecture. 'I wasn't a pacifist then,' recalls King, 'but the power of A. J.'s sincerity and his hardheaded ability to defend his position stayed with me through the years. Later, I got to know him better, and I would say unequivocally that the current emphasis on nonviolent direct action in the race relations field is due more to A. J. than to anyone else in the country."[60]

In the middle of the next decade Martin Luther King, starting with the Montgomery Bus Protest, began to lead his people to their freedoms as Americans and shapers of their own destiny. Through the power and strategies of nonviolence, he preached, taught and exemplified a high-principled movement, the American civil rights movement.

Near Philadelphia in 1949 Charlie Walker played a part in history, lighting the spark in a young leader that turned into a flame, a flame of peace and nonviolence that is today a beacon to oppressed people everywhere.

Nonviolently Tackling Racial Issues

Charlie wrote to Charles Parmer on November 29, 1949, at Stout Institute in Wisconsin, saying, "There was nearly a race riot in Coatesville recently…. There had long been friction between Negroes and whites (it's a terrible set-up on race in Coatesville), and one day it broke out into the open. For several hours all the students were milling around outside the school building, students refusing to get on the buses.

"Negro teachers from another school came to be on hand if anything started, but fortunately no violence did break out. Some of these days there will be a frightful harvest in that town of all the bitter seeds sown there for so long."

Then he switched to a story from another area of the country. "A remarkable incident occurred in Jackson Park in Chicago which you might find useful. There was discrimination there, had been for a long time. If Negro kids ventured in, the whites chased them out and frequently beat them up. A group committed to nonviolence wanted to do something about it, and decided to go in as an interracial group and play a game of softball.

"They did, and in another corner of the park, white boys started to gather. However, they were unprepared for a group that size, so nothing materialized. The next time the group went back, the [white] fellows were ready. They assembled quickly and started to run toward the softball field. Without even preliminaries, they started to slug and pound the players, but no one retaliated. They got up off the ground and said, 'What's the matter? We have nothing against you. We just came here to play a game of softball.'

"The rioters were taken aback by such unusual behavior, and then they started shoving the players around to try to get them to fight. Again, no retaliation but friendly responses. The incident ended with the rioters playing the interracial group a game of softball!

"But here's the amazing thing. Two fellows got their jaws broken in the fray, and a girl got her nose broken.... Yet they were able to discipline themselves to the point of such self-control, they won the day by nonviolent resistance.... The point is, this is not an esoteric doctrine, but can be worked out in America, and has been."[61]

Chapter 6

Taking Up Race Issues, Early 1950s

Especially in the field of race relations, the FOR has built up a body of experience which indicates Gandhian tactics are relevant to the American scene. We look forward to the time when as much detailed attention and generous resources are devoted to developing a "science of peace" as are usually spent on military science.

–Charles Walker, letter to Charles Parmer, November 1, 1949

A new decade, the 1950s, had begun with a new war in the offing—Korea. After World War II, Korea became divided with Russia occupying the north and the United States, the south. The United Nations made attempts in 1947 to unify the two parts, but Russia refused to allow the U.N. commission to enter the zone it held. The United States withdrew its troops from the South in 1949, but North Korean raids into democratic South Korea continued with greater frequency.[1]

Brotherhood Month

Charlie Walker looked on the fledgling civil rights movement with excitement and concern. If not kept nonviolent it could be a terrible bloodbath.[2] Therefore he felt glad his Fellowship of Reconciliation remained eager to be of assistance in race issues.

Charlie sat at his desk at the beginning of the new decade, typing his proposed plan for a new year. It was early January 1950, and having worked at his job for more than a year, he felt confident of the programs he was developing for the FOR. He planned to renew efforts in colleges in the Philadelphia area and obtain speaking engagements to bring in funds and mobilize people in the "evangelistic side of the program," as he called it.[3]

The Congress of Racial Equality's Call to Action during Brotherhood Month came to mind. James Farmer, who had left FOR to head CORE, had an idea for the month of February—a Brotherhood Pledge to fight

213

segregation using strictly nonviolent methods. CORE would ask people to work on brotherhood all year, not just limiting it to the month of February. Charlie's friend called it "voluntary noncooperation with jimcrowism." *Jim Crow* was a name given to traditions of segregation against blacks in the United States.

At the end of the previous year, support for this Brotherhood Pledge had been urged by George Houser, writing in an FOR memo that many "have felt that something with a little more punch was needed."[4]

Charlie picked up Farmer's Call to Action to reread it. "In a small town in North Carolina, the students at a Negro women's college never attend the local motion picture theater. The reason is that by local law and custom they would be forced to climb seventy-two steps on the outside of the theater to the second balcony entrance each time they were to see a movie. They would have to sit through a long film in the stuffy jimcrow quarters and have only a distorted view of the screen."

Farmer went on to say, "First, enforced segregation is a humiliating and degrading experience for the Negro. It makes him a second-class citizen and imposes the stamp of inferiority on him. Second, segregation is a basic moral compromise for the white person. By his cooperation with it he denies both the high truths of his religion and the claims of democracy. Third, race prejudice cannot be overcome as long as a system of segregation keeps people of varying races apart from one another." Charlie read on, considering various points.

The Pledge itself read:

> I wish to join with others in committing myself anew to an interracial way of life. In line with this commitment, I agree that, unless necessity demands it, during Brotherhood Month I will not use any facilities in which racial segregation is required. Concretely:
> 1. I will not attend theaters and other public places where segregation is demanded. I will use facilities where segregation is enforced only if I have no alternative choice and necessity demands it.
> 2. I will inquire about the policy of any facility I use, if there is doubt about its practice.
> 3. I will inform the management of facilities I do not use of the reason for my noncooperation.
> 4. I will maintain an attitude of nonviolent goodwill without self-righteousness in carrying out this commitment.[5]

Charlie decided to send these Pledges out to everyone on the FOR mailing list. Along with the Pledge came a description of National CORE, which had grown substantially in the last decade. The basis of CORE was a federation of mostly autonomous local groups.

Principles of CORE:

1. These groups are interracial, because they know the race problem is a human, social problem touching all people of every race. It is a social cancer which must be cut out from our social order through the cooperative efforts of all people who believe in the brotherhood of man.... Whites and Negroes must act together.

2. These groups believe in direct action.... They believe the most effective means for gaining full citizenship rights for all Americans regardless of race is to refuse to accept any barriers to that citizenship....

In carrying out their action program, these local groups follow the procedure of, first, investigating the suspected area of discrimination to ascertain all the facts; second, discussing the grievance with those seemingly responsible for the practice, in an effort to bring about a change of policy; third, appealing to a wider public for support in achieving a nondiscriminatory practice; fourth, attracting wide attention to the unjust racial practice through such demonstration as picketing or passing out leaflets; fifth, using noncooperation techniques such as organizing a boycott or strike, etc., to induce a change of policy.

Although the main emphasis is on direct action, at times these groups will use legal, legislative and political action in order to oppose race discrimination.

3. These groups believe in avoiding all violence of action or attitude in carrying out their program.... They believe that positive values result from a group's maintaining an attitude of good-will and reconciliation even in the midst of a noncooperation campaign. The experience of local CORE groups in action projects has proven that if members of the group maintain an attitude of goodwill, the support of the public is won, police will tend not to interfere, and often the friendship of the opposition is gained.[6]

After reading the above statements, Charlie thought, *No other group right now does what CORE does.* He signed his Pledge and sent it in.

The clickety-click of the secretary's typewriter sounded through the office wall, as Henrietta worked in the large room. Charlie realized with regret he would not be hearing that sound much longer. The National Office had decided to let go of the secretary as a cost-cutting measure, so Charlie would have to adjust his work habits.

His corner office, which he loved, faced the street. He looked for a moment out onto the city scene. It had a calming effect on him. He used this technique as often as possible to cope with the stress of long hours reading, writing, organizing conferences and attending meetings.

With characteristic optimism, Charlie had that day written a letter to Ken Cuthbertson, his old friend from Columbus who now worked for the American Friends Service Committee in Philadelphia, "The release of the secretary may prove to be a boon in disguise. My present plans call for the major part of the work this year to be put into 'concentrated field work.'"[7]

Charlie wrote a letter to Charles Rockel, chairman of the board of the Philadelphia FOR, which read, in part, "I just received a copy of John Swomley's letter to you this morning. I confess I was astounded when I learned that the staff and the Executive Committee recommended full salary for me. But I feel uncomfortable about taking the raise from an organization like the FOR, which is supported by giving which is often sacrificial.

"It doesn't seem fair to me to get the full salary—even if we could squeeze it out of the budget—when we are at the point of actually releasing a secretary. Let me say now that it doesn't take long to appreciate the full value Henrietta has been. At any rate, the salary decision is up to the Finance and Executive Committee."[8]

Later at home, Marian was indignant. "What do you mean, you don't think you deserve full salary? Of course you do! Putting in all those long hours. Working night and day. Traveling all over, putting your heart and soul into your work. And, it's awfully hard to keep a household going on your salary. Food and clothing for four kids doesn't come cheap, even if I don't buy expensive meats. Please don't keep refusing bonuses and what is due to you, because of some crazy idea that others need it more than we do!"

"But, Marian, the FOR budget is so tight."

"So is ours!"

———

A month later, Charlie pulled into the snowy drive and parked in front of the little house in Cheyney. He wished he had buttoned up for the short hustle to the side door, because as soon as he exited the car, the freezing wind peeled open the front of his coat.

Charlie entered the house in a flurry of stamping and flinging snow off his clothing. He took off his boots, placed his coat and hat on a coat hook and turned toward Marian with a smile. "Hello, Marian, I've been invited to Albright College in Reading[9] this Friday afternoon, to speak at their seminary. They are combining all their college peace groups just to hear me!"[10]

She returned his greeting. "That is exciting! Things seem to be opening up for you."

"The students in these groups are particularly interested in the work of the FOR. The pastor organizing this feels there's a good chance it will start an active group on campus. He promises a fair-sized group, around thirty-five, including some professors."

"Great!"

"They also said I should stay for supper at the parsonage and invite you to come along, but I already told them you couldn't come."

"Why on earth did you do that? I do like to get out of the house sometimes." Marian's easygoing husband had a tendency to make decisions without consulting her.

Charlie attempted damage control. "They apologized for the long wait between 10:00 a.m. and 4:00 p.m., saying I could bring paperwork with me to make it worthwhile. Anyway, what would we do?"

"Well, we could go out to lunch, see the campus. The town of Reading is nearby. Why not?"

"Well, we have four children now, and Allan is less than a year old. That seems like too many to bring along."

"Yes, but we've left them before with your mother or my mother. It's not impossible to make such arrangements if we plan ahead," Marian argued. "Being here with four children all the time gets a little tiresome. It would be nice to do something with you. You travel all the time. I get lonely."

He drew her close for a hug. "I'm sorry, I wasn't thinking."

She returned his embrace. "It's all right. I'd just like to be asked."

———

Charlie plunged into field work with renewed vigor, especially since his secretary was gone and staff time allotment overhauled. He wrote Emily Longstreth, "As you know, only one-third of my time thus far has been allotted to the Philadelphia FOR and of course, the Philadelphia group pays only one-third of my salary. So a good deal of work goes into college work for the National College program.... Now that we no longer have a secretary, office work will be cut down to a minimum, and thus we shall have to abandon any kind of project which requires much coordination or planning."[11]

Charlie scheduled Bayard Rustin, the FOR's College Work Director, to speak at Philadelphia's Race Street Friends Meeting House on February 26 on the topic "The Road to Freedom." A. J. Muste would speak at Fellowship House February 12, and on March 19 Dr. Howard Thurman, of the FOR's National Council, who had just released his book *Jesus and the Disinherited*,[12] was listed to speak in Germantown.[13] In March, Charlie made a point to go hear the prestigious Mordecai Johnson, first African American president of Howard University. Dr. Johnson came to speak at Race Street Meeting House on "What of Gandhism in India? In America?"[14] Was this the same speech by Johnson that Martin Luther King said "electrified" his interest in nonviolence? Fellowship House in Philadelphia where King heard Dr. Johnson was not a Quaker organization, although it had Quaker roots and stood for nonviolent solutions to social problems.

Homecoming for Bayard

Bayard Rustin was to have a "homecoming" in West Chester. Charlie greatly anticipated this event, not only because West Chester was Rustin's hometown, but also because the Walkers lived nearby, and Charlie's children would later attend West Chester High School.

The FOR did not sponsor this homecoming, but several of its members in the area, including Charlie, initiated the idea and did much of the planning. The first initiative came from Concord Friends Meeting's Peace Committee.[15] About 350 people came to the high school auditorium April 13 to honor the West Chester native son, who "made good" in more than the conventional sense. Groups from many neighboring towns came, and sponsors included persons prominent in education, businesses, churches and civic groups.[16]

Rustin took the microphone. "It's important in the twentieth century in the United States of America that one should stand up and outline how he came to believe what he believes." He told of growing up in West Chester with the race divide. One of his white friends could not invite Bayard home to visit, nor could he spend time at Bayard's home, because of their parents' attitudes. The only places they could meet were the high school gym and the library.

Rustin spoke of his move to New York where he tried out the Communist Party briefly, because it was a place to belong, after being shut out of so many. "They had me, others would not," he explained.[17] But he became disillusioned by Communism and broke with it in 1941[18] feeling that Russia now "is as bad as the rule of Hitler. Russia's attempt to usher in good with bad means failed."[19]

Bayard said he liked the ideas of the American Friends Service Committee, Quakers who "believe the only way to find real peace and freedom is to be peaceful and free. You cannot usher in democracy without the presence of it." He put forth his advocacy of nonviolence, saying it is always the persecutors and not the persecuted who receive the greatest harm from prejudice. "Out of violence there can only come more violence."[20]

Rustin had been a conscientious objector during World War II. Marian and Charlie gave each other a meaningful look during that part of the speech. Bayard spoke of a subject dear to their hearts, full of emotional memories.

Bayard explained he became a lecturer in Britain after the war, traveling to India, where he became a personal friend of Prime Minister Nehru. It was there he fell in love with Gandhian philosophies. He talked of participating in the Journey of Reconciliation in 1947, to test the Supreme Court ruling which allowed Negroes to ride in the front seats on interstate buses and being sentenced to a chain gang in North Carolina as a result of that Journey. He concluded his talk with a beautiful song, "There is a Balm in Gilead."[21] Charlie and Marian were delighted with the event.

The next morning Marian woke Charlie with, "Look at the front page of the *Daily Local News!* Bayard's Homecoming has a wonderful write-up!" The article reported the "Bayard Rustin story is one of nonviolence yet definite conflict, of peace through peaceful means, and of the sameness of every man, regardless of race, creed, or color.... With a 'meek shall inherit the earth' attitude, Rustin, who on many occasions has been cited as a troublemaker, advocated a policy of nonviolence in dealing with the current world situation."[22]

"This is great! Not usually front-page stuff!" Charlie exclaimed. The town which had previously shut Rustin out, had now welcomed him back with open arms and hearts. Charlie cut out the article. It would make a positive report for his next FOR meeting. He reported to the Executive Committee in May that it was the outstanding event of the previous month and Bayard had been in good form. "Forty-eight copies of Bayard's pamphlet on the Journey of Reconciliation were sold, and the expenses were liquidated successfully."[23]

At Charlie's request the Philadelphia FOR formed a committee, called the Exploratory Committee for United Schools in West Chester, which would take the initiative in finally breaking down segregation of the schools there.

In May came the welcome appearance of Gerald Heard at the Friends Conference on Religion and Psychology, at Haverford College and at a weekend retreat at Pendle Hill. "On most of these occasions, he received an enthusiastic response," Charlie reported. "Gerald Heard made a deep impression at Haverford at an evening talk rather than a chapel talk, speaking on 'Are Moral Values Relative?' Think he sort of out-flanked them and aroused an interest in some of the fundamentals of pacifist interpretation of history."[24]

War in Korea, Blood Banks, and Another Walker Move

On June 24, 1950, North Korean troops invaded South Korea, and war broke out. At once, Philadelphia FOR arranged a special luncheon, where A. J. Muste gave his analysis of this development. Forty people, on short notice, rushed to that meeting. "The theme of his message was that this was no 'new development' in the nature of police action or collective security, but represented an intensification of the power struggle, fraught with danger for the future."[25] War, power struggles, danger, all were abhorrent to Charlie.

Charlie received a letter late in August from Bill Willoughby, his Elizabethtown College friend, who had visited from Virginia. "Thanks ever so much for your gracious welcome in your small house," he wrote. "I believe our five-room apartment has more room than your house.... Although yours is a noble work, I believe you're contributing more to the Kingdom through your children than through the FOR. They're really a top-notch bunch of kids."[26]

When Charlie showed the letter to Marian, she was happy for the compliment about the children, and later often remembered the sweet sentiment, especially since she felt she was doing the lion's share of raising the children.

"Why didn't you tell me Ern was getting married?" Marian asked, holding up Willoughby's letter. He reported Ern Lefever had returned from his world journey, having had a private conference with Jawaharlal Nehru, the new Prime Minister of India, who had a background in Gandhian beliefs. "It says here he and Margaret are raring to go with their wedding and plan to spend their honeymoon in Venice."

Willoughby additionally wrote he thought Korea was going to be an unpopular war, and that things were heating up on the national scene and resentments getting stronger as officials blamed each other. He signed off with, "Yours, with many thanks for the food ... and the ball-game."[27]

In September FOR's National Staff approved continuing to work on the Brotherhood Pledge and recommended the Executive Committee grant permission for preliminary work on race workshops in Washington and St. Louis.[28]

To people who inquired about the FOR, Charlie described it as a religious pacifist fellowship of people who wished to work directly on preventing war, as well as eradicating its causes. He wrote to one such seeker, "We include a variety of religious faiths in our membership and try to avoid any semblance of sectarianism. Especially in the field of race relations, the FOR has built up a body of experience which indicates Gandhian tactics are relevant to the American scene. We look forward to the time when as much detailed attention and generous resources are devoted to developing a 'science of peace' as is usually spent on military science."[29]

Able to afford private school because of scholarships for Quaker children, Marian and Charlie enrolled Winnie at nearby Westtown Friends School, when they first moved into the area. They had taken this step, strongly desiring their children learn Quaker values,[30] and now Winnie enjoyed second grade, while Larry attended kindergarten. A carpool of Tanguy mothers took turns driving their children to Westtown, and Marian found her "new" car was plenty big for all the children in the car pool when it was her turn to drive.

At this time, they realized Ada George's rental house in Cheyney had become too small to house four children and two adults. With winter approaching, squeezing into the cramped space looked less and less appealing.

So, when Charlie looked through the mail and found a letter from their landlord requesting they move out, he took it as a matter of course. "Ada George says she's retiring, Marian, and needs to move in here now. She'd like us to find another place as soon as possible."

"John Ewbank has wanted us to move to Bryn Gweled,"[31] Marian offered "He lives up there and loves it. We could go look at houses there."

"Okay, Marian. Let's do it, and also look around here. The only thing I ask is that it's bigger!"

They settled on a place in nearby Thornton, on the way to Concord Meeting. Marian did not want to move to Bryn Gweled. "The houses are expensive, and we'd have the worst house on the block. I'd rather have a nice house around here."

The rental house was a little white stucco with a long lane, which headed past the home of the people they rented it from. "Three bedrooms, Charlie, this is wonderful," Marian exclaimed, and they began the process of packing and moving. It was not easy with four little children underfoot. On moving day, Charlie's brother Herb, home from the war, arrived from Gap to help, and they borrowed a pick-up truck for the short move.

They lived close to the school, so Marian arranged for a Westtown School bus to pick Winnie and Larry up every day.

Mid-October, Charlie called George Houser, still Racial-Industrial Secretary of the FOR along with Bayard. "George, at Temple University, I got involved in the issue of blood banks and bloodmobiles that go around collecting blood donations.[32] Universities and colleges are popular spots for these things, because students are usually in good health and always in need money."

George believed that to be the case.

"Well, the Red Cross wanted to come on campus with their bloodmobile to get pints of blood for Korea, especially. But for the second year in a row, the student body voted it down, the reason being that the blood is segregated according to race."[33]

George answered, "Yes, we had a campaign in Chicago in the early '40s against the segregation of blood during the war. The Red Cross was segregating blood at that time, and I think our campaign had an effect."[34]

"You did? That's really interesting! Because this is going on at Temple this year," Charlie continued, "and the administration tried to put pressure on a number of key student leaders to let the Red Cross in, but was still unable to swing it."[35]

He continued, "Now, the students have decided to invite the Red Cross to come in and conduct their program on a nonsegregated basis."

"I'm glad they're taking a stand, Charlie," George said.

"It occurs to me," Charlie proposed, "this could be an issue which might be good to raise on other campuses … as a way of putting them to work on an issue where they could exercise leadership and involve a large sector of the college community."[36]

Houser agreed this issue had possibilities, as scientific evidence was incontrovertible that human blood did not differ by race and was "simply human." He added, "I don't think we would oppose the campaign on the issue of the need for blood in the Korean War. Segregation is the issue."[37]

Bayard Rustin and A. J. Muste

One cool November evening after colorful leaves had mostly fallen from the trees, Marian commented after dinner, "Charlie, my mother called and wanted to make sure we were coming to Thanksgiving at their place in Lancaster this year. I told her I thought so, but wanted to check with you."

They took a minute to watch little Allan toddle around and fall. He laughed at his own antics almost as much as his parents did. Standing up immediately, he tore off in another direction and fell again.

"Thanksgiving at your folks should be fine, Marian." Charlie folded his arms on his chest and leaned back on the couch. It was great to enjoy some respite from his busy schedule with time at home with the family. He sighed and smiled. Winnie was seven, Larry five, Brenda three, and Allan one year old.

Then he remembered something. "Speaking of mothers, I just got a letter from Bayard today asking me if I could pick up his Mama, Julia, in West Chester and drive her up to New York on November twenty-first for some event at which he is speaking. I'm supposed to go, too, but it depends on whether our car is fixed on time. If it isn't, I'll have to catch a train and not be able to take his Mama. Since she is quite elderly, she cannot walk to and from train stations."[38]

Marian laughed. "Bayard always leans on you when he needs transportation either for him or his mother." Bayard called fairly often, asking Charlie to pick him up and take him somewhere, such as to Cheyney College for a speaking engagement or an appointment with the President, Dr. Hill.

"Yes, he does," Charlie admitted, "but like all of us in this line of work, he's strapped for funds. I'm happy to help."

"Do you remember the time Bayard wanted us to pick up his mother and take her to a meeting in Philadelphia, and I agreed to do it? Ruth Edwards drove, and we took Julia somewhere near Sixty-Ninth Street where Bayard was singing or speaking."

Charlie's eyes bugged out. "Ruth Edwards was driving?" Ruth, of Concord Meeting and Tanguy, was known for driving fast.

"Yes, don't you remember that? That was the scariest part of it. Ruth had her pedal to the metal, as they say." Marian giggled. "Ruth and I picked Julia up and then brought her home. I didn't say anything to Ruth afterwards, and neither did Julia in the back seat, but she'd been pressing the floor boards, like she was trying to apply the brakes!"[39]

"Good grief, Marian, we're lucky Bayard's Mama didn't have a heart attack!"

"Yes, but we love Ruth and her willingness to help. She's a wonderful worker for peace."

Charlie couldn't resist a big grin, teasing, "Except maybe for peace on the roads."

The Philadelphia FOR had concentrated its work on local colleges and found success at many of them. Charlie said in his end-of-year report that individual FOR members had continued to be active on behalf of pacifism at Crozer Theological Seminary,[40] the institution from which Martin Luther King graduated the following year.

Charlie and Bayard wrote each other the same day, December 13. A peace group met regularly at Swarthmore College, and Charlie had scheduled Bayard to speak at their big Christmas meeting. Bayard wrote, "It would be a very good thing if you could pick me up at my house [his childhood home in West Chester] on Sunday and take me over to Swarthmore."[41]

At the same time, Charlie reported on his talk at Bryn Mawr College on December 6. "A small group, maybe twenty or so were expected. Instead, seventy-five showed up to fill a good-sized lounge; a number of them were profs."

Charlie concluded by adding a thank-you from the young lady, Betsey Repenning, who had chaired the meeting: "Thank you again for your most interesting and thought-provoking talk last nite (sic). You will be happy to know that your discussion seems to have aroused a great deal of concern. Discussion lasted till after midnight in several halls—a very heartening sign to those who know how rarely such interest is generated over anything at Bryn Mawr."[42]

———

Charlie loved the writings of his boss, A. J. Muste, one of the most inspiring essayists of his day. At the age of six, Muste arrived from Holland with his immigrant family and soon became a naturalized US citizen. A graduate of Hope College near Grand Rapids, Michigan, he became a minister for the Dutch Reformed Church, but later resigned, feeling he was not in line with the church's strict theology. He moved to Rhode Island, became a Quaker minister in the Providence Meeting, resigned from that and then in 1919 became the spokesman for the Lawrence textile strike, where he implemented nonviolent techniques. After rising to head of the new Amalgamated Textile Workers Union, he became a recognized union leader and in the 1920s and 30s became very active in new union organizations. In 1936 he broke with socialists and communists, with whom he had worked at times, and returned to the Christian pacifist position, determined to combat Marxism and proclaim Christianity. The inherently violent beliefs of communists put them opposite to Christian laws of love and nonviolence, and Muste became dedicated to writing about and teaching the differences between the two.

In the November 1950 issue of *Fellowship* magazine, published by the FOR, Muste had written about overcoming fear.

> Jesus' greatest strength was that there was nothing he wanted of the world, nothing of which it could deprive him, that he was not entirely willing to let go.... He had overcome the world because it could no longer hurt him.
>
> The dictators and the stirrers up of hatred and hysteria all work from the knowledge that people are "attached"—attached to money, ease, a job, pleasure; to other people, to fame, to a reputation for being a solid citizen. These things can be taken from them. Therefore, they can be terrorized, made to conform, sign loyalty oaths, goose-step, and stand by silent when freedom is stoned to death.
>
> Jesus, although having the power to kill, chose instead to suffer and pay the ultimate price. At first men never believe that. They cannot "see" it, for it seems absurd. The Cross is foolishness. He explained the concept of Divine Foolishness. Jesus, who had seemed foolish, had after all been infinitely wise. He who had seemed weak would reign among men throughout time. Whenever a man follows in Jesus' footsteps—

even of you and me this is true—he walks the earth without fear, and where he is, life is renewed. This is not a counsel of passivity, indifference or cheap success. It is a summons to sanity and moral heroism.[43]

Charlie had long been fascinated with the idea of nonattachment furthered by Gerald Heard, and there it was again, pounded in beautifully by Muste. He resolved to become less attached to things which could cause him to live in fear, where he would be susceptible to spiritual blackmail. *Moral heroism*, he thought. *Not passivity or cheap success, but a hard-won peace with the self.*

Africa, Interracial Workshops

Bayard Rustin wrote describing an inspiring struggle for freedom that erupted in Africa's Gold Coast (now Ghana), giving hope and courage to leaders in the country of South Africa and foreshadowing the American civil rights movement. Rustin had interviewed American-educated Dr. Kwame Nkrumah and other leaders in the movement, as well as "simple men" who were shot at and imprisoned. The story began in 1949, when Nkrumah established the CPP (Convention People's Party) whose slogan was "Self Government Now."[44]

On November 20, 1949, the CPP held its first mass meeting, attended by 90,000 people, where the leaders called for radical reforms. The government laughed at the demands and British officials called it "drum beating." But, Bayard wrote, "The British were soon to discover that the 'African dog' bites as well as barks. Nkrumah went to villages and towns calling for boycotts, strikes, civil disobedience and noncooperation."

The day of the first strike, a Sunday, military veterans planned to march to the governor's house to present a petition of grievances to the governor. The government gave permission for a parade and the route was agreed to.

"Sunday afternoon came," Bayard wrote. "The veterans were marching abreast toward Government House. They were followed by thousands of bush and towns people, many of whom had traveled miles to the capital to witness the beginning of the general strike. As the veterans, marching slowly and with great discipline, reached a spot near the sea about one half mile from the Governor's palace, they were met by a British officer … in command of several scores of African police and soldiers with guns and fixed bayonets. The war veterans began to sing, and marched on.

'Shoot,' cried the officer.[45]

Not one African soldier or policeman fired. "Shoot! Shoot!" he cried again. As the veterans continued on, the African soldiers ... would not fire upon their brothers and cousins, who merely marched and sang—and carried no weapons. "The bewildered officer opened fire. Four men lay mortally wounded or dead upon the ground. Most of the veterans continued forward."[46]

On February 22, Nkrumah and all the executive members of the CPP were arrested en masse and jailed with the charge of inciting an illegal strike.[47] Bayard wrote, "By March the curfew and martial law were lifted. The CPP told the people that only their actions could release their leaders. They were encouraged not to hate the British but to go to the polls for independence, for Ghana and for God. On April 1, CPP voters swarmed to the polls and won the local elections. At Accra, the seat of the government, 'the capital was taken without a gun.'"[48] In 1951, the CPP, with the imprisoned Nkrumah at the top of the list, swept to victory.

On March 20, 1951, the Legislative Assembly opened with Africa's first black Prime Minister, Dr. Kwame Nkrumah, and a new government, while the men imprisoned with him became *ministers of state*.[49] Charlie could not agree more with Bayard's conclusion, "A handful of black men have demonstrated once again that no array of guns and prison walls can prevent men from pursuing freedom and justice when they have rejected guns and depend on that spiritual power which springs from forgiveness and an indomitable will."[50]

George Houser, working on Interracial Workshops sponsored jointly by CORE and FOR, for college students and young adults to take place in July in Washington, DC, organized them for the purpose of training and nonviolent action for combating discrimination. Many swimming pools, municipal and private, throughout the nation had closed in recent years rather than face racial integration. Racial clashes took place in 1949 when some of them opened on a nonsegregated basis. CORE was convinced that these clashes could have been averted if there had been educational campaigns among the public. The following summer two pools targeted by the CORE plan opened and operated all summer without interracial clashes.[51] Helping to keep these pools operating would be part of the workshop tasks.

Also in the mix would be integrating restaurants. This campaign had gained considerable notice the previous summer following the arrest and conviction of fifteen workshop participants who peacefully sought service at Sholl's Cafeteria in Washington, DC. The case was now on appeal. In May, Charlie received a letter from the New York FOR, informing him Houser would be in Europe till the first week in July and Charlie needed to recommend attendees, as it lacked participants.[52]

Although workshoppers learned most through participation in action projects, a key aspect of the program was group discussions led by persons prominent in the race relations field, such as Mary McLeod Bethune of the National Council of Negro Women. Additionally, each group, housed together in one building near the Negro community, would have first-hand experience in interracial living. Learning to write press releases, radio scripts and progress bulletins were important to participants, who also received training in meeting with community leaders and negotiating with theater owners, restaurant officials and personnel directors.[53]

Walker Baby Number Five

A new Walker would arrive in late summer, prompting a move to Tanguy Homesteads in 1951. All of Bill Willoughby's jokes about Marian and Charlie's small house had hit home, so to speak, and they started looking for another house in the area to rent.

In Philadelphia Charlie strode the pleasant walk from the train station to his office, delighting in the crisp, spring day. "We've had girl-boy-girl-boy, and now it's time for a girl. I guess I'll concentrate on girl names," Charlie mused. Lofty clouds floated in a blue sky above skyscrapers, while the city's waking up from a long winter brought a lightness to his step. The stately statue of Quaker William Penn on top of City Hall, the tallest building in the city, made him feel a certain pride. Penn, founder of this city! As flawed as it was, this country still was partly a reflection of the work of the Friends and of Penn.

The work of the Quakers is largely ignored by historians. Why they were given so little credit, Charlie did not know. But, when the citizens of Boston confiscated the Quakers' "dangerous" books in 1656 and burned them, they were decrying ideas that now are part of American law and history. The Quaker ideals of "conscience" and "human brotherhood" are now commonly accepted. Penn's Frame of Government influenced much of our Constitution.

The nation's courts allow the use of an affirmation instead of an oath, because the Quakers took the Bible's admonition seriously.[54] One can now swear or *affirm* to tell the truth in court, because the Quakers believe truth is sacred at all times, not just under oath. When Penn's colony was established, Penn made his historic treaty with the Native Americans. He bought, not confiscated, land for his settlers. This treaty, said the French philosopher Voltaire, was the only one between the white men and Indians never sworn to and never broken.[55]

Quakers were the first religious sect to set free their own slaves. Quaker conductors and stationmasters in the Underground Railroad—like Charlie's ancestor Lindley Coates—gave Harriet Beecher Stowe much of the material she used in *Uncle Tom's Cabin*. And, after the Civil War, Friends established many schools for freed slaves in the South.[56]

Quakers have generally been two to three hundred years ahead of their time.

Charlie felt rich indeed. Rich in family, in friends, profession and purpose. He certainly was not wealthy, but he felt he was the richest man around.

He thought of the popular saying, *Quakers came to the New World to do good, but they did well.* However, when one studies the real history, one realizes that Quakers not only did well, they did an enormous amount of good. Yes, Philadelphia grew into the biggest and richest city in the colonies for a time, but Quaker values and ethics helped the colony prosper into the free and democratic system we live under today, and that is our inheritance from the Quakers.

———

In April Bayard Rustin had been invited to speak at the home of humanitarian Pearl Buck, who had won the Nobel Prize for Literature for novels like *The Good Earth* and *East Wind: West Wind*. Charlie wrote, "You are invited by Frank Keller of Souderton to come down the morning of May 1, and he will take you to Pearl Buck's home. He has already asked her, and she will be glad to see you." Charlie joked, referring to her book title, that Bayard must have made some fortuitous remark in passing and having "sown the wind," was now "reaping the whirlwind" of being asked to Pearl Buck's house. He added, "The program will last one hour and fifteen minutes, and you will have the entire time. They want you to talk about race relations and nonviolent direct action in that regard. A question period is also in order." [57] Buck had grave concerns about race relations and after this meeting continued to speak about it locally and nationally.

––––––––––

In spring the Pond House at Tanguy became available, after the Guthrie family moved to their new house on the other side of the old barn. Bob Wilson, one of the founders of the cooperative community, strongly wanted the Walkers to join, feeling they would be a great addition to Tanguy's diverse and cooperative life.

"I'd like to live at Tanguy," Marian told Charlie, when he proposed they move there, only a few miles away from the Thornton House. "The people there are wonderful, and the kids have no friends here to play with. I have to take them everywhere. Besides, the driveway would be short and flat."

Another reason for the move was difficulty with the long, hilly driveway at Thornton. The not-so-new car battery was in bad shape, and to jump-start it they would let the car drift down the driveway into a small creek valley. However, even after starting, it would often stall on the ascent up to Cheyney Road. So it sat in the valley until the milk man came and pushed it up the hill with his truck, which he did many times without complaining. They realized depending on the good nature of the milk man could not be the best plan, but had little money to replace the battery.

"But, you're due soon, and it would be tough on you to move in the heat of summer."

"I can do it, Charlie. Let's move to Tanguy."

Tanguy Homesteads had been founded in 1945 by about a half-dozen families, mainly Quaker, who wanted to live out Quaker testimonies of racial harmony, social justice and peace. It still functions as a cooperative community with about forty families. It boasts a community center, a pond, and some twelve acres of dedicated open space.

In 1951 several black families lived at Tanguy, and they took part in all social functions, causing controversy in the West Chester area. At that time blacks and whites were not permitted to socialize.

Any family who planned to move to Tanguy generally needed a place to stay while their house was built. Therefore, many had lived temporarily at the Big House, the large home of the original Tanguy family. The Pond House presented another option, a former outbuilding down the hill from the big House near an old, roofless stone spring house that might have been used for processing the milk produced by the farm. The Walkers chose the Pond House.

The main road, or dirt path at the time, snaking through Tanguy was called Twin Pine Way, as Twin Pines were a symbol for cooperatives.

One evening before they moved, Charlie had some good news for his very pregnant wife, "Marian, some participants at my latest work camp learned we are moving and we need help, so they've volunteered to paint our new home!"

"That's marvelous, Charlie!" She sat, holding her big tummy, exhausted and frazzled from trying to pack up her household. "When can they start?"

"This weekend."

Marian was grateful. The work campers came and when they left, the house looked better, but the paint job was not finished. Finishing the painting would require Marian to climb high ladders. Displeased but determined, she did it anyway and they were ready to move in. Again, Charlie's brother Herb helped with the move, along with some Tanguyites.

Marian unpacked in the heat, careful not to carry heavy boxes or furniture. She was good at organizing and telling helpers what went where. The new house contained no attic or basement and was small. But it had one big room, where two sets of bunk beds lined one wall, making a great place for four kids to play and sleep. The older children slept on top bunks, with little ones on the bottom. Though rather tiny, the house sat in the middle of a community Marian strongly wanted to be part of. She quickly made friends.[58]

A large field in front of the Pond House became a fun place for children to hide in tall grass. The red barn behind the Big House hosted barn dances, bobbing for apples, hide-and-seek in the hay, and jumping off high rafters into haymows. The kids loved it.

On July 16, Charlie wrote to his friend, Francis Hall, "I am indeed sorry to have to say I can't come for the committee meeting on the Spiritual Life of the Fellowship on Sunday-Monday. For one thing, the baby isn't here yet, and I can't leave either just before or just after." Charlie offered some thoughts on Spiritual Life, adding, "The ultimate objective of our committee's work, I imagine, would be to get more members of the Fellowship to engage in prayer and spiritual disciplines regularly.... As FOR people attend these retreats, they will ... be driven to a more mature ...

understanding regarding the importance of the life of prayer to the peacemaker."[59]

––––––––––

Baby number five came out a girl, as Charlie had predicted, blonde and cute. Valerie Clare Walker came into the world at Chester County Hospital in West Chester. The name Valerie means "strong," and the root word, valor, also means "personal bravery" and "strength of mind or spirit that enables a person to encounter danger with firmness."[60] Clare is a French word for "light." Her parents had a vision of a brave and clear light to the world in this child. She came into the world shortly after the move to Tanguy Homesteads, and the couple made room for a crib in their bedroom.

Working with Bayard Rustin for the FOR

In December, Charlie attended a Student Volunteer National Conference Quadrennial, sponsored by the Student Volunteer Movement for Foreign Missions, at the University of Kansas in Lawrence. He and Bayard Rustin served as staff and delegates to this conference, which brought together 2,200 students, including about 200 foreign students, with the theme "Christ's Kingdom—Man's Hope."[61]

Charlie felt the platform speaker was way over the heads of the students![62] He commented to Bayard that the speaker on India saw fit to spend the first fifteen minutes in an esoteric discourse on philosophy. "Although he displayed an impressive virtuosity in the field, and juggled the names of Locke, Hobbes and Freud with dazzling dexterity, he was handicapped by the fact that nobody knew what he was talking about!" Bayard agreed, smiling.

"And when he finally came soaring down out of the ozone, he still moved along on such a lofty plane that I can remember only the two words, 'particularity' and 'Jinnah.' Or maybe it was 'Jinnah sais pas.'"[63] Charlie chuckled at his own French joke.

But the big issue at the conference was race. It grew out of an incident when an interracial group was refused service at a restaurant in downtown Lawrence. This group included two Indian students, a Canadian, Bayard, the Chicago FOR secretary, and a white minister. The Indian students were deeply affected.

Several of the group prepared a statement to be given to the Steering

Committee proposing three things: (1) that a list of nondiscriminatory restaurants be made available to conferees, (2) that a delegation visit restaurant owners in the spirit of Christian concern, and (3) that future conferences be held only where there is a civil rights law which is reasonably effective.

The statement made a difference. The conference had at no point yet really come to life, and conferees had been swimming in a sea of abstractions. Here was something concrete.

"I think the main factor was the foreign students," Charlie decided. "They had been distributed around in discussion groups (150 such groups) so that each group had one or two foreign students in them. Thus, it was assured the issue would be widely discussed. Then there was the Negro constituency; several unfortunate incidents had occurred on the way to the conference, and a few days earlier, an African student had been denied a hotel room downtown."[64]

The foreign students wanted to hold a protest meeting at once. After raising the issue, the next task was to get the facts, and then act responsibly in terms of the conference. The Steering Committee spent hours on the issue. A strange fact emerged: while many on the Steering Committee had wide experience in interracial education, as the various forces in this incident started swirling around, they found it extremely difficult to move ahead with confidence.

When by Sunday no clear-cut action had been taken, *all* of the African students refrained from going to church under fear of discrimination. At one of the churches a black man was separated from his white companions by the usher, maybe by mistake. When the minister made a reference to "some conspicuous guests," the black man was ready to leave. Later it was found the minister was referring to several in the front row who were wearing clerical collars!

"That is the kind of thing which can easily happen in these tense situations,"[65] Charlie mused. The Steering Committee brought some constructive suggestions to a fireside meeting where about four hundred people came out, including some townspeople. The meeting became very tense. A white student, in effect, called a black student a liar.

But the decisive point in the meeting came, Charlie felt, when Bayard, with more than his usual eloquence, pointed out this was not so much a matter of rights for Negroes, as it was man's injustice to man. He told of a white mob that wrecked the home of a black man in Cicero, Illinois, burning his furniture and marriage certificate. On the South Side in Chicago, a Negro real estate man would charge eighteen dollars a week for an unpainted room in a cellar, with hardly any toilet facilities, to a family with five children. This brought a note of contrition into the picture, and the group soon endorsed the Steering Committee's suggestions.[66]

"Success comes," Charlie concluded, "with a constant test of our resourcefulness, our energy and our willingness to give ourselves to people in countless discussions. What opens people up finally, however, is not so much argument, as example—and commitment. We tend to forget how much we were moved once by someone who, with little but the certainty of suffering before him, nevertheless committed himself to the way of nonviolence."[67]

Charlie experienced an extraordinary discussion on the way back from Lawrence to Chicago. "We rode on a special train, which also picked up other passengers. Some students wanted to talk further about problems raised at the conference. A time was set, and they went up and down the train drumming up interest. Finally, a group gathered in the lounge car. There were by actual count eighty-five people there, though it seemed like more, including several soldiers, business men and porters who seemed to find reasons for stopping by frequently. At one end of the car was a water cooler, so fortuitously designed as to enable Bayard to sit up on it. I stood below down in front. We dealt for two hours with questions that were raised, trying to keep both the religious and the political implications in the picture instructively. It was an intensely dramatic situation and probably, for that reason, a receptive one."[68]

Charlie wrote to A. J. Muste, "We are drawing up a Christmas card to be mimeographed on holiday red paper, with a strong pacifist message, to be distributed near Christmas as we sing carols." Muste approved the idea.[69]

As a result the Philadelphia FOR office produced a card, folded in four parts, with a hand-drawn bell and holly on the cover with the message, "Peace On Earth, Good Will To Men," and it was signed by "The Carolers." Inside read:

> The First Christmas—We sometimes forget what kind of world it was to which it was proclaimed: 'Peace on earth, good will to men.' It was a world of tyranny and oppression. A nation in bondage awaited a Deliverer who would lead in driving out the conqueror. But the Child,

when he grew up, did not use the sword for deliverance. He taught the way of love, even of enemies. He so lived and taught not because He was indifferent to the suffering of His people, but rather because only by goodness can evil be overcome. Truly the Prince of Peace had been born.

Christmas, 1951. The best Christmas present the world could receive is—PEACE. We talk about peace, not acts of WAR in the name of PEACE. But the genuine peace for which the people of the world have been seeking and longing. Whether or not a cease-fire in Korea comes by Christmas, declare your own cease-fire. Lay down the weapons of war, and join with others who have "put up the sword" and seek a better way. Only by constructive and nonviolent methods can a world of peace and justice be built.

We sing the Christmas tidings in the spirit He brought 1951 years ago. For we believe it to be the "wisdom" to which the Magi paid tribute, and by which the world might be led out of its darkness and travail into the light of peace.[70]

Muste, Gandhi, and John Raitt

In January 1952, Charlie again searched for a part-time secretary. "While a secretary will not find herself catapulted into the higher income brackets, the position does offer an excellent opportunity to learn more about the peace movement," he wrote in his ad in the Philadelphia FOR newsletter.[71]

He also reported in the newsletter, "A U.P. Dispatch quotes General Van Fleet, commander of the 8th Army in Korea: 'Korea has been a blessing. There had to be a Korea to put our defenses in good shape.' The people in Korea may be less inclined to feel they have been blessed."[72]

"Charlie, we have good news for you!" A. J. Muste greeted his young colleague when Charlie visited the FOR National Office in early January, 1952. Muste ushered Charlie to a seat and told Charlie that, because of what needed to be done out of the Philadelphia office, the budget committee had recommended, and the Executive Committee subsequently adopted, a record budget of over $6,000! "Now, this is because of the vigorous program, especially in the church and high school fields, that you have undertaken," Muste explained. "I hope you are okay with continuing in 1952 on a two-thirds-time basis."[73]

"Of course! That's wonderful!"

Charlie, extremely happy to hear the news, felt it a fulfillment of his passionate desire for funds for the needed and exciting programs the FOR conducted in the Philadelphia area. He noted the New York office gave a large vote of confidence to his program, yet kept him at part time. Then Muste asked about the upcoming year.

"As far as plans for January go," Charlie told Muste, "I'm planning a Gandhi Memorial Meeting for January 30, on the fourth anniversary of Gandhi's assassination."

"Good idea," Muste agreed.

"The influence of his philosophy and programs is still very much alive, not only in India but in many parts of the world."[74]

"I'd suggest Cherian Thomas as a speaker," offered Muste, "since he was an active worker in the Gandhian movement and has seen firsthand the impact of nonviolence on India. He also was a former official in the Indian Congress Party and is now on the staff of the Indian Legation here in New York City."[75]

"I'd like to schedule Bayard, too," Charlie added, "He was recently given the Jefferson Award for his work for racial justice and can testify to the power and relevance of nonviolence on the American scene. You know, A. J., pacifists seem to 'talk to themselves' too much, but here is an opportunity for outreach, for inviting nonpacifists to a program with wide interest."

Muste agreed.

"I plan to hold this Gandhi Memorial Meeting at the Friends Meeting House on South 12th Street in Philadelphia," Charlie explained, "and get more sponsors for it."[76] Muste thoroughly approved of Charlie's ideas.

After more discussion of plans for the new year, Charlie showed his mentor a letter. "It's from Irwin Shaw from Random House publishers, author of *The Young Lions*, a book about the fate of three soldiers during World War II.[77] He sent me this reply to my letter, 'I hope deeply for a final reconciliation with you. I am sick at the thought of violence. But the professed advertisement of nonviolence, I am sorry to say, seems to me, in this world, merely to be an agreement in advance to play the role of the victim in a savage drama of extermination.'"[78]

Muste considered a moment and told Charlie he'd like to make a reply to the letter himself. Although surprised, Charlie welcomed Muste's help in the matter. Later, he received a copy of Muste's letter to Shaw, saying in part: "My young friend and colleague, Charles Walker, was good enough to let me see the letter that he wrote you some time ago and your note to him of Jan. 5, 1952. Though I have no special right to intrude on your time, I am moved to send this letter for a number of reasons.[79]

"For one thing, you may or may not recall that a few years ago, you gave me permission to quote from your short story, 'Preach on the Dusty Roads,' and, if I wished, to use it as the title of a book of mine which Harper's was publishing. As it turned out, Harper's turned down the title and the book was called instead, *Not By Might*.... My main purpose is to comment on your rejection of Charles Walker's suggestion about resorting to nonviolence.... You, as is the case with so many of us, are 'weak at the thought of violence.' But because we have not the imagination and the faith to resort to nonviolence, we are drawn deeper and deeper into counter-violence, which is less and less to be distinguished from the violence which we abhor. Somewhere, there must be an end to that process."[80]

The Korean War weighed heavily on all pacifists' hearts. Thus Charlie felt heartened by a request for reading materials from a Korean man studying at the University of Michigan. Along with the materials, Charlie sent a letter urging nonviolence in the present situation over establishing a permanent cease-fire in Korea:

> The United States will be unable to perform much of a constructive role in the future of Korea unless it is first willing to forgo any ambition for establishing—or trying to establish—a power position in the Orient. As in the case of the British in India, having renounced the imperialist role it is possible to re-enter as a friend and co-worker.
>
> While we shall try to identify ourselves in any way open to us with the people of your country, even more, we hope to work even harder to prevent new Koreas elsewhere. As we are bidden to pray, "Thy will be done," I cannot believe it is God's will for us that we should slaughter each other.[81]

Kilsoo Ken Kang replied, "How I thank you, I don't know.... As a matter of fact, I have been struggling with the 'possibility of dealing with violence by nonviolence,'... so that I can be [of] service to prevent the slaughter-each-other business."[82]

Quakers had given up plain, gray clothing. Most had stopped using "plain speech." However, some of them retained it, if they worked for Quaker organizations or had been raised in Quaker households. One day in February, Charlie received a letter with a request from a Joseph Karsner, Director of the Speaker's Bureau for the Friends Peace Committee. It did not surprise Charlie to see the quaint "thee and thy" in the Friend's speech.

"I'm writing," Karsner began, "to ask if thee would speak at Richland Friends Meeting in Quakertown, on Fifth Month 11, at 2:30 in the afternoon. We are having a Forum sponsored by the Meeting."

Charlie checked his schedule. That should work out.

"The person for thee to contact is Lillian H. Shaw. Thee will receive thy expenses for the trip." Karsner indicated it would be on a First Day, or Sunday in layman's terms.

"If thee wishes to go up in the morning, Meeting for Worship is at 10:30. The subject of thy talk will be, 'Our Role in Today's World.'"

Charlie made a note to respond favorably. The letter concluded, "Thank thee very much for taking this assignment, and I look forward to seeing thee then. I'll send a confirming letter to thee soon."[83]

"Marian, how would you like to attend the Quarterly Meeting of the FOR March 4th in Philadelphia? I've arranged for Culbert Rutenber to speak, author of *The Dagger and the Cross*. You've heard me talk about his book on Christian pacifism? It's said to be the most important book to appear in this field since the Second World War!"

"Yes, I've read it and I'd like to go." Marian wiped counters after the evening meal.

"The frosting on the cake is that I've secured John Raitt, singing star of "Oklahoma" and "Carousel", to provide entertainment for the evening!"

"John Raitt! How did you do that?"

"Well, he's a member of the FOR and an anti-war man. Since I'm a sports fan, it was interesting to find out that besides his Broadway talent, Raitt was a member of the American Olympic track team."

"No kidding! Where is this meeting going to be?"

"It'll be held in the Sunday School Room of First Baptist Church, which can hold several hundred."[84]

"Count me in, Charlie. Let me call my mother to see if she'll take care of the children."

When Charlie invited ministers in the Philadelphia area to the meeting who were interested in peace, he urged, "It is imperative that conversation between pacifist and nonpacifist Christians goes on more searchingly if the church is to have a clear voice to raise in these dark and troubled times."[85]

When Marian and Charlie headed for the Raitt-Rutenbur Quarterly Meeting, the evening's March snow storm was characterized as "one of the worst nights for a long time." Despite that, over one hundred people attended, and a very pretty, dark-haired Mrs. Raitt accompanied her husband on the piano.

Charlie and Marian both believed John Raitt was "magnificent." They loved Broadway shows and songs. At one point, John sang, "The sun is a-shining to welcome the day. Hi, ho! Come to the fair!" It was a number Marian had learned in high school, and she sang along with gusto. John turned in her direction and smiled at her as he sang. Marian became self-conscious and sang more softly. Later in the concert, Raitt jumped off the stage to interact with the audience, and Marian worried he might hurt himself. Then she remembered his Olympic background![86]

John Raitt and his wife stayed the entire meeting, talked with quite a few people, and left among the last. This successful event helped raise funds for the FOR's work.

In his March report about the Rutenber talk titled, "An Adequate Religious Basis for Christian Pacifism," Charlie commented, "As we claim to be Christian pacifists, it is important for us to understand why the great bulk of the Christian community rejects the stand we take."[87][88]

By now, Charlie had found a second job working one-third time as Executive Secretary for the Friends Medical Society of Philadelphia. The FMS would pay the FOR $250 a year for his office use, typewriter, mimeograph, telephone and minor office supplies. Salary for Charlie would be $1,200 and an additional $50–$100 would be marked for FMS travel and overhead expenses.[89]

A knock on his office door took Charlie's attention from reading the March issue of *Fellowship*. He called "Come in!" Joy Marshall, a former FOR secretary, entered with a baby on her hip. Both bundled up for the cold day, they soon unwrapped and the little girl bounced happily on her mother's knee.

"Just came to say 'hi' Charlie, and let you meet my little girl. You know, I used to think your children were wonders, but that was before Sylvia arrived," she gushed. "I expect great things of her. She is now talking at ten weeks, in the best FOR tradition. So help me, her first word was 'Gandhi'!"[90]

They both laughed as the baby grabbed Charlie's finger with one of her little hands.

"Today she suddenly said 'apple,' and she was eating applesauce at the time. Einstein, take a back seat!"[91]

"You're probably right," Charlie countered. "The first words Winifred spoke were 'Why the heck do I have to go to bed at 7 o'clock?'"[92]

"Ha. Ha. You know, I think babies are wonderful," Joy added, "I advise them as the cure-all for all ills, physical and mental. Now that I have one which takes up all of my time, I wonder how your wife manages her life."[93]

"She seems to do amazingly well, I think. But you mention babies as a cure-all, and this is enough to make a strong man shudder like an aspen. There are times, you know, when the cure is worse than the disease."[94] Charlie chuckled at his own joke.

"Well, my husband stays home nights and helps me!"[95] Joy enjoyed the tit-for-tat with her former boss and his quick wit. She knew she could tease him about being gone from home a great deal because of his work.

"Well, when Number Four came along, I told Marian, 'This is absolutely the last. Any more and I throw in the towel.'"[96] Charlie let out a belly-laugh.

Joy laughed. They talked about old times and then the subject came around to the new secretary, Mrs. Fulford. Joy commented, "Dawn seems to be doing a good job. But, what a pity she's pregnant now! I thought it was middle-aged spinsters for you from now on!"[97]

"I tried to hire an older lady, however it was not to be!"

"I believe you tried, Charlie, but good secretaries are difficult to find. Oh, by the way, we saw "Three Wishes for Jamie" at the Shubert Theater starring John Raitt! Imagine a singer like that being a FOR member! Somehow, we all seem to be peculiar misfits."[98]

"I think you misread the situation. FOR people are so danged normal, ordinary and adjusted that they don't stand out against this misfit civilization."[99]

Joy's eyes twinkled. "I do miss you all. And didn't we have good times and do great works, of course?"[100]

"Of course! But if you miss us that much, over there is a sizeable pile of envelopes to address."[101]

"I don't miss you that much!"

South African Nonviolent Resistance

In March 1952 Charlie sent out a memo titled "Background on the South African Non-Violent Resistance Campaign."

On April 6, a history-making campaign of nonviolent noncooperation against unjust racial laws will be launched in South Africa. For the first time, groups representing the masses of native African, Indian and colored communities are joining in united action. Resistance will be directed especially at Pass laws, which make it illegal for Africans to go outside a certain area; the apartheid regulations, which enforce segregation in train stations, post offices, etc.; and in rural areas against the government's policy of limiting livestock....

The campaign was agreed upon December 17, 1951. The government was asked to repeal these laws.... The ... government, however, has made it clear it will take strong action against this movement. Manilal Gandhi, son of Mahatma Gandhi, has already begun a three-week fast.

On January 30 the *South African Free Press* quoted Prime Minister Malan warning a Bantu tribal organization, the African National Congress, that the government had no intention of repealing these laws, [declaring]: "It is self-contradictory to claim as an inherent right of the Bantu, who differ in many ways from Europeans, that they should be regarded as not different, especially when it is borne in mind that these differences are permanent and not man-made. If this is a matter of indifference to you and if you do not value your racial characteristics, you cannot in any case dispute the Europeans' right ... to take the opposite view and to adopt the necessary measures to preserve their identity as a separate community.[102]

Charlie ended the background memo with his own commentary. "The fact that this movement is being launched as a nonviolent one could have historic significance for the whole struggle for freedom and self-determination. This could be the 'revolutionary instrument' which could serve the true interests of justice."[103]

A June 13 memo from A. J. Muste said the action scheduled for April 6 in South Africa did not come off, but that small groups would be trained to carry out nonviolent actions against segregation and be prepared to accept imprisonment. "It should be kept in mind that there is some Communist infiltration in the leadership of one or two of the organizations of non-whites in South Africa. It would seem unwise on that account to cease our interest in the struggle, since that is simply abandoning the field to the Communists. It is especially important under the circumstances that in anything we do, nonviolence should be emphasized as the only right and effective method of struggle.[104]

John Swomley, Associate Secretary in the FOR National Office, sent a letter in early July asking if Charlie could use Bayard Rustin for a speaking tour after he returned from Africa. The FOR had spent a large sum on

Rustin's Africa trip, and they needed to recoup the money. "If you could guarantee fifty dollars for each day of Bayard's time and could actually get seventy-five a day, we would be willing to have the additional sum go into your own budget."[105]

Swomley added a joke: "I hear from Glenn Smiley the Communists are picketing Forest Lawn Cemetery out there. The sign reads, 'It's a Capitalist Plot.'"

Later in July, Charlie wrote to Morgan State College in Baltimore, "Inasmuch as Bayard Rustin, Director of College Work for the FOR, is now in England and will later be in Africa, I am pinch-hitting to make inquiry about the Christmas conferences.... Bayard, incidentally, will have been returned only a brief time from Africa, where he will have conferred with revolutionary leaders there, seeking to win them to nonviolent revolutionary methods in their struggles (as you know the Communist Party is making rapid headway), and in some cases where the group is already committed to non-violence, to give of our experience with nonviolence in the racial field in America. Thus he might give some really fresh perspective regarding the African situation in the section on the world struggle."[106]

The Philadelphia FOR Executive Committee, including John Ewbank, Wayne Dockhorn and Miriam Pennypacker, met on July 14. Disgusted that so many meetings had been canceled because some of the officers could not attend, Charlie suggested that another person be designated to run the meetings. It was no surprise, then, when they asked him to run the meeting in place of the absent president. He reluctantly agreed.

Treasurer John Ewbank reported the main appeal for the summer salary fund brought in less than $200. "The financial situation is poor and will probably result in having no secretary for Charles Walker in the fall." Considerable discussion of the economic outlook included talking about what more could be eliminated. Meetings? Speakers?[107]

Volunteering at the FOR

One perfect day in mid-October, Marian and Charlie headed by car to the FOR office in Philadelphia.

Charlie felt blessed in his children. He remembered how he had told Gene Exman in a recent letter, "I think they 'wax in wisdom and stature and in favor with man'—and I hope with God. The thought of how much children are influenced by their parents is a continually terrifying thought, though it shouldn't be. We influence people around us all the time. Coworkers have the advantage of being able to get up and leave, but kids can't."[108]

Dawn Fulford had left to have twins, and no funds were available to replace her. With no secretary again for Charlie, Marian had offered to come in one day a week to type and answer the phone. Her typing skills were exceptional, and she enjoyed the change. A Tanguy Homesteads woman, Ellen Bleecher, took turns at the job, and Amy Kurkjian gave a hand. They were paid little but any amount was a help. Marian brought her vegetarian food with enough for Charlie. For him, it meant one more meatless meal a day, and Marian noted he was not crazy about that.

"Charlie, I just love the trees when they're flaming reds and yellows like this," Marian exclaimed, feeling energized to be on the road. She loved her world right then. "Valerie's walking and talking and just the cutest, sweetest baby."

Charlie halted for a red light and started up again. Then he changed the conversation to a more serious subject. "By the way, Bayard Rustin is back from Africa. He wrote a memo to those who made his trip possible and sent me a copy. He said, 'From the Mediterranean to the Cape of Good Hope, every imaginable form of resistance is being used to break three hundred years of various forms of European domination. The methods vary from the nonviolence of South African Resisters to the arson, murder and juju of Kenya.'"

"What's juju?"

"It's the magic ascribed to charms or amulets used by Africans. Bayard thinks everywhere in Africa, nationalism is rising, but he's also convinced that peaceful solutions in some very real degree will depend on the nature of the response that the American people and government make to these very sincere peoples' revolutions. Time did not permit his fulfilling all the requests made by African leaders to speak on nonviolence. Because of this urgent demand, he's been invited to return to Africa for a year or so."[109]

"A year?" Marian was incredulous. "A whole year away from his work here?"

"Yes, and even though it's a long time, he feels inclined to go. But only if the FOR becomes convinced this work in Africa would serve the cause of peace and racial justice more than other things he might do."

"What did he ask you to do?"

"No more than give prayerful consideration of his situation."[110]

———

On December 8, Charlie received a thank-you letter from James H. Duckrey, president of Cheyney State Teacher's College. "This note of appreciation is from the faculty, staff and students who were the beneficiaries of your significant contribution to our Religious Emphasis Week. I personally considered this week's program to be one of the most stimulating events I have witnessed in the life of our College. It is our hope that we may ultimately be successful in our search for ways of exemplifying in practice the wholesome and constructive thoughts that you … brought to us."[111]

Charlie and his Philadelphia committee discussed establishing a "regional pattern" in the Middle Atlantic. His boss, John Swomley, suggested some evaluations of his work might be needed and that Charlie should not expect to be the person to run this regional office. He also said Charlie might think of working elsewhere for the FOR. So Charlie sent requests to some key people for evaluations to be sent to Swomley. [112] It turned out to be a misunderstanding on Charlie's part that Swomley needed him to provide these evaluations, but they give some insight as to how highly Charlie's colleagues thought of him.

On Christmas Eve, Red Schaal of the American Friends Service Committee in Philadelphia composed a letter to Swomley saying, "I have Charlie Walker's letter, relating to a personnel check-up, which seems to me to be a peculiar procedure, but I will conform to the pattern you have set, except I am sending a copy of this letter to Charlie also. As a representative of the pacifist position, Charlie Walker rates very high. He has the sort of devotion and commitment to the job of being a pacifist that lends integrity and force to everything he does. I have not observed him making long speeches or addresses, but I assume from what I have heard he is quite effective at that point. He certainly can make himself understood on an effective level in the meetings where I have seen him operate. As to his organizing ability, I do not think it is his strong point, although I believe he has improved considerably at it. In public relations one finds him a very easy person to work with.

"Charlie has been placed in a very awkward position [because the FOR could only hire him part time, and of necessity he had to work other jobs to support his wife and five children], … in his work with the FOR, but personally I have found him very reasonable and easy to work with in spite of this situation, which is no fault of his. I am concerned that the FOR—national and regional, as well as in Philadelphia—ought to do something more than it is doing for Charlie if we hope to keep him working effectively. If we can't furnish him a full-time job then we ought to encourage him to look elsewhere for one. He is too good a man to depress and confuse by having him work in an impossible situation.... I should think with the people available and the funds available in Philadelphia, something better ought to be possible. I hope this letter will not embarrass either of you, but it is how I feel this Christmas Eve and it carries my judgments and convictions in the situation."[113]

Violence and Nonviolence

A new year rolled around, and Charlie had found a part-time job to replace the one with Friends Medical Society. He wrote in January 1953 to George Houser, "I start today on a new part-time job, which is coaching basketball (assistant) at Westtown School.[114] The basketball job will be okay in some ways, will give me much-needed exercise and be close to home. However, it ties me to a very rigid schedule."[115] Charlie also coached soccer at Westtown and before this had been a night watchman for the school.

Finances at Philadelphia FOR were looking up. Charlie told Swomley their gross income for 1952 listed at $8,000 and income was steadily rising. "I hope such a felicitous trend continues." He related that when his article in the *Friend*, introduced by another party, stated that Charlie "questioned scientific conclusions as a representative of the Gerald Heard school of philosophy," he was upset at being misquoted. "That strange grinding noise you hear in the background is CW gnashing his dentures."[116]

Rustin and Muste at Odds

Bayard Rustin was a homosexual.

This trait had been known for quite some time, but the FOR had tried to keep a lid on it. They wanted to keep a premier speaker, writer and organizer working for peace and racial justice. He was one of their two African American representatives in the field of race relations, Jim Farmer being the other. Bayard's sexual orientation was an embarrassment to the FOR. There were laws against homosexual activity, and Bayard had been jailed a number of times for breaking the law. Since this was a problem which weakened the Fellowship, A. J. Muste had warned Bayard to cease these relationships. Bayard had assured Muste he would do so, but found he could not.[117] Now Bayard was incarcerated in California for an incident in January, and the high degree of publicity reflected once again on the FOR.[118]

Charlie received a February 24 letter from a disappointed A. J. Muste, who had offered to substitute at speaking engagements which Charlie had procured for Bayard at two Quaker colleges, "I gather that Swarthmore and Haverford are not having me. In both cases, they learned about Bayard from American Friends Service Committee and it was before I had any opportunity to write them that we were willing to supply a substitute. Under the circumstances, I thought I had better let it go."[119]

As Rustin biographer Jervis Anderson observed, Muste reasoned that the Christian pacifist message of the FOR was a moral one and one of self-discipline. "It was imperative, Muste emphasized, that Rustin restrain his sexual behavior whenever or wherever he appeared as a representative of the FOR. Surely that wasn't an unreasonable demand."[120]

This was difficult for Muste, as he had thought of Rustin as his adopted son. In the office, the two affectionately had been called "Muste and Rusty." After Bayard was released from jail in March, 1953, Muste, with much regret, felt it necessary to relieve Bayard of his position and asked for his resignation. Thus, Bayard's tenure at the FOR was over.[121]

Even as fellow employees knew Bayard was on his last legs at the FOR, Charlie was undaunted in his support of Bayard, and upbeat in his attitude, as shown by his letter to Bayard in jail, "It was a great delight to get your letter, and to learn of your thinking about the present and future. If many have written you, you can be assured that many more have been thinking of you—not to mention talking about you.... The dominant mood has been the hope that ways will open up for you to apply your gifts and to serve the movement.

"I am looking forward to your release and trust you will let me know at the earliest opportunity when you will be around."[122]

———

Charlie happily reported to his Executive Committee on the success of a conference on Non-Violence and the World Struggle held in Philadelphia at the University of Pennsylvania on March 6 and 7. The event "dominated all other activities this month.... We got excellent news coverage, with the promise of more to come in the Negro press. The FOR name has gotten around town."

A large crowd had appeared to hear Clarence Pickett from the AFSC, and from the FOR, A. J. Muste and Charlie Walker. Resistance in South Africa had been a big draw, along with Korean issues.

"Reactions to the meetings were highly favorable, so far as we heard them," Charlie boasted. "A modest estimate is that forty Negroes were in attendance.… This was a terrific program item: to activate the members, to get our name around, to arouse interest in Africa, to make good publicity possible, that I personally feel the entire project was of great service to our work and relatively cheap for the results we got." Charlie reported increased efficiency and activity with the new secretary, Ethan Nevin, on board.[123]

"Be still and cool in your own mind and spirit from your own thoughts and then you will feel the principle of God." George Fox, the founder of Quakerism, wrote these words in 1658, three hundred years before Charlie Walker read them and scribbled them down on lined notebook paper.[124] Charlie had been doing much soul searching, and wanted to put down his reasons for belief in pacifism. Fox's admonition came from the past, and from this kind of "still and cool" center Charlie produced the following writing, *On Pacifism*.

> Pacifism to me is a way of believing and acting which is implied in the law of love. "Be not overcome of evil, but overcome evil with good" (Romans 12:21).
>
> I think of pacifism as operating on three levels. One is the level of means and methods, of tactics for dealing with tension and conflict. Stated negatively, pacifism imposes limits.… These limits apply not only to the use of force, but to truthfulness, our livelihood and our dealings with people in many ways. Stated affirmatively, 'Love conquers all,' for it is the ultimate reality. Nonviolence as an instrument of reconciliation is based on fearlessness, disinterested concern, the search for justice, and the deep-going belief that no difference, no conflict should dissolve the bonds of brotherhood which unite us.
>
> A second level at which pacifism operates is that of policy. Every problem has its loose ends, its ambiguities, its inheritance of good and evil intermixed. As we cannot rely only on tactics, neither can we rely only on ideals.… Pacifist policy is the middle ground which begins with basic commitment but is still adaptable within limits.…
>
> The first two levels have to do mostly with overcoming evil in its outer and social aspects. The third level is pacifism as a spiritual discipline. It has to do not with outer struggles, so much as with what happens inwardly, as we confront Him whose name is Love. Most of us live in a tepid middle world where good and evil either mean little to us, or are not matters of great soul-searching. But as we actively see the

good, the deadly power of evil, within as well as without, is more clearly revealed to us. The ultimate nature of evil can be seen only in the light of the ultimate good.

Our first response in the presence of God is repentance—for our addictions to pride and greed and prestige, and the subtle "violence" we employ to hold onto them. These stand between us and "the great works" of reconciliation we would do. They keep us from responding whole-heartedly to the love of God. The spiritual discipline is "mortification," the "dying self" which is no death at all but liberation, the gift of eternal life.

Our response finally is grateful service to all God has created. The forgiveness we have experienced in being still called to newness of life flows out to our fellows.... Life is a seamless garment, which if weak or torn at any point, is affected in its entirety. Thus, I find it impossible to abstract pacifism out of the total claims under which I try to live.[125]

Charlie sent the above words to Ern Lefever, hoping to reach him with cool and logical persuasions. But the debate continued to be heated. Ern wrote:

"Violence is evil." Muste, Churchill and Niebuhr know and recognize that, but by so characterizing this factor by no means removes it from an active role among other factors in a complex situation.... Violence is not an unmitigated evil, in the sense that it may be employed for relatively good or relatively bad ends. You will have to admit that violence at the hands of Stalin is a greater evil than in the hands of a city policeman.

Human selfishness is ever-present and even our best saints ... are painfully aware of it. In personal relations and international the same principle applies: the lesser of two evils, or if you prefer, the greater of two goods. Example:... Frau Schmidt needs food. I have more food than I need. If I share, my pride is fostered. To foster pride is evil. If I share not, Frau Schmidt suffers; that is also evil. So I send a CARE parcel (which includes several other evils), hoping that the total good will be greater than the total evil. If this is "prudential politics" make the most of it.[126]

Charlie could not convince everybody and had to live with it. But it was especially hard if the person was an old friend.

———

April 22, Charlie wrote to A. J. Muste, "You may recall that some time ago, I broached the idea of a seminar of pacifists and non-pacifists using Gandhi as the pivotal theme. I have not abandoned all hope that such a get-together could be extremely worthwhile." He added Bayard worked on the idea as well, consulting with big names.

"What could be accomplished?" Charlie asked. "The very holding of such a seminar with names [such as Ralph Bunche,[127] who had expressed interest] would help to put nonviolence a little more on the intellectual map." Charlie suggested some central questions such as: "To what extent was Gandhi a 'special case' or was he a universal figure?... Turning to the American scene, what strands in the American thinking are congenial to Gandhian ideas? In what way is the experience of CORE-FOR race work relevant?"[128]

Charlie had in mind some of Gandhi's inspiring statements: "Nonviolence in its dynamic condition means conscious suffering. It does not mean meek submission to the will of the evil-doer, but it means the putting of one's whole soul against the will of the tyrant. And so I am not pleading for India to practice nonviolence because it is weak. I want her to practice nonviolence being conscious of her strength and power.... Let me not be misunderstood. Strength does not come from physical capacity. It comes from an indomitable will."[129]

Muste responded favorably, sending suggestions of people to contact.

"Let's Talk It Over" and "Mr. Average Citizen Views the News"

Charlie and Marian had been living at Tanguy long enough that they needed to pick out a lot and make a plan to build. One evening in early spring, they sat in the living room with the windows open while the children slept in their room. The talk was about staying or leaving.

"I like Tanguy," Marian said. "The children love it here, but Valerie is getting too big for a crib, and this Pond House is getting too small for five children."

Charlie agreed but was of a different mind on the idea of purchasing a lot. "My business is meetings and committee meetings and more meetings. And Tanguy holds lots of meetings—too much of the same kind of thing. I really don't think I want to be a member here."[130]

"If we move nearby, we can be associate members," Marian offered. "Then we can still come to events and picnics. We can still be part of it." She was disappointed, but they really did not have money to build a house. So, it was decided. The Walkers would hunt for a place to rent again.[131]

Charlie brought up a new subject. "I thought you'd be interested to know the FOR has bought thirteen weeks of time on local radio, Coatesville's WCOJ, for a program called *Let's Talk It Over*. Ed Randall agreed to help us. He's been in the radio business for more than twenty years. We'll bring in local citizens to be interviewed, as well as 'visiting experts.'"

"How exciting. I can tell everybody to tune in! When does it start?"

"September 6 is the opening program, and it runs till the last Sunday in November. Tell your friends to tune in to 1420 on their dial."[132]

"I sure will!"

In August, Charlie arrived home with more good news. "I heard of a new place for us to rent, a former hotel named Tanglewood with possibilities of being made into a pacifist center of some sort."[133]

"Where is it?"

"Here in Cheyney, a few miles away. It's a very large building up in the woods with lots of room for the children."

On a beautiful summer day, Charlie took the family to see the edifice on a hill off Cheyney Road. The car chugged up the narrow driveway and up the steep, steep hill. Heading still upward toward the huge, gray-stone building on the left, they traveled a charming tree-lined drive with an old barn on the right. Roomy but somewhat run-down, the place sat in an extremely woodsy location. A large tree branch extended over the third-floor porch, almost touching its railings.

After stopping in the backyard, they piled out of the car. The children eagerly investigated the house. Marian and Charlie liked its spacious front areas, but the kids seemed to claim the back of the house where the hotel staff had made their quarters. The couple ultimately decided to live in the back section, mainly because they could better afford to heat it. Its small living room contained a humungous fireplace next to a roomy kitchen, while a spacious family room, formerly for hotel storage, offered an abundance of cupboards.

It turned out to have been a dormitory used by Cheyney College during the war, and a hotel before that. The owner, Dr. Rose, agreed to terms. With stone porches and large balconies, it was reminiscent of opulent days gone by. A huge master bedroom suite the family never used took up the third floor. Tanglewood became a wonderful home for the Walkers for six years. Charlie held some meetings at the house, but it never became a peace center.

The family moved there in August, 1953. The day they moved in, the children raced through the area their parents had cleaned and made ready.

Ten-year-old Winnie claimed her own room; Larry and Allan would share bunk beds in another room, while Brenda and Valerie's room abutted the back stairs. The moving of furniture and household items became hectic, so the children played inside and out, exploring the woods and grounds.

Tanglewood became a great place to play indoors in any weather and, on nice days, to run outside through the woods. A tree in the backyard became a favorite hangout, as children in those days spent many hours in trees—talking, daydreaming, reading, and relaxing.

In September, Charlie received a letter from Bill Willoughby, his old Elizabethtown College roommate, now living at Bridgewater College in Virginia, saying he had visited Ern Lefever and new wife Margaret in New York City. At the end he said, "Best wishes to you in your new fifteen-bedroom house. Is Marian enthusiastic about the idea of fifteen children?"[134] She was not, but enjoyed his joke.

The September meeting of the Philadelphia FOR Executive Committee began with a reel tape playing of the radio series *Let's Talk it Over.* September 6 had been "Why Talk It Over?" September 13 had been "What Can One Person Do?"

After the committee listened to the September 13 program that had aired the day before, one committee member asked, "Why can't we present more of the peace point of view?"

"Are you sure we can call the interviewee an 'expert'?" someone else questioned.

Another frowned. "Couldn't the answers be more specific and concrete?"

Charlie took in the suggestions and finally spoke up. "All these are good points, but I think it's more important to preserve the unrehearsed quality of the program. When it's unrehearsed, it's impossible to get in all the items you'd like them to say, but we are all learning. It is a very big job to arrange these programs, and experience is improving them. The total cost of each program has averaged about $24, including station fee, tapes, travel, phones, printing, etc. We hope to raise this money from special gifts and so far have had three gifts totaling $70. If we get an audience built up, the station may be willing to continue us as a sustaining program."[135]

John Ewbank moved that the program be continued. It was approved for the full thirteen weeks. Charlie asked if an advisory committee could be appointed to work with him on this project. Chairman George Walton agreed to appoint such a committee.

A flyer asking for contributions to this project pointed out, "This is an experiment in peace education, affording an opportunity for reaching a new audience. We have been fortunate in securing expert technical advice, and have already gained valuable radio experience. These programs are not designed for those already of our persuasion. The largest segment of the audience will know little about pacifism, perhaps little about world affairs."[136]

At the conclusion of the thirteen-week radio series, the radio station invited Charlie to conduct a fifteen-minute weekly commentary on the news.[137] [138] It was to be called *Mr. Average Citizen Views the News*. He would not be paid, but neither would the FOR need to pay for it. At the December 8 Executive Committee Meeting Charlie played the first radio show, and the comments, this time, were uniformly favorable. Here was an opportunity to obtain a wider audience.[139] This popular radio program continued into the 1960s.

Charlie wrote an October 26 memo to George Houser regarding an upcoming conference. "Can you give me a couple of more days to make a final decision on the Detroit conference? I noticed just recently, with some sense of shock that the National Council [in New York] precedes Detroit, and that in effect I would have to spend more than a solid week away from Philadelphia at a critical time. Furthermore, transportation is no longer available. The Philadelphia FOR is a fiscal wreck—almost—and the 'help' from the Friends Peace Committee toward travel promises to be modest in the extreme (it might be possible transportation by ox cart, provided the ox didn't eat anything along the way!)[140]

As the year came to a close, Charlie hearkened back to the fact that he had been at FOR five years. Many young people, awed by A. J. Muste's powerful intellect and intuitive grasp of the world scene, intensely idolized him despite his being in his sixties. He had become an excellent recruiter of the young and idealistic. They poured into his organizations.

Charlie had been asked to give some remarks on his boss at an FOR Commemorative Meeting honoring A. J. Muste. "As you know," he said,

"A. J. has an affinity for baseball, like I do. He's in his later years, and can still hit fairly well but can't run. I was sometimes his designated runner. For years now, I feel that in the world of organization, I'm A. J.'s designated runner. No matter, because whatever role one plays in working with him, it is always that role—slash—colleague. He speaks clearly in tense situations, is excellent at avoiding ugly confrontations, and makes situations manageable."[141]

He smiled over at A. J., as everyone affectionately called him.

"He's a great listener. This requires enormous self-discipline, for many reasons. He uses it at times for tactical reasons, but it's become a style of interaction. He seeks a common ground upon which the other needs to recognize and come to. And then they can argue or embrace. But somehow they know they are in a common enterprise together."

He looked down at his notes, since his eyes were misting up.

"Thomas Traherne wrote in *Centuries of Meditation*: 'To think aright is also to worship in the Inner Court.' A. J.'s mind, superbly analytical, is more than that: it is in the service of those great causes which are the lodestars of his life. All of us at the FOR are testimony to those causes which have called A. J. and us together into their service."[142]

Chapter 7

Supreme Court Decision of 1954

The opening signal, the equivalent of the "shot heard round the world," sounded [May 17, 1954]. It was the Supreme Court decision on school desegregation.... This action generated an electric effect for millions of black people, charging them with new hope and expectancies. They looked "in wild surmise" at what might be in the making. Many white people were no less startled.... Many sensed that a new era of social activism was at hand.[1]

— Charles Walker, *Lessons from the Civil Rights Movement,* Monograph for Center For Conflict Resolution, Haverford College, Haverford, PA, 1973

The Korean War ended in mid-1953. Now, the Fellowship of Reconciliation staff began working more energetically on race issues along with establishing a new regional office in Philadelphia. The landmark Supreme Court ruling in Brown v. Board of Education of Topeka declared that racially segregated public schools were inherently unequal. This overturned the old 1896 Supreme Court case Plessy v. Ferguson, which had said that equal segregated facilities could be provided. The new decision declared segregation under "separate but equal" to be unequal, citing a clear disparity between US public schools for whites and blacks.[2]

New Regional Office

John Swomley, one of Charlie's bosses at the FOR's National Office, indicated the organization's early involvement in the history of race issues by writing in February 1954:

> When World War II ended, there was a revolutionary atmosphere in the world. Gandhi had demonstrated how millions of brown-skinned Indians [plus Indonesians and Burmese] could gain their freedom from England. In Africa an African National Congress came into existence to fight European control. Everywhere around the world freedom and

equality became words of explosive meaning.

This mood was not confined to Africa and Asia. It flourished also in the United States. Negroes said they were tired of fighting for freedom in armies that were segregated by race. They were fed up with sitting or standing in the rear of buses, with having to give up seats to white people, having to use separate drinking fountains, eat in the kitchen or take food out in a paper bag, because they were not permitted to eat in a restaurant that served white folks. Above all, they were aroused by the low estimate whites had of them—so low that a Negro could be flogged or lynched or brutally murdered like the 14-year-old Emmet Till.... In some Negro colleges where I spoke, students were saying, "The only language the white man will understand is force." Some were beginning to buy guns or to get them on trips into the North.[3]

Charlie read Swomley's provocative paper with concern. *So, how are the Negroes of this nation going to choose?* Charlie wondered. *Will it be violence or nonviolence?* Nonviolence seemed a long shot, but Charlie was hopeful and willing to work hard for it.

He busied himself at colleges, high schools, churches, and other groups. Charlie sent out a post card asking his constituency to write to radio station WCOJ with opinions on his Sunday morning radio program, *Mr. Average Citizen Views the News*. He encouraged them to mail cards and letters, as the series was scheduled through December, 1954, but would need to show support for it to continue. "Tell your friends to listen in."[4]

A small group met in the Jane Addams House on Walnut Street in Philadelphia in early February. The weather outside was snowy and cold, while the Executive Committee of the Philadelphia Fellowship of Reconciliation inside, had important decisions to make concerning the future of the FOR. Charlie Walker had tendered his resignation.[5]

Committee Chairman George Walton spoke first. "We have come to an important juncture in the development of the Philadelphia FOR," Walton stressed. "For the past six years, Charles Walker has been our Executive Secretary, for the most part on a two-thirds salary basis. All the difficulties of securing additional income to maintain family needs have accumulated to the point where he can no longer afford to work for us, despite his desire to remain, and ours to keep him.... It would mark a step backwards if we lost an experienced staff person just near the time of a possible regional expansion."[6] The new region would consist of a large chunk of southeastern Pennsylvania, portions of northern Maryland, northern Delaware and eastern Jersey.

Treasurer, George Hagner, interjected, "The Philadelphia FOR alone cannot undertake a full-time salary. It seems clear we cannot go beyond present commitments."[7]

Walton countered, "It seems to me the solution is to recommend the National FOR establish a Middle Atlantic Region with Charles Walker devoting *full time* to a combination of local and regional work."

Vice-Chair Wayne Dockhorn suggested soliciting from their membership and former members, pledges for the next two years for the extra funds that would be needed. "We would only need to raise half, as National will match what we raise."[8] Dockhorn's mentioning the funds from National radically shifted the mood in the room from cautious to hopeful.

"I move," declared Ernest Kurkjian, "that we put Charles Walker on full salary, on the basis of $450 per month [$5,400 per year]." Lyle Tatum suggested an alternative program in case National did not see its way clear to go ahead.

The motion carried unanimously, and pledge sheets mailed.[9] It was not a full third increase, but it was enough for Charlie. He wrote to a friend about the new region, "As you know, there used to be a Middle Atlantic Region.... This was always an easy item to lop off the budget when things got tight, unfortunately. But there is great potential in this area. Another factor was that I found it impossible to continue as Philadelphia Secretary on a two-third time basis, for we [he and Marian] were going into debt too fast. However, the Executive Committee held up my resignation till they could explore the possibilities of going regional. I am by no means an indispensable man, but the Committee felt my leaving would mean in the immediate situation a loss program-wise in the confidence we have built up."[10]

Charlie sat in his office at home at Tanglewood. He had decided to locate it away from the family area, so it would be relatively quiet. A sunlit, little room, it featured a backyard view and white walls covered with pictures and papers. Ensconced at his typewriter, he wrote thoughts on "The Prayer of a Righteous Man," a topic given to him by a church group for an upcoming talk. It was now spring and he opened a window to hear birds chirp outside. Other signs of life stirred in the woods at the end of the yard. What a great time of year, when the snows recede and the sun warms the earth to bring forth deep greens of luxurious lawns, gardens and flowers! Speaking of bringing forth new life, Marian had told him the night before she was suspicious she was a few months pregnant. Six children to support!

"I hope this new salary increase helps our family finances," he thought out loud. "We're going to need it." So, he dutifully bent to the task at hand but did not come up with anything he liked. Then he remembered he could be more creative if he wrote by hand. So he put aside the typewriter and took from a drawer a long, lined yellow tablet.

"The Prayer of a Righteous Man," he penned, in part:

> Those deeply serious about prayer believe it has to do with motives, purposes, decisions and self-discovery. It helps us find who we are and what we are to do. And, as we know, in James 5, (KJV, James 5:16) "The effective, fervent prayer of a righteous man availeth much." I personally believe that man has been long convinced there is more to the self than the I-ego.
>
> Each man is unique. This is confirmed by facts of biological diversity. Nature has taken great pains to make each person unique. There is that of God in every man. There is a BEYOND WITHIN— the light which lighteth every man. We are not just the "dust of the earth." We are born in a particular time and place, which is our social inheritance. Each has a calling, a unique purpose, a destiny in the Providence of God.
>
> Therefore, the quality of our prayer is affected by what we *do*. Do we invoke blessing or greed? Can we pray that evil befalls another? Jesus said if you have anything against your brother, go to him and talk it over. Action and prayer are interrelated.
>
> The first level of prayer is purgation, or purging yourself of evil. It is dying unto the self. Which self? The inflated, pride-inflamed ego, the trio of "me, myself and I." This is a two-fold task—discipline mixed with prayer.
>
> The second level is inter-relation of prayer and action. Gandhi said act on the measure of light you have. Buber said "you will be given enough light that it will not blind you." In Isaiah, God said "stand up and I will speak through you. You will be empowered." This experience is something of which you should not be possessive. It is an offering, a ritual of thanksgiving. We act because we have been acted upon. As the worm is transformed into a butterfly in the chrysalis, so is the enemy transformed by our prayers. So also are we changed into a new form, a liberated form closer to God.
>
> As we go about our work, we must listen to the inner prompter. As Fenelon said, "How rare it is to find a soul quiet enough to hear God speak!" And as Isaiah 50 (RSV) tells us, "The Lord God has given me the tongue of those who are taught, that I may know how to sustain with a word him that is weary. The Lord God has opened my ear, and I was not rebellious, I turned not backward."

The prayer of a righteous man availeth much.[11]

Glenn Smiley, National Field Secretary for the FOR, planned to hire three new workers in the South. The need was great, as race relations had become more important. For instance, the FOR pioneered the first interracial work camp, setting the pattern which Quakers and others subsequently adopted.[12]

The Shot Heard round the World

The landmark Supreme Court ruling in May 1954 overturned previous laws and made it clear that "separate but equal" was anything but. The Brown v. Board of Education decision was the start of a whole new era for Charlie. As its ripples started the first national waves of the national civil rights movement, he quickly saw its significance.

Charlie later observed:

> The opening signal, the equivalent of the "shot heard round the world," sounded [May 17, 1954]. It was the Supreme Court decision on school desegregation in 1954.... This action generated an electric effect for millions of black people, charging them with new hope and expectancies. They looked "in wild surmise" at what might be in the making. Many white people were no less startled; they had just witnessed the ravages of McCarthyism, the "silent generation" on campus and the stultifying impact of the Cold War at home and abroad.
> Many sensed that a new era of social activism was at hand. The first reaction among Southern whites was not defiance and resistance, but surprise and head-shaking. The unthinkable was happening before their eyes![13]

The Walkers' friend and neighbor, Louis L. Redding, the first black civil rights lawyer working in Delaware, in 1951 had filed and won *Bulah v. Gebhart*, a dispute from one of the four cases presented in the 1954 decision.[14] Ruth Redding, his wife, and Marian had become very good friends, and worked together over the years locally to further civil rights. In fact, Marian advocated for the hiring of Ruth as the first black teacher in the West Chester school system.

Little by little, school desegregation began to be implemented. As Charlie said, black people were waking up and looking around them with new expectations. They started to hope.

In the meantime, Charlie publicized the FOR's commitment to nonviolence in race relations. In one FOR pamphlet, he declared, "We support PEACE—In Season and Out. Only with peaceful methods can peace or justice ever be achieved.... We support *nonviolent resistance*. It combines the social power of the strike and boycott with the moral power of voluntary suffering. This is not appeasement. It is a kind of resistance which 'overcomes evil with good.' Gandhi was the great pioneer in this method."[15]

He reported to the Executive Committee that he'd be working full time for the new Middle Atlantic Region, beginning the first of May with a membership of about 600. "Am to try to place Glenn Smiley, National Field Work Director, at a church on May 16. Any ideas?"[16][17]

———

Much of the American civil rights movement gained its inspiration from Gandhi and his stellar work in the nonviolence field. Charlie felt indebted to Gandhi, so one day wrote down some "Selections From Gandhi," from a book *The Mind of Gandhi* to keep by his desk:

> I have been practicing, with scientific precision, nonviolence and its possibilities for an unbroken period of over fifty years. I have applied it in every walk of life—domestic, institutional, economic and political.... I know of no single case in which it has failed. Where it has seemed sometimes to have failed, I have ascribed it to my imperfections.
>
> It is the acid test of nonviolence that in a nonviolent conflict there is no rancor left behind, and in the end the enemies are converted into friends.
>
> In my opinion nonviolence is not passivity in any shape or form. Nonviolence, as I understand it, is the most active force in the world. Nonviolence is the supreme law. During my half-century of experience I have not yet come across a situation when I had to say that I was helpless, that I had no remedy in terms of nonviolence.[18]

Another Gandhi quote Charlie liked was, "If we are to make progress, we must not repeat history but make new history."[19]

New Baby Coming, Training and Progress

Summer is a lazy time of year, but Charlie was never lazy. In the summer of 1954, he busied himself making FOR's new Middle Atlantic Region successful. He had concerns about the expenses of another child. Marian was indeed pregnant. Charlie contemplated the fact that they had two boys, Larry and Allan, and three girls; Winnie, Brenda and Valerie. If they had another boy, it would make the family evenly distributed and thus perfect. With anticipation, he suggested the Walker family name "James" to Marian. Jimmy Walker sounded good to him.

One afternoon in July, as Marian washed and then ironed baby clothes left-handed in the large family room at Tanglewood, six-year-old Brenda contemplated her mother's big tummy. She watched as her mother folded tiny blankets. "Is it going to be a boy or a girl?" she asked.

"We don't know, but if it's a boy we'll name him James, and if it's a girl, we'll call her Gloria."

"Was I a beautiful baby, Mommy?"

"All my babies were beautiful!" Marian declared with a lovely smile.

Around that time, Charlie wrote a paper describing how soldiers train daily to conquer fear and suggested pacifists work as diligently to conquer that same fear:

> We are primarily creatures of conditioned reflexes; we react out of our training, our ingrained habits, our deepest beliefs. The pacifist aims not only at the conquest of fear but at the discipline of [controlling] anger. He, too, must train—daily, carefully, patiently. He also must learn that high resolve alone cannot change habits or character.

He then described his belief that mankind cannot have progress without purpose, analysis without synthesis, nor material gain without spiritual direction. That man has not been able to match his power over the environment without a corresponding power over himself:

> Civilization cannot continue a stable advance unless two aspects of experience are kept in focus. All growth is characterized by two principles: the power to expand and the power to cohere during expansion.... Thus it is that we cannot keep admitting more experience than for which we can make sense and give meaning....
>
> Civilization must therefore progress not only in sense but in sensibility; it must not only expand and become more complex, but it must cohere during expansion and make unity of the complexity. Otherwise, collapse is inevitable at the very time when it seems at the height of power.[20]

National Association for the Advancement of White People

"Good morning, friends. This is Mr. Average Citizen." Charlie Walker's voice went out over the air waves at 10:45 a.m. He never said his actual name, preferring to keep it anonymous and stress the "average citizen" angle. He welcomed this valuable experience and the chance to put forth some of his concerns.[21] Although a heavy drain on his time, it helped him keep abreast of current issues and reach a radio audience every week.[22] With a voice both self-assured and intelligent, he reached out to the citizens of Chester County on Sunday mornings.

"Since it's going to be impossible to keep this whole question out of politics this election year," Charlie commented over WCOJ one morning in

1954, "there are some indications there might be a move to get an anti-lynching bill through Congress, and abolish the poll tax, which is used to prevent many from voting."[23]

It was October 3, 1954 and Mr. Average Citizen was on the air.

Good morning, friends. Let's take a look at the news of this last week, at the stories behind the headlines. And when I say behind the headlines, I don't mean behind the keyhole.… I mean what the news looks like after you forget about the headlines, the fancy speeches and the slogans of the moment.…

It surely looks like a fouled-up situation down there in Milford, Delaware, on the issue of segregation in the public schools.… The editor of the local paper said, in his whole lifetime he couldn't think of a single piece of trouble they'd ever had between black and white. Yet there is trouble today. And, in spite of the editor, there was trouble before, too, but too many white people didn't see it, just because people weren't getting hit over the head. There was trouble there in the many open and subtle ways our society still makes second-class citizens out of our Negro citizens. Then comes the day when the ugly truth is revealed, and people can't understand how all this trouble suddenly appeared.

At first, things in Milford seemed to be working out smoothly.…

Then came the demonstrations, and a group called the National Association for the Advancement of White People and a man named Bryant Bowles. A large wooden cross was burned across from the school entrance. A motorcade went up and down the streets urging parents to keep their children home from school. The drivers in this motorcade were teenagers, and the signs said, 'Kick 'em out.' Even little children six or eight years old were sent out to carry signs on their backs reading 'Hate Thy Neighbor.' People don't do this kind of thing when there has, quote, never been any trouble, unquote. Finally, the newly-elected school board voted to take the eleven Negro children out of the school and send them to an all-Negro school.

Here's what the Delaware Police have to say about Bryant Bowles, the key man kicking up all this rumpus. On May 12, 1953, Bowles was arrested by the Baltimore City Police on five charges of false pretenses. He was found guilty and fined $25 apiece on each of the five charges. He was wanted by the police in Tampa, Florida, for passing bogus checks. Later he made restitution for the bad checks, and he is no longer wanted by the Tampa police. A warrant was on file at the Sheriff's Office in Harford County, Maryland, in April, 1954, but the charges were nolle prosequi. That means the person who made the charges decided not to pursue them further." Charlie went on to say that reaction to such incidents divides into five general groups: a relatively small group determined to do the right and decent and democratic thing, another small group who believes in white supremacy, a great majority who doesn't care one way or another about any public issue, a segment who is somewhat concerned but doesn't know enough of the facts so can be buffaloed by threats and loud talk, and a final segment in the middle who can't make up their minds one way or the other.

So, the largest group—those in the middle—do nothing, while at the same time they hold the balance of power. So a lot depends upon who takes the initiative. It is only too true that many will go along with the mood of the moment."

Charlie's persuasive voice continued to fill the airways that Sunday morning. "If those who believe in justice for everyone no matter what color or religion they happen to be—if these people take a strong initiative, the middle majority go along and so do the white supremacy advocates, even though they grumble a lot. But then there are times when those who believe in white supremacy take the initiative, although sometimes it's concealed under the slogan 'separate but equal.' As the Supreme Court said, in the nature of the case, separate can't be equal when the whites do the separating, just as it couldn't be equal if the Negroes did the separating....

"I might say I get impatient with these cartoons and speeches which say how terrible this race hatred is in Milford, because it gives the Russians more ammunition. Yes, it does that, but we should be practicing racial justice, not because of what [Soviet Premier Georgy] Malenkov might say, but because it's the right and decent and fair thing to do. Any time we are tempted to be self-righteous and preach to the rest of the world, we should remember Milford, not down in Georgia or Alabama but in neighboring Delaware. Then in humility we may realize we still have, as a people, a long way to go before our practice of democracy is as good as our preaching."

Then Mr. Average Citizen turned to a lighter note. "Did you hear or see the World Series? While I'm no hysterical Giants fan, the wonderful thing about their winning was it upset the odds. If everything in life went according to the odds, just according to the figures and the predictions, we would be in bad shape. Any time the underdog comes out on top, in spite of the so-called reasonable predictions, we demonstrate again that life isn't just statistics, but an adventure."[24]

Shortly after the above broadcast, on October 9, Charlie went personally to the Baltimore area to observe an NAAWP rally, because Bryant Bowles had said he planned to come to Philadelphia. Charlie wrote a detailed report.

> The meeting was held at a race track outside Baltimore.... A fair estimate of the crowd would be between 350 and 400 people. It was to have been announced by way of airplane loudspeakers over the city. Bowles reported to the crowd this didn't get done because the pilots ran

low on fuel and had to return to Washington. This sounded implausible, for what kind of pilot wouldn't know how much gas it takes to go to Baltimore and back?...

Hatred is an ugly thing. I had never seen so much of it at one time. Mothers were trying to out-do each other in vilification of Negroes and those who would defend them. One said to the woman beside her: "If they try to bring those n-----s in, it'll be pure murder." Apparently, her neighbor remonstrated mildly, for the first one turned on her and burst out: "Wouldn't you rather have a race war than live with those j--s?"

Bowles had come in early, driving up from Washington. He had hardly arrived before he was served with a warrant having to do with taxes withheld from employees in a firm he operated. The government wants to know what happened to that money. Bowles said he didn't know anything about it; his accountants would have to straighten it out....

Finally the meeting got under way. He began by pointing out this was a private meeting and therefore the press could be ejected.... Bowles asked if the crowd wanted the reporters and photographers to leave. The crowd screamed yes, adding choice expletives. But then Bowles said they would just be requested to leave, but would not be forced to go. Apparently, this was all a maneuver to get the crowd started off on the right emotional track, for the speakers cooperated with cameramen throughout!

Bowles obviously hadn't thought about what he was going to say, and his speech was sadly disjointed. Most of the time was spent rallying the crowd to their pet hates—Negroes, politicians, the NAACP—and defending himself against the many charges against him.

"I've been accused of being anti-Negro," he said. "That's not true. I'm pro-White!... Another [Bowles] pet peeve, mentioned before, is the "politician," the man who plays along (in his view) with the terribly influential Negro groups who rule the roost. Some are "bad." Some are just afraid to speak out their true feelings because the white people are so unorganized as he put it. A favorite device of his is to refer to some official: "I don't know what color he is. (snickers) But if he's white it's only skin deep."

Bowles urged that public schools be abolished, and that three systems be set up instead: white, black and "indifferent." The state would then subsidize each child to go to the private school of its choice.[25]

Charlie elaborated on attempts to get people in attendance to sign up for Maryland and Delaware chapters. Conversation around him indicated people were reluctant to join for fear of reprisals—the same reason, he observed, why many liberal-minded people won't get involved in the other direction. The crowd seemed to be one which felt looked down on by "old line whites" and looking to find somebody else even less fortunate to kick around. The people were saturated with suspicion and paranoid tendencies.

This is an ugly situation where many people who formerly thought this way but felt they had no support now are coming out in the open, with all the drive and exhilaration of a great crusade. But it's a crusade of hate. Bowles is wrong: He's not so much pro-white as he is anti-Negro.... What has happened is the NAAWP has revealed the actual situation, and the job, after the fireworks have died down, has just begun.[26]

Charlie reported to his Executive Committee, "Mr. Average Citizen had the information about the police record of Bryant Bowles, before it was published in the *Enquirer!* I plan to go to Baltimore on Friday and Saturday, working with the FOR group there on a mass meeting of the NAAWP Saturday. It is doubtful if Bowles will come to Philadelphia as threatened."[27]

A Terrific Storm

Marian found herself near delivery of their sixth child when Hurricane Hazel made its ugly mark on the Pennsylvania countryside. Hazel had raged across Haiti and the Bahamas before turning north and tearing across the Carolinas and Maryland. Hazel, labeled a Category Four hurricane, headed toward Pennsylvania. Charlie was away on business. Hearing of the approaching storm, she lay in bed, worriedly reading books about midwifery in case the baby came early. The next day, while the children played outside, the wind picked up and Marian knew Hazel was near. "Come in right away!" she called.

"What is it?" they asked anxiously as they put away their bikes and hurried inside.

"It's Hurricane Hazel." Soon the great storm raged and shrieked, like several great locomotives outside the strong stone walls of their old mansion. The lights had gone out, so they huddled in the dark, waiting for the storm to abate. For hours Hazel unleashed her furious attack before finally heading toward Canada. The children gingerly stepped outside.

What a terrible sight! Many of the beautiful trees they had played in and loved had been ripped up and tossed down. The tree-lined driveway now looked a twisted wreck, the helpless victim of faceless fury.

"Marian, are you all right?" Concerned about the young mother's welfare, two men from Tanguy, Howard Yates and Harry Bleecher, ran up the driveway, after parking their car as close to the house as possible. Tanguy mothers knew phone and electric lines had been knocked down, and Marian remained alone with the children. So they sent their husbands to see if she was okay. Marian, relieved to see their smiling, caring faces after such an ordeal, happily assured them all was well. The men returned to Tanguy to deal with their own families' problems of downed trees and power outages. Hazel turned out to be one of the deadliest and costliest storms of the twentieth century.[28]

Soon after the storm, Gloria Lynne Walker greeted the world from Chester County Hospital in West Chester. No particular meaning was attributed to this name; Marian and Charlie simply thought it was beautiful. The younger children again stayed with family members, while the two eldest, Winnie and Larry, remained at Tanglewood so they could continue with classes. Brenda, age seven, resided temporarily with Marian's Grandmother Shank and Aunts Mary and Grace. Allan, five, and Valerie, three, stayed with Grandma Mina Walker, who now owned and lived at Sunset Cabins in West Grove, a very low-budget motel. She sold penny candy, along with other items, at the little office store in front of her living area.

Charlie, excited over the arrival of Baby Gloria, embraced her and sang tender lullabies, crooning in his soft tenor, "Tell me why the stars do shine...."

During this time, Charlie had come across Nels F.S. Ferre's *Strengthening the Spiritual Life.* He wrote a summary of the chapter on "Family Devotions," which became part of his family values and beliefs on raising children.

> "Jesus grasped the right formula for a new life," Ferre said. Make the tree good. The good life can bear good fruit, not only in thoughts and deeds, but especially in good children. The most important crop to care for is the family fruit. The surest way to strengthen the spiritual life is to strengthen the spiritual life of the family. Children, to become creative and cooperative members of the family, need to experience genuine love at home from their early infancy.
>
> "Blow-outs" can be forgiven and erased ... but lack of love kicks the emotional underpinning from under the child. For the children's sake—and they constitute the coming world—the parents must therefore find love. The test of such love is whether each carries the concerns of the other in his [/her] heart, whether he wants to shield his partner from blame, or to blame her when something untoward has happened, whether he subordinates his personal desires to the family welfare, or whether he wants what he wants when he wants it, whether he disciplines and eradicates personal faults or rationalizes them into virtues.[29]

All his life, Charlie quoted Ferre and the Bible to his children. "You will know them by their fruits" (Matthew 7:20 KJV), as a measuring stick for the wisdom of a possible path or the worth of a questionable friend. His philosophy fostered a "cheerful expectancy" in the home. He listened to, lifted, loved, and taught his children. Yes, Charlie loved all his children deeply and worked to abide in that love in his dealings with them.

1955: A New Year

The Angora Civic Association had been trying to keep African Americans from moving into certain parts of West Philadelphia. Charlie recruited people to observe their meetings and report back to FOR. He also planned for the Philadelphia FOR again to pass out Christmas cards on the street and possibly do some caroling.[30]

Charlie ended the year feeling great progress had been made. The radio station, WCOJ, commended Charlie twice for his *Mr. Average Citizen* program, with especially good comments about his Bryant Bowles segment.[31]

The year 1955 began with Charlie's vigorous plan to decentralize FOR meetings to suburban areas. Meetings in February and March in places such as Media, Germantown, Abington and Haddonfield would replace the usual midwinter conference. Hoping speakers on current topics would attract FOR members and guests, he lined up George Willoughby, Chairman of the FOR's new Middle Atlantic Region, as the speaker for Haddonfield meeting."[32]

In April Charlie decided he might visit Europe that summer. He called Marian to excitedly report that if so, he could attend the International FOR conference in Switzerland and another world conference the first weekend in September.

"I would have to raise the money myself, I mean from non-FOR sources, almost entirely personal—family and a few friends," he hurriedly explained. "I figure the final decision will be whether I could get some staff job on a student ship, thereby taking care of travel expenses. It would be nice if the National office could help, but it's in trouble financially. It not only has problems that led to reducing staff, but the Far West office put up such a protest after being severed, that the decision has been reversed. That's going to mean more of a financial pinch than ever before."

"How long would you be away, Charlie?" Marian asked anxiously.

"It would mean a seven-week period with no one in the office here, since my secretary is usually gone over the summer. That's an extra month, along with my three weeks of vacation. But I'm asking for time off *with pay*, such as was given to other staff members who went overseas."

"But then there would be no summer vacation with me or the kids." Marian had a sinking feeling.

"But it would help give a boost to my undistinguished background."

"What do you mean, undistinguished? You're distinguished!"

"Well, I believe I'm still quite undistinguished in education and accomplishment. I can sell other speakers to groups, but am not in demand myself. This is my best chance to get to know key people from the rest of the world. A trip of this kind would help me in getting background for analysis, in getting speaking engagements, in doing the radio job, and so many things. Think of it as a great opportunity I can't pass up."[33]

She agreed to think about it that way and tried to be happy for him. In May the FOR National Council approved a four-week leave of absence to be added to Charlie's three weeks of vacation. Now he could start planning.[34]

———————

Glenn Smiley wrote Charlie in June a "Letter to a New FOR [Regional] Secretary," explaining in part,

> Ours is more than a job, more than a means of earning a livelihood—it is indeed a calling, a commitment of one's all. If I were asked to say what characteristic is most important in a secretary, I would unhesitatingly say "The love of people,"… one who would point men by precept and example to a forgiving God who will help me to build again the old walls.
>
> Wives are people, too, but you would never guess it by the way some FOR wives are treated! Happy indeed is the secretary whose wife is committed in the same sense in which he is to the task, but one need not be surprised if a wife shows up some day with the idea that her husband's job should be sued for alienation of affection.

Glenn, who was married, followed this with two suggestions to help with the FOR secretary's family situation: "He will be held accountable if he brings peace to the whole world and yet has war at home because of his neglect," and to "make every step to see that his wife has the same opportunities for growth that he does. If there are small children, she may be too tired to read, or cannot attend meetings, and thereby miss the constant stimulation to growth which you may take for granted. Again, you may be weary of FOR when you get home and just want to rest or forget.

But she is eager to know what has happened." He also suggested the stenographic secretary is also a human being and should be left a place to express her own initiative and creativity, especially since she would not take a job of this sort without having, too, felt a sense of calling.[35]

Although Charlie had enthusiastic support from his family for his work, his children now recall him being gone a great deal from the family scene and not around for their big events, awards and programs. Charlie read Glenn's suggestions carefully, but did not heed as well as he might have.

European Trip

Charlie managed to raise enough funds for his European trip through friends, Peacemakers and letters such as the one A. J. Muste sent out, urging, "It is very important to have some live, younger US delegates" at the International FOR conference. "Charlie Walker, Middle Atlantic Regional Secretary of the FOR and active Peacemaker, will come back with fresh contacts and insights, and equipped to contribute more than ever to the cause of nonviolence and peace."[36]

Glenn Smiley wrote, "I think there is no one who would either enjoy or profit by a trip of that sort more than Charles Walker, as he has that peculiar type of perception and sensitiveness that would make it valuable to him and to the movement."[37]

The trip would be from July 27 to September 21, 1955, and would include visits to Holland, Germany, Austria, Yugoslavia, Italy, Switzerland, France and England. Traveling by "economy ship," he planned to see his brother in the Army in Germany and FOR centers in Berlin, Vienna, Geneva, Paris and London. After attending the Conference of the International FOR in August, he would be a US representative of Peacemakers at a conference in London in early September. Charlie told friends that Marian, with the six children, would keep the home fires burning and would welcome notes or visits in the absence of her husband.[38]

Charlie traveled to Europe on a Dutch economy ship to return on a Canadian line. He began his trip in Rotterdam, and met some FOR and Women's International League for Peace and Freedom people in Berlin.

"Hey, Walker, your brother's here from the States!" Younger brother Bill Walker, serving in the US Army in Wiesbaden, Germany, jumped when

Charlie appeared in his barracks, grinning from ear to ear.

"Charles!" Bill was delighted to see his older brother. After much back-slapping and hand-shaking, Bill introduced him to some of his comrades-in arms and then asked, "What are you doing here, Brother?"

"I want you to come to Switzerland with me. Let's go! I have it all arranged."

"Great!—Oh, no! I'm on duty this weekend. But, I'll go talk to the captain." He went off, hopeful and excited.

Luckily, the commanding officer sat in the same room with the captain. Bill boldly entered to ask a favor. "Sir, my brother just popped in from the United States! He must have called my mom and found out where I was, because I didn't know he was coming. He just walked in! Is there any way you can get me off duty?"

After some questions and discussion, the commanding officer barked, "Hey, here's a three-day pass. Go. I'll get somebody else to take your duty."

So Bill packed a bag and off they went. When the brothers reached the train station, someone informed them they were late. As they purchased their tickets, the ticket agent warned in German, "You're not going to make it. That train's pulling out!" They knew enough German to get the idea.

"Come on!" Bill yelled, and they took off jogging on the platform by the tracks. The train had, indeed, begun to leave the station. Throwing caution to the wind, the brothers started sprinting with their travel bags in hand. Both men, in great physical shape, turned on the speed. Managing to hop on the steps just in time, they entered the train car.

"Where did you come from?!" an astonished conductor asked in German as they hurried inside.

"From the train station," Bill panted in English.

"Half a block down the rails!" Charlie added. Sitting down, they caught their breath, chests heaving.

"This train must have been going twenty miles an hour." Bill grinned. "We're lucky there wasn't a tower or something to knock us off." Exhilarated, they rejoiced in their good fortune and upcoming trip.

Once their heartbeats had calmed, Charlie told Bill he had just realized that since *they* were in Germany and *brother Herb* was in England in the Navy, Mina was the only immediate family member left in the United States. Bill's tour of duty spanned 1954 to 1956, mainly in Germany, directly after basic training.

"You know, Mom and Aunt Pearl had totally different reactions to my coming here." Bill took off his jacket and settled in. "When I wrote to them telling them I was going overseas, Pearl wrote to me. 'I was hoping you wouldn't have to go overseas, that you would just stay in the States the whole time.' But Mom writes me a letter saying, 'Isn't that wonderful news? You'll get to go to Europe! You'll probably never get to go overseas the rest of your life. What a wonderful opportunity!' And she was right. I'm getting to see Europe!"

They traveled to Geneva and then Bern, where they stayed at an FOR member's house. Charlie took Bill up a ski lift—a whole different experience in the summer time. Bill came away from the trip feeling Charlie must know just about everybody in the whole world.[39]

Around the time he picked up Bill, he spoke at the IFOR Council in Switzerland after attending the IFOR Conference in London. He also represented Peacemakers at a conference in London for an organization called Third Camp, in which he and Muste were involved. Besides his conferences, he visited AFSC work camps in Berlin and Salzburg; a Quaker Meeting in Vienna; Friends Centers in Geneva, Paris and Versailles; and peace agencies in London. He spoke of FOR work in Freundchaftsheim (Friendship Home) at Buekeburg, Germany.[40]

He had the unexpected pleasure of meeting an Indian friend of his by chance at a train station in Zagreb, Yugoslavia, on his way to an AFSC Seminar in Kranj, Yugoslavia. At the FOR conferences, Charlie shared the FOR's future plans for debates. He said it was an inspiration to meet "the storied people in our movement." He felt especially gratified to be able to entertain London-based FOR members, as they, in turn, visited Philadelphia."[41]

"Good morning, Friends," Charlie's cheerful voice intoned on September 25, 1955. "It's good to be back, after this interlude, talking over the news with you. I did a lot of traveling this summer. You know, when you're traveling, it takes a lot of effort to keep up with the news, even the headline events, not to mention the rest of the story. You hear radio newscasts only once in a while, even with a radio in the car. You can pick up a national news magazine once a week, but there's every chance the important angles of the news pass you by."[42]

In his office back in Philadelphia, Charlie talked on the phone with A. J. Muste in New York. "My first trip abroad sure was an educational adventure," he chuckled. "Yes, the finances worked out, although when I arrived home, I had less than a dollar in my pocket![43]

"Oh, and did you see that the *Christian Century* printed my report of the IFOR Conference? That's terrific! But surprisingly enough, my most vivid memory is of the war ruins in Berlin. I could not help but imagine Philadelphia in a similar state someday—God forbid!"

In his "Reflections on a Summer Abroad," Charlie wrote, "Street after street, even ten years after the war, give mute evidence of the ravages of war. People get used to seeing these ruins, as people get used to any tragic experience in their lives, but the scars remain."

> The omnipresence of officials during travel brings to mind the many ways the police intrude themselves into the lives of the people. In Switzerland, when I registered at a hotel, I noted a place on the registry to state where I was going next. When I asked the clerk what this was for, she said it was for the police. I told her personally I thought it was ,no business of the police where I was going, and asked what would happen if I left that space blank. She shrugged and said, 'Let it go.' And nothing seemed to come of it. But in Yugoslavia, when I stayed overnight at the AFSC Seminar, the officials had to be notified of my being there, and there is a heavy penalty for failing to so advise. And when I talked about it to an Indian friend, he startled me by saying the same was true in India for foreign visitors.44

Charlie's views of his own country had changed. "It was true for me, as with many others before me, that the trip abroad gave me a new appreciation of America, or some aspects of America. The difference between a little freedom and little more freedom is tremendous. We may rightly decry the inroads made in our liberties, and we may well take a dim view of the political health of our land today. Nevertheless, each of these freedoms remaining, or to be re-won, is a precious matter for those who benefit by them, recognized all the more by those who have suffered under tyranny."[45]

Charlie concluded his reflections, "I'm so grateful for this opportunity I had in going on this trip and hope the FOR will be repaid for the time off by fresh vigor on the job, more insight into some problems, and increased dedication to our common task for which so many have labored so long *and so sacrificially.*"[46]

Charlie included in his October FOR newsletter, *Pacifist Notebook:*

> Nonviolence cannot be understood as a sudden act out of context. It must be integrally related to justice, to the unity of the human family, to living situations. In one sense it is a gift. In a socio-logical sense, nonviolence is also a long and complicated process. Even as violence may be a reaction, nonviolence requires initiative, freedom won at the high cost of discipline; it reverses the descending spiral, and enthrones the person, one endowed with choice and spiritual freedom.[47]

Emmet Till

In the Deep South the murder of a black Chicago youth, Emmett Till, became a new concern. In August 1955 fourteen-year-old Till, while visiting a relative and unaccustomed to the ways of Mississippi, foolishly took a dare to flirt with a white woman. He wolf-whistled at her, angering her husband and family, who took it upon themselves to kidnap the young man. They beat and shot him, throwing his body into the river.[48] This first big racial story after the *Brown v. Board of Education* decision made national headlines, especially when a jury acquitted the two men arrested on murder charges in September. Later a grand jury considered kidnapping charges, but did not indict.

In November, "Mr. Average Citizen" tackled the situation. "A grand jury in Greenwood, Mississippi, failed to indict J.W. Milam and Roy Bryant for kidnapping Emmett Till, the 14-year-old Chicago boy. I was interested to note that the foreman in the Till case this week, Mr. Broadway, said he would like to make a statement about the case, but that he was sworn to secrecy for six months.... There have been shootings in Florida and more trouble in Milford, Delaware. What is happening in the South is that a way of life is breaking up. The die is cast, and the doctrine of separate but equal is finished."[49]

Racial integration was coming, opposition or no.

Charlie then made an unusual statement. "What the South needs today is a Gandhi, someone who will help in leading the Negro people to ever increasing freedom and opportunity, but do it in such a way as will undermine the fear of the white southerners, as Gandhi won the confidence of the British."[50]

Charlie Walker's foretelling of then-unknown Martin Luther King Jr. was uncanny. The following month in Montgomery, Alabama, a protest began against segregation of city buses. It would bring King's phenomenal leadership abilities to national attention.

Author's Note

The story doesn't end here. In fact, it's just the beginning. Volume 2 of *A Quaker Behind the Dream: Charlie Walker and the Civil Rights Movement* is on the way and should be out this coming year! Written in the same style as Volume 1, this book begins with Charlie's visit to the Bus Protest in Montgomery, where he officially meets Dr. King. Charlie announces on his *Mr. Average Citizen* radio show, "Let me give you some more of the story about Montgomery, Alabama, and the passive resistance movement there. Almost everything the bus company and the authorities did to try to break that boycott served only to strengthen the determination of the Negro...." This volume includes exciting correspondence between Dr. King and Charlie Walker.

Walker recruits, organizes and trains for the sit-ins and Freedom Rides in the early '60s. He helps organize the March on Washington in 1963 and stands on the dais with Dr. King as he makes his historic "I Have a Dream" speech. The magazine Charlie co-founds is the very first to print, nationwide, Martin Luther King's "Letter from a Birmingham Jail." Additionally, Walker serves as a staff trainer for the Mississippi Freedom Summer of 1964.

Becoming a premier expert on nonviolence, he codifies what is known about nonviolence, cowriting one handbook in 1957, and then authoring and publishing the first handbook of its kind, *Organizing for Nonviolent Direct Action* in 1961, to be used in the movement in the 1960s. These books detail the Three Levels of Nonviolence, the Seven Steps to Nonviolence and the Ten Benchmarks of Nonviolence.

Walker explains, "In loving his white adversary, the Negro does not necessarily express a desire to spend an afternoon at a concert or the ball game with him. Rather, he wishes the white man well; he does not intend to do to the white man what the white man has done to him. The white man, too, is a victim of the same system which degrades and debases them both.... Therefore the Negro is willing to undergo hardship and suffering on behalf of the white man, recognizing ... that their struggle for liberation is a common struggle."

Walker believes nonviolence to be more than tactics, writing, "When you are calling people to struggle and to suffering, one must do more than show tactical or even strategic relevance. One must invoke something at a much deeper level in a human being if he is to endure what must be endured."

Walker says on his radio show, "So it may be that in the Dexter Avenue Baptist Church, a 27-year-old man, branded a criminal and an agitator who stirs up the people, who nevertheless preached: 'This is not black against white but justice against injustice,' this little church may come to loom larger in history than the State House in Montgomery, just as at an earlier time, it was not an empire that counted so much as a stable."

Walker organizes and conducts the nonviolence workshops for the Poor People's Campaign in 1968, writing, "Training is one of the anchor points of the nonviolent movement. It is both a tool for and child of organization. It is a morale factor. It is one of the more concrete elements in [the] field."

He deplores in later eras, the trashing of the 1960s and spends much time and effort defending the many good things that happened during that decade.

The *Epilogue*, which only appears at the end of Volume 2, is a tender story written by the author regarding her father's passing, which appeared in *Guideposts* magazine.

Readers may look up a Wikipedia article on Charles Coates Walker and can follow developments for Volume 2 at http://www.brendabeadenkopf.com.

About the Author

Author and Quaker historian Brenda Walker Beadenkopf works tirelessly to promote her father's work with Dr. Martin Luther King during the American civil rights movement. At conferences and many other venues in the United States and Kenya, she has spoken and led workshops about the importance of nonviolence in the successful protests of the 1950s and 60s. With a deep concern to promote race relations in the Unites States, she believes "nonviolence is the teachings of Jesus in a practical form."

Beadenkopf graduated from Southwestern Michigan College's journalism program with 4.0 GPA and was chosen for SMC's first Wall of Fame. Award-winning editor of the *Berrien County Record* newspaper in Buchanan, Michigan, she has been published in *Friends Journal*, *Guideposts*, and *Highground*.

Beadenkopf has nine children and sixteen grandchildren. She lives with her husband, William, in Michigan.

Endnotes

Prologue

[1] Charles C. Walker, "The March on Washington," *Gandhi Marg* magazine, India (Oct. 1963), 5.

[2] Charles Walker, letter to Dr. Enus Wright, President Cheyney State College, Sept. 25, 1984 (CCW)

[3] Organizer and leader of the Brotherhood of Sleeping Car Porters, the first predominantly African American labor union.

[4] Charles Walker, letter to Lena Walker, Cheyney, Penna., Jan. 6, 1984, 2; signed in Charles Walker's handwriting at bottom of CW's copy of, "The March on Washington," *Gandhi Marg* magazine, New Delhi, India (Oct., 1963), 5. (CCW).

[5] Charles C. Walker, "The March on Washington," *Gandhi Marg* magazine, New Delhi, India (Oct. 1963), 2.

[6] Ibid., 3.

[7] Ibid., 5.

[8] Ibid., 1.

[9] Ibid., 1.

[10] Martin Luther King Jr., *Why We Can't Wait* (New York: Harper and Row, 1963), 62.

[11] Charles C. Walker, "The March on Washington," *Gandhi Marg* magazine, New Delhi, India (Oct. 1963), 1.

[12] King, *Why We Can't Wait*, 23.

[13] Ibid., 22–23.

[14] Ibid., 25.

[15] Ibid., 37.

[16] Charles Walker, "The Man of Montgomery," article for special MLK issue of *Gandhi Marg* magazine, published in India by the Gandhi Peace Foundation (Jul., 1968), 77-83. (CCW)

[17] Walker, "The March on Washington," 3.

[18] Larry Walker, personal taped interview by the author (Aug. 6, 2001, at Walker home in Cheyney, Pa.), unpublished manuscript; Marian, Larry and Valerie all state they saw Charlie Walker before the beginning of the program, come out to the edge of the speakers dais and look over the crowd.

[19] Walker, "The March on Washington," 3.

[20] Ibid.,4.

[21] Walker, "The March on Washington," 4.

[22] King, *Why We Can't Wait*, 123.

[23] Walker, "The Man of Montgomery," 77.

[24] Walker, "The March on Washington," 4.

[25] Walker, "The March on Washington."

[26] Walker, "The March on Washington."

[27] Ibid.

[28] Ibid.,5.

Chapter 1

[1] Charles C. Walker, original poem in *Friendly Agitator* (Friends Suburban Project newsletter), 1970s.

[2] This building still exists on the left.

[3] Now Chestnut Street.

[4] Ibid., 191; M. Blanche Cochrane, S. Kauffman and E. Glenn Kauffman, *Bridging the Gap, 1701–2001: A Celebration of 300 Years of History* (Gap, Pa., 2001), 5.

[5] Gerald S. Lestz, "Penn Spring at Gap," *Lancaster New Era* (Oct. 31, 1978).

[6] There were three bridges. The middle bridge is the only one remaining today.

[7] The last Lancaster to Coatesville trolley ran in 1932.

[8] Charlie's great-grandfather Isaac Walker Jr. helped buy the clock in 1872 and put it in a tower in the old town hall. By 1887, since that tower was about to be torn down, some townspeople climbed the stairs in the middle of the night and stole the clock. They hid it in an ice house for five years. Then they built this tower for the clock on Isaac Walker's land and put it back in 1894. Source: Cochrane, *Bridging the Gap*, 15–16.

[9] Carolyn Neuhauser Keneagy, *A Gap in My Memory* (Gap: PA, 1996), 19.

[10] Now Route 30.

[11] Arthur L. Reist, *The Conestoga Wagon—Masterpiece of the Blacksmith* (Lancaster, PA: Brookshire Printing, 1975), 32.

[12] Cochrane, *Bridging the Gap*, 12.

[13] "History." White Horse Inn website: http://mcqueenswhitehorseinn.com/history.html (Sept. 19, 2013).

[14] The Clemson Gang holed up in the old nickel mines up near Mine Road. They kidnapped slaves escaped from Maryland and took them back over the state line just south of Gap for bounty money. The Clemson Gang was named after Amos Clemson, who owned a tavern, their hangout, in Gap. He dug a tunnel from the tavern basement out into the hills, so the gang

could escape the law or bury people they'd killed. They'd steal horses, paint over their markings and sell them. Gap was known as a den of horse thieves. The town organized a posse in the 1850s and almost stopped them, but it wasn't until the 1890s that a Constable Kauffman from Phoenixville disguised himself as a hobo, joined the gang in the nickel mines and spied on Til Clemson, head of the thieves at the time. When he had enough evidence, he arrested them and that put an end to the Gap Gang. Cochrane, *Bridging the Gap*, 14-15.

[15] Ibid., 33-35.

[16] Ibid.

[17] Ibid., 24–28.

[18] William Walker, interview with author, Aug. 5, 2001.

[19] Born May, 1930; Herbert J. Walker born Apr., 1925.

[20] William Walker, interview with author, Aug. 5, 2001.

[21] William Walker, interviews with author Aug. 5, 2001, Mar. 11, 2002 and Jan. 22, 2015.

[22] Keneagy, *A Gap in My Memory*, 19–20, 30–31, 43, 48, 54, 60.

[23] William Walker, phone interviews with author Mar. 11, 2002 and Jan. 22, 2015.

[24] The Gap farm house cistern collected rainwater from gutters at the edge of the roof and piped it down to a cool cement pool in the cellar.

[25] These were the days before seedless raisins.

[26] Now Pequea Avenue.

[27] Now Newport Road.

[28] *History of Lancaster County*, 1056.

[29] A plain wagon with a board seat on springs.

[30] Marian Groff Walker, *Charles Walker's Life as Remembered by Marian Walker* (unpublished manuscript, Jan. 4, 2002).

[31] Keneagy, *A Gap in My Memory*, 30–31.

[32] Pearl Albright Mendenhall, interview by the author at Coates Family Reunion, Quarryville, PA, Aug. 18, 2002.

[33] Precisely 150 years before the September 11, 2001, terrorist attacks on the United States.

[34] Margaret Bacon, *Rebellion at Christiana* (New York: Crown Publishers, Inc., 1975), 74.

[35] Ibid., 101.

[36] Rettew, *A Charge of Treason?*, 15.

[37] Bacon, *Rebellion at Christiana*, 121.

[38] Rettew, *A Charge of Treason?*, 23.

[39] Ibid., 21.

[40] Ibid., 25.

[41] Ibid., 27.

[42] Ibid., 6.

[43] Ibid., 28.

[44] William Walker, interview by author, Aug. 5, 2001.

[45] William Walker, phone interviews with author Aug. 5, 2001, Mar. 11, 2002 and Jan. 22, 2015.

[46] Warren Ammon had married Charlie's cousin Christine Walker, who was ten years older than Charlie.

[47] William Walker, phone interviews with author Aug. 5, 2001, Mar. 11, 2002 and Jan. 22, 2015.

[48] Pearl Albright Mendenhall, interview by the author at Coates Family Reunion, Aug. 18, 2002.

[49] Lena Walker, (Herb's wife) phone interview by author, Feb. 11, 2002.

[50] Arthur and Lila Weinberg, eds., *Instead of Violence* (Boston: Beacon Press, 1963), 353.

[51] Ibid, 381–382.

[52] Ibid, 378–389.

[53] Ibid, 379.

[54] Salisbury High School, *The Blue Bag*, printed program for senior class school play (White Horse, PA, 1936). Ray Shirk played the man searching for the blue bag and Don Neuhauser was his chauffeur. Ida Worst was hotel maid, and Ralph Thompson eloped with the maid. To compound the plot, Clara Hendry thought she was eloping with Ralph. John Graham and Pauline Simmons were also looking for the bag. Dorothy Shirk played an actress staying at the hotel and Don Martin was a customs officer.

[55] The ruins of Lindley Coates' burned barn's stone foundation can still be seen near Christiana.

[56] Smedley, *History of the Underground Railroad*, 30, 31, 32, 33, 34, 80, 83. Levi Coates was related to and worked with Levi Pownall, Jeremiah Cooper, Asahel Walker, and Joseph Dickenson of Sadsbury Meeting. Charlie Walker is likely related to Dickenson Gorsuch of the Christiana Rebellion through the Quaker Dickensons who moved to Maryland. Other Quaker abolitionists and Underground Railroad conductors/stationmasters in the area to whom Charlie Walker is related are Daniel Gibbons, Isaac and

Dinah Mendenhall, Truman Cooper, Thomas Hood, Allen Smith, Jeremiah Moore, Joseph Brinton, Joshua Brinton, Joseph Moore, Charles Moore, James Moore, Joseph and Caleb Hood, and William Jackson.

[57] Ibid., 86.

[58] Thomas Clarkson, a British Quaker, is credited with beginning the anti-slavery movement.

[59] Smedley, *History of the Underground Railroad*, 88.

[60] Ibid., 89.

[61] Ibid., 34,84.

[62] Margaret Bacon, "Abby Hopper Gibbons: Prison Reformer and Social Activist," *Friends Journal* (June 2001), 24.

[63] The house where Charles Coates had lived was called the Henderson Place, because Hendersons lived in it at one time. Charles Coates had deeded or sold it to his children and their spouses and it was then deeded to Mina from a group of eight Coateses, Albrights and Zimmermans for $1,275 in 1936.

[64] Violet Baker, phone interview with author, Apr. 20, 2002.

[65] William Walker, interview with author Aug. 5, 2001.

[66] An expression for picking beetles off the plants to prevent damage to the plants.

[67] Coates family reunion records in the possession of William H. Walker.

Chapter 2

[1] Chet Williamson, *Uniting Work and Spirit, A Centennial History of Elizabethtown College* (Elizabethtown, PA: Elizabethtown College Press, 2001), Chapter 3:1.

[2] Now Wenger Center.

[3] *Lancaster New Era* (May 1936).

[4] Williamson, *Uniting Work and Spirit*, 146–155.

[5] Ibid.

[6] Ernest Lefever, interview with author, Jul. 27, 2001.

[7] Unpublished autobiography, Ernest L. Lefever, used with permission., 3:3.

[8] *The Etonian*, yearbook of Elizabethtown College (1938–39), 60.

[9] Lefever, interview with author, Jul. 26, 2001; autobiography, 4:4–6.

[10] Ibid.

[11] Lefever, interview with author, Jul. 26, 2001.

[12] Ibid.

[13] William Walker, interview with author, Aug. 5, 2001; diary of Mina C.

Walker in the care of William Walker.

[14] William Walker, interviews with author, Aug. 5, 2001, Mar. 11, 2002, and Jan. 22, 2015.

[15] Wilmer Fridinger, interviews with author, Apr. 2, 2003, and Jul. 22, 2003.

[16] Lefever, autobiography, 4:9.

[17] *The Etonian* (1938–39), 60.

[18] The fourth dimension is generally considered to be "time" or "something out of the ordinary experience of man." Charlie may have been referring to a reality of the Spirit.

[19] *The Etonian* (1938-39), 60.

[20] Lefever, autobiography, 4:5.

[21] William Walker, interview with author, August 5, 2001; diary of Mina C. Walker in the care of William Walker.

[22] Charlie said he earned 10 cents a day, while brother Bill said it was a quarter.

[23] William Walker, interview with author, Aug. 5, 2001.

[24] Walter R. Miller, "Courageous Confederate Nurse Is Honored By Marker At Gap," *Christiana Ledger* (Mar. 15, 1956), 1; and Christine Walker Ammon, interview with Valerie Walker Peery, Oct. 16, 1991; son of author Brenda Beadenkopf, Ron Beadenkopf, underwent military training at Fort Gordon in Georgia.

[25] Ernest Lefever, "Catty Tales," *The Etownian*, student newspaper of Elizabethtown College (Oct. 20, 1938).

[26] Lefever, autobiography, 4:9.

[27] Fridinger, interview, Apr. 2, 2003.

[28] "Armistice Day Peace Call, Nov. 11, 1938," editorial in *The Etownian* (Nov. 5, 1938).

[29] Ibid.

[30] Lefever, autobiography, 4:4.

[31] Lefever, autobiography, 4:5.

[32] Ernest Lefever, email Feb. 17, 2003.

[33] Lefever, autobiography, 4:10.

[34] Bethany Biblical Seminary was later renamed Bethany Theological Seminary and relocated to the campus of Earlham College in Richmond, Indiana.

[35] President Franklin Delano Roosevelt.

[36] Lefever, autobiography, 4:14–18.

[37] Ibid., 4:19–20.

[38] Charles C. Walker, "Peace Talk," unpublished paper (circa 1939) donated to the author by Ross Coulson.

[39] William Willoughby, letter to Charles Walker, Jul. 16, 2003.

[40] Marian Groff Walker, interview with author, May, 2001.

[41] General Edward Hand's historic home on the Conestoga River is open to the public.

[42] "We Look at War," "Transient Observations," *The Etownian* (Oct. 19, 1939).

[43] Lefever, "The Religious Man," *The Etownian* (Mar. 25, 1938).

[44] Fridinger, interview with author, Apr. 2, 2003.

[45] William Willoughby, interview with author, Jul. 16, 2003; *The Etonian* (1940–41), 86.

[46] Lefever, autobiography, 4:13, 14.

[47] Lefever, interview with author, Jul. 26, 2001.

[48] *The Etonian* (1940–41), Juniors Section.

[49] Ibid.

[50] Ibid.

[51] Ern never became a millionaire, but did become a national figure. He was foreign affairs consultant to Senator Hubert Humphrey and did similar work for the National Council of Churches. He was senior researcher for the Brookings Institution, and in 1976 established his own think tank, the Ethics and Public Policy Center, in Washington, DC. In 1981 President Ronald Reagan nominated him for Assistant Secretary of State, but two of his brothers opposed the nomination, testifying against him before Senate hearings. After the Senate Foreign Relations Committee voted to reject his nomination, he withdrew his name, citing character assassination. Devoting himself to his Ethics and Public Policy Center, he wrote many books, articles and letters to the editor, surviving his friend Charlie Walker by five years until his death August 4, 2009.

[52] Unpublished autobiography, Ernest L. Lefever, used with permission, 4:23.

[53] Ibid., 4:22–24.

[54] "Lefever and Willoughby Extend Vacation," *The Etownian* (Oct. 7, 1940), 1.

[55] Ibid.

[56] "Campus Capsules," *The Etownian* (Oct. 7, 1940), 2.

[57] Ibid.

[58] "Coach Herr Starts to Realize Results of Ten Year Building Program," "Phantoms Trip up Wagner; 48–30 Score," *The Etownian* (Feb. 26, 1941).

[59] "Debating Revived After Two-Year Dormancy," *The Etownian* (Feb. 26, 1941).

[60] "Ping-Pong Tourney Proclaims Victors," *The Etownian* (Apr. 1, 1941).

[61] "Candles Select March 29 For Banquet Date," *The Etownian* (Feb. 26, 1941).

[63] Marian Groff Walker, interview with author, May 2003.

[64] "Gray Ghosts of Etown Avenge Earlier Defeat By Trimming Indians," *The Etownian* (May, 1941).

[65] "Elizabethtown Rallied to Trip Moravian." *The Etownian* (May, 1941).

[66] "Elizabethtown College Fights Hard to Nip Penn Military College 4–3," *The Etownian* (May, 1941).

[67] "Piano and Voice Recital Closes Musical Program," *The Etownian* (May, 1941).

[68] "Faculty Feted By Senior Class in Gymnasium," *The Etownian* (May, 1941).

[69] "Seniors Honored at Annual Banquet Held at Diff's," "Campfire Services for Volunteers," *The Etownian* (May, 1941).

[70] Today called Chickies Rock, where the Chiques Creek meets the Susquehanna River.

[71] "Joint 'Y' Sponsors Doggie Roast at Chiques Rock," "Students Enjoy Annual Outing at Mt. Gretna," *The Etownian* (May, 1941).

[72] "42 Receive Degrees," *The Etownian* (May, 1941). "The Thirty-Ninth Annual Commencement of Elizabethtown College" program, May 26, 1941. Although the program says Handel's "Largo," as does the article, Marian distinctly remembers Charlie playing Beethoven's *Moonlight Sonata*.

[73] "The Thirty-Ninth Annual Commencement of Elizabethtown College" program, May 26, 1941.

[74] "42 Receive Degrees," *The Etownian* (May, 1941).

Chapter 3

[1] The mill and buildings are still standing today near Mill Creek.

[2] Now the Old Mill Shoppe gift store.

[3] Letter June 3, 1941, signed by A. J. Muste and John Nevin Sayre.

[4] "Message of Annual Conference F.O.R., 1940." (SCPC)

[5] "The Conscientious Objector under the Selective Training and Service ACT of 1940," NSBRO Pamphlet, (Washington, D.C., Rev. Oct. 1944), 13–16.

[6] Biographical Notes on Rev. A. J. Muste.

[7] Richard Gregg, "Non-Violent Resistance," (New York, NY: Fellowship of Reconciliation pamphlet).

[8] John Nevin Sayre, "What Pacifism Proposes," (New York. NY: F.O.R. pamphlet).

[9] "Two Examples of Nonviolent Campaigns in India," unsigned, 1940s (CCW)

[10] Larry Walker, "Our Mother's Recollections on Charles Walker's Life," Cheyney, PA, Jan. 5, 2002.

[11] Sandusky trip story from Larry Walker, "Our Mother's Recollections on Charles Walker's Life," Jan. 5, 2002; Compilation of Interviews with Marian Walker, 2001.

[12] Herbert G. Bohn, "We Tried Non-Violence," *Fellowship* magazine, (Jan., 1937), 7, 8.

[13] Grading papers story from Larry Walker, "Our Mother's Recollections of Charles Walker's Life," Jan. 5, 2002.

[14] Arthur S. Link, and David S. Muzzey, *Our American Republic* (Boston, New York, Chicago, Atlanta, Dallas, Palo Alto, Toronto: Ginn and Company, 1966), 607.

[15] "Why War," An Exchange of letters Between Albert Einstein and Sigmund Freud, (Jul. and Sept., 1932).. (CCW)

[16] Charles F. Boss Jr., "The Case for Methodist Conscientious Objectors," Executive Secretary, General Conference Commission on World Peace, (Chicago, IL: Methodist Episcopal Church, circa 1937)

[17] Charles Walker, "On Pacifism," unpublished paper (1940s). (CCW)

[18] Aldous Huxley, *Ends and Means*, (New York and London: Harper and Brothers, 1937), 1.

[19] Ibid., 28.

[20] Charles C Walker obtained a copy of his FBI file many years later through the Freedom of information Act. (FOIA)(CCW)

[21] *Friends in Civilian Public Service, Quaker Conscientious Objectors in World War II Look Back and Look Ahead*, from a conference held Nov. 4–7, (Wallingford, PA: Pendle Hill, 1996), 26, 27.

[22] Ibid.

[23] Marian Walker, interview with author Jul. 18, 2006.

[24] Marian Walker, interview, Feb. 26, 2002.

[25] James Farmer, "The Race Logic of Pacifism," *Fellowship* (Feb. 1942). (SCPC)

[26] Ernest L. Lefever, unpublished autobiography, used with permission.

[27] Ibid.

[28] The release of a prisoner temporarily (for a special purpose) or permanently before the completion of a sentence, on the promise of good behavior.

[29] Charles Walker, "*Saga of a C.O,*" original poem, 1940s. (CCW), mailed to the author by Ross Coulson.

[30] Marian Walker, interview with author, Nov. 1, 2006.

[31] Marian Walker, "Our Mother's Reflections," interview by Larry Walker, Jan. 4, 2002.

[32] Charles Walker, letter to Ross Coulson from Springfield State Hospital, Sykesville, MD, Mar. 7, 1943. (CCW)

[33] *Friends in Civilian Public Service*, 28.

[34] Lowell Reidenbaugh, letter to Charles Walker, 1943. (CCW).

[35] Charles C. Walker, "On Leaving CPS," unpublished paper, (Oct. 6, 1943). (CCW)

[36] Ibid.

[37] A. J. Muste, "National Council Meets, Discusses Peace Plans, CPS, other Matters," (*Fellowship*, June 1943), 116.

[38] Robert E. Cushman, "Conscription of Conscience," pamphlet by Mulford Q. Sibley and Phillip E. Jacob (Cornell University Press, 1952); Charles C. Walker Editor, "Quakers and the Draft" (Phila., PA: Friends Coordinating Committee on Peace, 1968), 18.

[39] William Walker, interview with author, Aug. 5, 2001.

[40] World Peace Brigades in 1962 and Peace Brigades International in 1981.

[41] Charles C. Walker, self-published pamphlet, "Pacifism Confronts a World at War," June 3, 1943. (CCW)

[42] Walker, "Pacifism Confronts a World at War." (CCW).

[43] Marian Walker, interview with author Nov. 3, 2006.

[44] Marian Walker, interview with author, Feb. 26, 2002.

[45] Charles Walker, unpublished paper probably written for draft board, "On Leaving CPS," Oct. 6, 1943. (CCW)

[46] Charles Walker, handwritten "Chronology Re: Draft," 1942–44.

[47] Charles C Walker obtained a copy of his FBI file many years later through the Freedom of information Act. (FOIA)(CCW)

[48] Ibid.

[49] Margaret Rice Good Shank, married to John Fry Shank.

[50] Marian Walker, interview with author Feb. 26, 2002.

[51] Ibid.

[52] Frederick Faber, Henry Hemy and J. G. Walton, "Faith of Our Fathers," *A Hymnal for Friends*, (Phila., PA,: Friends General Conference, 1955), 69.

[53] Walker, "On Leaving CPS."

[54] Walker, "*Saga of a C.O.*"

[55] August Meier, and Elliot Rudwick, *CORE A Study in the Civil Rights Movement* (NY, London, Urbana, IL: University of Illinois Press, 1975), 6.

[56] Ibid.

[57] James Farmer, *Lay Bare the Heart: An Autobiography of the Civil Rights Movement* (New York: Arbor House, 1985), 97–99.

[58] Farmer, *Lay Bare the Heart*, 102,103.

[59] Farmer and Houser differ slightly in founding of CORE. The author combined information from Farmer with August Meier, and Elliot Rudwick, *CORE, A Study in the Civil Rights Movement* (New York, London, Urbana, IL: University of Illinois Press, 1975.)

[60] Bayard Rustin, letter to Norman Whitney (Oct. 19, 1943). (CCW)

[61] Charles C. Walker, "The Impact of Gandhi on the U.S. Peace Movement," chapter in *Gandhi, His Relevance For Our Times*, eds. G. Ramachandran and T.K. Mahedevan (New Delhi, India: Gandhi Peace Foundation, Kapan Printing Press, 1964).

[62] Glenn Smiley, letter to Mrs. Kay Shannon (June 13, 1967). (SCPC)

[63] "Charles C. Walker," author unknown, article based on interview with Walker at time of Haverford's Center for Nonviolent Conflict Resolution, 1970s. (CCW)

[64] Charles Walker, letter to the editor, *Harper's Magazine*, (April 9, 1954). (CCW)

[65] "A Few Small Candles: War Resisters of World War II Tell Their Stories," section written by John H. Griffith, edited by Larry Gara, Lenna Mae Gara, *War Resistance in World War II* (Kent, Ohio: Kent State Univ. Press, 1999), 4–13, 114, 115.

[66] John Griffith, email to author, Jul. 12, 2006.

[67] John Griffith, letter to author, June 29, 2001.

[68] John Griffith, email to author, June 6, 2007.

[69] Charles Walker, *Cryme in Rhyme*, original poems, (1943). (CCW)

[70] "Hunger Strikes in Prison," *PCCO News*, [Phil. Council for Conscientious Objectors] Nov. 1944. (SCPC)

[71] Ernest Lefever, interview with author, July 26, 2001.

[72] "Important! A significant landmark has been reached!" *CORE Comments*, CORE newsletter June 25, 1943, Vol. I, No. II. (CORE Archives, U of Wisc, Series 3, Exec. Sec. File, Box 4, Folder 1, File 1940s)

[73] Ernest Lefever, interview with author July 26, 2001; (Unpublished autobiography, Ernest L. Lefever, used with permission.), 4; handout from Stoner's Restaurant Final Strategy Meeting, Procedure "Project at Stoner's Restaurant Saturday, (Chicago, IL: CORE, June 6, 1943).

[74] Ernest Lefever, interview with author, Jul. 26, 2001.

[75] A. J. Muste, letter to Marian Walker, Apr. 4, 1944. (CCW)

[76] Ibid.

[77] Marian Walker, letter to NRSB (National Religious Service Board), May 3, 1944.

[78] Author unknown, "Charles C. Walker," article or part of monograph, based on interview with Walker at time of Haverford's Center for Nonviolent Conflict Resolution, 1970s. (CCW)

[79] http://www.nebraskastudies.org/0800/stories/0801_0107.html, Feb. 20, 2016.

[80] Charles Walker, "*Saga of a C.O.*," original poem, 1940s. (CCW)

[81] The Walker family is working to locate this old deed and would be happy for any leads.

[82] William Walker, interview with author, Aug. 5, 2001.

[83] Charles C. Walker, "A Discipline for Peacemakers," Jan. 14, 1945. (CCW)

[84] Charles Walker, letter to relatives, Nov. 1945.

Chapter 4

[1] Arthur S. Link, and David S. Muzzey, *Our American Republic* (Boston, New York, Chicago, Atlanta, Dallas, Palo Alto, Toronto: Ginn and Company, 1966).

[2] Charles C. Walker, "Captive of the Spirit," *Motive* (Methodist Student Journal. 1946) 26, 27.

[3] Margaret E. Hirst, *The Quakers in Peace and War* (London: The Gresham Press), 43.

[4] Ernest Lefever, "A Message From Ernest Lefever," *Motive*, (Methodist Student Journal 1946), 30.

[5] Robert Fangmeier, Advisory Section of NSBRO, letter to Charles Walker, Aug. 2, 1946. (CCW)

[6] Columbus period based on interviews with Marian Walker, Nov. 1, 2006, Oct. 11, 2014, Mar. 1, 2016; and interview with Larry Walker.

[7] August Meier, and Elliot Rudwick, *CORE A Study in the Civil Rights*

Movement (NY, London, Urbana, IL: University of Illinois Press, 1975) 32, 33.

[8] Charles Walker, *Cryme in Rhyme*, original poems, 1940s. (CCW)

[9] Charles Walker, post card to Marian Walker, Oct. 19, 1946. (CCW)

[10] Howard H. Brinton, *Friends for 300 Years* (Wallingford, PA, Pendle Hill: 1965), 90, 132, 150.

[11] Charles Walker, letter to President Harry Truman, Nov. 29, 1946. (CCW)

[12] Charles Walker, letter to Ernest Lefever, Feb. 21, 1947. (CCW)

[13] "A Message to Men and Women of Goodwill," letter to Fellow Americans, circa 1946. (AFSC)

[14] "AFSC Undertakes Program in Finland," "From the Children of Nimes," AFSC newsletter, circa 1945. (AFSC)

[15] Meier and Rudwick, *CORE A Study in the Civil Rights Movement*, 34, 35.

[16] Meier and Rudwick, *CORE A Study in the Civil Rights Movement*, 34.

[17] Congress of Racial Equality letter dated 1947 and signed by George M. Houser and Bayard Rustin.

[18] Meier and Rudwick, *CORE A Study in the Civil Rights Movement*, 34.

[19] Ibid, 36, 37.

[20] John Raitt later became a close friend of Charlie and Marian. His daughter, Bonnie Raitt, is a well-known singer.

[21] "Child Is Hurt in 40-Foot Fall," article in Columbus, OH newspaper, summer 1947. (CCW)

[22] Winifred, a very popular 'War Baby' name, meaning bringer of peace.

[23] Adrienne (last name not listed), letter to Charles Walker, Sept. 1, 1947. (CCW)

[24] Charles Walker, letter to Adrienne (last name not listed), Sept. 8, 1947. (CCW)

[25] Charles Walker, letter to Molly Blackburn, Sep. 29, 1947. (CCW)

[26] "Aspects of Current American Foreign Policy," (Washington, DC: The Department of State, Oct. 20, 1947), 3.

[27] Ibid., 4.

[28] Ibid. 4-7.

[29] "A Declaration to the American People," flyer for Peacemakers signed by Charles Walker, Ohio, AFSC newsletter, (New York, Liberation Press) 1947. (CCW)

[30] Sanderson Beck, "Quakers: Fox and Penn's Holy Experiment," *Guides to Peace and Justice from Ancient Sages to the Suffragettes* (Santa Barbara, CA: World

Peace Communications, Jul. 2005), 354.

[31] Beck, *Guides to Peace and Justice from Ancient Sages to the Suffragettes*, 360–362.

[32] Paulette Meier, "Knowing and Sharing our Faith and its Historical Influence," *Friends Journal* (Mar. 2007), 38.

[33] "The Spiritual Life Retreat," informational sheets, 1947. (AFSC)

[34] "Workshop in Rehabilitation," informational sheets, 1947. (AFSC)

[35] "Service Committee Shares Nobel Award," *North Central Area News,* AFSC Columbus newsletter, (Nov. 1947).

[36] Ibid.

[37] Charles C. Walker, "Conciliation and Direct Action: A Time for Collaboration," paper about Friends and the international scene, 1970s, (Haverford Research Project). (CCW)

[38] Jack Sutter, AFSC Archivist, "AFSC in History," Nobel Peace Prize Curiosities, Stories from AFSC's Past, "About AFSC," article on AFSC website December 2000.

[39] A. J. Muste, "Notes on National Conference Themes, 1947," (1947).

[40] Charles Walker, letter to Ernest Lefever, Jan. 2, 1948.

[41] Ernest Lefever, letter to Charles Walker, Feb. 2, 1948.

[42] Charles Walker, letter to John Ewbank given to the author by Marjorie Ewbank, Feb. 3, 1948.

[43] A. J. Muste, "Call For a Conference on More Disciplined and Revolutionary Pacifist Activity," Call to Peacemakers to attend conference Apr. 2–4, 1948 in Chicago.

[44] A. J. Muste, Holy Week 1948 Message to the National Executive Committee of the Fellowship of Reconciliation.

[45] Charles Walker, letter to Eugene Exman, May 11, 1948. (CCW)

[46] Eugene Exman, letter to Charles Walker, Apr. 4, 1946. (CCW)

Chapter 5

[1] Wilma Hosholder, Swarthmore Peace Collection Staff, from an introduction to the *College Program and Student Movement Files*, description in FOR files, FOR Archives, Swarthmore College Peace Collection, description of material in Boxes 9, 10, 13, 17, Swarthmore, PA (SCPC)

[2] John Swomley, letter to Charles Rockel, Sept. 30, 1948. (SCPC)

[3] FOR Exec. Comm. Mtg., Nov, 7, 1948. (SCPC)

[4] John Swomley, letter to Charles Rockel, Sept. 30, 1948. (SCPC)

[5] Charles Walker, letter to Richard Richards, Sept. 20, 1948. (SCPC)

[6] Charles Walker, memo to John Swomley, Sept. 24, 1948. (SCPC)

[7] Charles Walker, memo to John Swomley, Sept. 28, 1948. (SCPC)

[8] Charles Walker, memo to John Swomley, Oct. 1, 1948. (SCPC)

[9] Charles Walker, memo John Swomley, Oct. 9, 1948. (SCPC)

[10] "The Social Creed of the Methodist Church 1948," Commission on World Peace of The Methodist Church, Charles Boss Jr., Executive Secretary (Chicago, IL, 1948). (CCW)

[11] John Swomley, letter to Charles Walker, Oct. 18, 1948. (SCPC)

[12] Charles Walker, letter to Charles Parmer, Nov. 1, 1948. (CCW)

[13] Pronounced TANG-gee.

[14] Pronounced CHAY- Nee.

[15] Charles Walker, FOR memo to John Swomley, Oct. 18, 1948. (SCPC)

[16] Charles Walker, letter to Herman Will, Nov. 20, 1948. (SCPC)

[17] Dorothy Detzer, "We Tried the United Front," reprint *Fellowship*, (New York: Journal of the Fellowship of Reconciliation (Oct. 1948). (CCW)

[18] The building has since been torn down.

[19] Arlo was brother to Lyle Tatum, whose family became friends to the Walker family. Arlo became Brenda Walker's later employer at a conference center in New Jersey.

[20] Charles Walker, letter to Richard Richards, Dec. 20, 1948. (CCW)

[21] Charles Walker, letter to Rev. Worth, Dec. 18, 1948. (SCPC)

[22] Marian Walker, interview with author, June 2, 2009.

[23] Ernest Lefever, letter to Charles Walker, given to author, Jan. 1, 1949.

[24] Charles Walker, letter to Reed Smith, Jan. 4, 1949. (SCPC)

[25] Reed Smith, letter to Charles Walker, Jan. 16, 1949. (SCPC)

[26] "YWCA Columbus," "History," ywcacolumbus.org/site/Page Server?pagename=about history (May 6, 2015).

[27] John Swomley, memo to Charles Walker, Jan. 31, 1949. (SCPC)

[28] "Mr. Charles Walker to Address SCA Feb. 15," "Dr. McCorkel Guest Speaker at SCA," *The Susquehanna*, Feb. 8, 1949.

[29] "An Ohio College Conference, Theme: "Training for Campus Peace Action," program for conference at Oberlin College for Feb. 18–20, 1949. (SCPC)

[30] Charles Walker, letter to David White, Mar. 3, 1949. (SCPC)

[31] Howard Alexander of Michigan FOR, letter to Charles Walker, Mar. 9, 1949. (SCPC)

[32] Charles Walker, memo to John Swomley, Mar. 22, 1947. (SCPC)

[33] Charles Walker, letter to Emily Longstreth, Apr. 5, 1949. (SCPC)

34 Charles Walker, letter to FOR membership, Phila. Branch, Apr., 1949. (SCPC)

35 John Swomley, letter to Charles Rockel cc. Charles Walker, Apr. 20, 1949. (SCPC)

36 Charles Walker, letter to Carolyn Neuhauser, Jul. 6, 1949. (CCW)

37 Charles Walker, letter to Robert James, Jul. 7, 1949. (SCPC)

38 Bayard Rustin, memo, Aug. 4, 1949. (SCPC)

39 Robert James, letter to Charles Walker, Jul. 12, 1949. (SCPC)

40 Charles Walker, letter to Mrs. Richard S. Miner. (SCPC)

41 Charles Walker, letter to James A. McQuail Jr., Jul. 21, 1949. (SCPC)

42 Emily Anne MacDonald, letter to Charles Walker, Oct. 13, 1949. (SCPC)

43 JoAnn Ooiman Robinson, *Abraham Went Out: A Biography of A. J. Muste* (Phila., PA: Temple University Press, 1981), 277: Charles Walker, letter to Dr. Enus Wright, Sept. 26, 1984.

44 Charles Walker, letter to sister-in-law Lena Walker, "Your asking me about my relationship with the work of Martin Luther King Jr.," Cheyney, PA, Jan. 1984, 3. (CCW)

45 Footnote for letter from Martin Luther King to Charles Walker, *The Papers of Martin Luther King, Jr., Vol. III Birth of a New Age*, December 1955–December 1956, ed. Clayborne Carson (University of California Press: 1999), 464.

46 Marian Walker, interview with author, Mar. 26, 2001.

47 Charles Walker, "The Impact of Gandhi on the U.S. Peace Movement," chapter in book *Gandhi: His Relevance for Our Times*, ed. G. Ramachandran and T.K. Mahedevan (New Delhi, India: the Gandhi Foundation, Kapur Printing Press, 1964).

48 Cynthia Fisk, "Nonviolence: The Law of Love," "Viewpoint," *Friends Journal* (June 2001), 5.

49 Charles Walker, memo to Bayard Rustin, Nov. 14, 1959; Swarthmore College Peace Collection, Swarthmore, PA, Fellowship of Reconciliation Records, Section 3, Series C, Box 10, Folder "Charles Walker, General Correspondence, 1948–1953.

50 Robinson, *Abraham Went Out: A Biography of A. J. Muste*, 277.

51 Charles Walker, letter to Lena Walker, Cheyney, PA, Jan. 1984. (CCW)

52 Charles Walker, letter to David Garrow, Dec. 15, 1986. (CCW)

53 David J. Garrow, *Bearing the Cross: Martin Luther King, Jr. and the Southern Christian Leadership Conference* (New York: William Morrow & Co., 1953).

54 Charles Walker, letter to Lena Walker, Jan. 6, 1984.

[55] Charles Walker, letter to David Garrow, Dec. 15, 1986. (CCW)

[56] A preeminent university primarily for African American students.

[57] Martin Luther King Jr., *Stride Toward Freedom, The Montgomery Story* (New York: Ballentine Books, 1958), 76: http://explorepahistory.com/hmarker.php?markerId=1-A-367, 3/5/2014.

[58] Charles Walker, letter to Lena Walker, Jan. 6, 1984.

[59] Robinson, *Abraham Went Out: A Biography of A. J. Muste*, 277.

[60] Nat Hentoff, *Peace Agitator: The Story of A. J. Muste*, (New York: MacMillan, 1963), 17, 18.

[61] Charles Walker, letter to Charles H. Parmer, Nov. 29, 1949. (CCW)

Chapter 6

[1] *Encyclopedia Britannica*, Volume 13 (Publisher William Benton, 1768–1970, Chicago, 1970): 460–461.

[2] Marian Walker, interview with author, Mar. 21, 2009.

[3] Charles Walker, "Proposed Program for the Phila. F.O.R. in 1950," (Phila., Jan./Feb). (CCW)

[4] George Houser, letter to FOR workers, "Charlie" handwritten at top in pencil (National FOR, New York, Nov. 17, 1949), 1. (SCPC)

[5] Ibid., 2.

[6] National CORE publication (Chicago, Jan. 1950). (SCPC)

[7] Charles Walker, letter to Ken Cuthbertson, Jan. 10, 1950. (SCPC)

[8] Charles Walker, letter to Charles Rockel, Jan. 24, 1950. (SCPC)

[9] Pronounced "Redding."

[10] Rev. Richard Dettrey of Grace Methodist Church and Union Seminary, letter to Charles Walker, Feb. 1, 1950. (SCPC)

[11] Charles Walker, letter to Mrs. Walter Longstreth, Feb. 3, 1950. (SCPC)

[12] As FOR board member, Howard Thurman urged his former student, James Farmer, to establish the separate organization, the Congress of Racial Equality (CORE), upon whose board he also sat. From *A Strange Freedom: The Best of Howard Thurman on Religious Experience and Public Life*, eds. Walter Earl Fluker and Catherine Tumber (Boston: Beacon Press, 1998), 6.

[13] Charles Walker, "Well-Known Pacifist Speakers Coming to the Greater Phila. Area," FOR schedule, Feb., 1950. (SCPC)

[14] "What of Gandhism in India? In America? First-Hand Reports on World Pacifist Conference held in India, December, 1949," advertisement for a meeting featuring Mordecai Johnson, with Lewis Hoskins of AFSC presiding, AFSC, Mar., 1950. (SCPC)

[15] Charles Walker, "Report to the May Executive Committee Meeting" (Phila. FOR, May 8, 1950). (SCPC)

[16] Charles Walker, "A Report of the Year's Activities of the Phila. F.O.R." (Phila., 1950). (SCPC)

[17] "Rustin Calls Non-Violence Solution to World's Ills: Negro Leader Returns to West Chester; Describes Philosophy Evolved During Life-Long Effort Against Prejudice," *West Chester Daily Local News* (West Chester, PA, Apr. 14, 1950), 1. (SCPC)

[18] Walter Naegle, email to author clarifying the year Rustin left the Communist Party, "It was actually after Hitler invaded Russia (1941) and the CP here changed their anti-war stance. They asked Bayard to dismantle his committee on race, and support the war effort. He would not, of course, do that," Apr. 15, 2004.

[19] "Rustin Calls Nonviolence Solution," *West Chester Daily Local News* (Apr. 14, 1950), 1. (SCPC).

[20] Ibid.

[21] Ibid.

[22] Ibid.

[23] Charles Walker, "Report to the May Executive Committee Meeting, Phila. FOR, May 8, 1950. (CCW)

[24] Ibid.

[25] Charles Walker, "A Report of the Year's Activities of the Phila. F.O.R.," Phila., 1950. (SCPC)

[26] William Willoughby, letter to Charles Walker, Aug. 25, 1950. (CCW)

[27] Ibid.

[28] "Minutes of F.O.R. Staff Meeting, National Office (New York, Sept., 20–21, 1950). (SCPC)

[29] Charles Walker, letter to Edward Kinslow, Oct. 2, 1950. (SCPC)

[30] Marian Walker, interview with author, June 2, 2009.

[31] A cooperative community north of Philadelphia, similar to Tanguy.

[32] Charles Walker, memo to Bayard Rustin and George Houser, Oct. 12, 1950. (SCPC)

[33] Ibid.

[34] George Houser, email to author, June 6, 2009.

[35] Charles Walker, memo to Bayard Rustin and George Houser, "Blood Banks or Blood-mobiles," Phila., FOR, Oct. 12, 1950. (SCPC)

[36] Ibid.

[37] George Houser, email to author, June 6, 2009.

[38] Bayard Rustin, letter to Bessie LeBon, c.c. Charles Walker, Jamaica, NY, Nov. 14, 1950. (SCPC)

[39] Marian Walker, interview with author, Mar. 21, 2009.

[40] Charles Walker, "A Report of the Year's Activities of the Phila. F.O.R., Phila., 1950. (SCPC)

[41] Bayard Rustin, memo to Charles Walker, handwritten "Important - Charles Walker," "Swarthmore Engagement, Dec. 17, 1950, Dec. 13, 1950." (SCPC)

[42] Charles Walker, memo to Bayard Rustin, Dec. 13, 1950. (SCPC)

[43] A. J. Muste, "Overcoming Fear," *Fellowship* (New York: Nov., 1950), 4–7.

[44] Bayard Rustin, "Report on trip to Africa," FOR report, Oct. 20, 1952. (CCW)

[45] Ibid., 2.

[46] Ibid., 3.

[47] Ibid., 4.

[48] Ibid., 4,5.

[49] Ibid. 5,6.

[50] Ibid., 6.

[51] "Interracial Workshops Washington D.C and St. Louis, MO," sponsored by FOR and CORE, for Jul. 1–31, 1951, brochure (FOR New York, CORE, NY). (SCPC)

[52] Ibid.

[53] Catherine Raymond, Secretary at the N.Y. FOR, letter to Charles Walker, May 25, 1951. (SCPC)

[54] But above all things, my brethren, swear not, neither by heaven, neither by the earth, neither by any other oath: but let your yea be yea; and *your* nay, nay; lest ye fall into condemnation. KJV

[55] Howard H. Brinton, *Friends For 300 Years* (Wallingford, PA: Pendle Hill Quakerback, 1965), 156-159.

[56] Ibid., 147, 148; R.C. Smedley, *History of the Underground Railroad*, (NY, Arno Press and *The New York Times*, 1969), 84.

[57] Charles Walker, memo to Bayard Rustin, Phila. FOR, Apr. 11, 1951. (SCPC)

[58] Marian Walker, interview with author, June 4, 2009.

[59] Charles Walker, letter to Francis Hall, Phila. FOR, Jul. 16, 1951. (CCW)

[60] *Webster's Ninth New Collegiate Dictionary*, 1987, (Merriam-Webster, Inc., Springfield, MA.): 1302.

[61] Charles Walker, "Report on Pacifism at the Student Volunteer National Conference," at University of Kansas at Lawrence, Dec. 1951, in cooperation with Bayard Rustin, Phila. FOR, Jan, 1952, 2.

[62] Ibid., 2.

[63] Ibid., 2.

[64] Ibid., 3.

[65] Ibid., 4.

[66] Ibid., 5.

[67] Ibid., 6.

[68] Ibid., 5.

[69] Charles Walker, memo to A. J. Muste, Phila. FOR, Dec., 1951. (SCPC)

[70] Copy of Christmas card, Dec. 1951, written or co-written by Charles Walker, Phila. FOR, 1951. (CCW)

[71] Charles Walker, FOR newsletter, (2006 Walnut Street, Phila., Jan., 1952, 1. (SCPC)

[72] Ibid., 2.

[73] Ibid.

[74] Ibid.

[75] "Non-Violence: India and America," flyer FOR, Phila. Branch, Jan., 1952. (SCPC;) A Legation is a diplomatic office.

[76] Ibid.

[77] Later made into a movie of the same name starring Marlon Brando.

[78] Irwin Shaw, letter to Charles Walker, Jan. 5, 1952. (CCW)

[79] A. J. Muste, letter to Irwin Shaw, Jan. 16, 1952. (CCW)

[80] Ibid., 2.

[81] Charles Walker, letter to Ken Kilsoo Kang, Jan. 9, 1952. (SCPC)

[82] Ken Kilsoo Kang, letter to Charles Walker, Jan. 12, 1952. (SCPC)

[83] Joseph Karsner, letter to Charles Walker, Second Month 6, 1952. (SCPC)

[84] Charles Walker, letter to Rev. Ivan Murray Rose of First Baptist Church, Feb. 7, 1952. (SCPC)

[85] Charles Walker, memo to "Friends of Peace Among Philadelphia Ministers, - #1, "Rait-Rutenbur Meeting," Phila. FOR, Feb., 1952. (SCPC)

[86] Marian Walker, phone interview with author, June 13, 2009.

[87] Charles Walker, Phila. FOR, "Report to the Executive Committee By the Executive Secretary on the Quarterly Meeting," Mar. 10, 1952. (SCPC)

[88] Charles Walker, letter to Rev. Dr. Murray Ivan Rose, First Baptist

Church, Feb. 7, 1952. (SCPC)

[89] Charles Walker, ed. *Friends Medical Society newsletter*, "Executive Secretary Appointed," (Phila.: Feb., 1952). (SCPC)

[90] Joy Marshall, letter to Charles Walker, Mar. 23, 1952. (SCPC)

[91] Ibid.

[92] Charles Walker, letter to "Dear Friends, the Marshalls," Mar. 25, 1952. (SCPC)

[93] Joy and Bob Marshall, letter to Charles Walker, Mar. 23, 1952. (SCPC)

[94] Charles Walker, letter to Joy Marshall, Mar. 25, 1952. (SCPC)

[95] Joy Marshall, letter to Charles Walker, Mar. 23, 1952, 2. (SCPC)

[96] Charles Walker, letter to Joy Marshall, Mar. 25, 1952. (SCPC)

[97] Joy Marshall, letter to Charles Walker, Mar. 23, 1952, 2. (SCPC)

[98] Ibid.

[99] Charles Walker, letter to Joy Marshall, Mar. 25, 1952. (SCPC)

[100] Joy Marshal, letter to Charles Walker, Mar. 23, 1952, 2. (SCPC)

[101] Charles Walker, letter to Joy Marshall, Mar. 25, 1952. (SCPC)

[102] Charles Walker, Phila. FOR Executive Secretary, memo on South Africa, "Background On The South African Non-Violent Resistance Campaign," Mar., 1952, 1. (SCPC)

[103] Ibid., 2.

[104] A. J. Muste, "Memo to F.O.R. Staff from A. J. Muste," June 13, 1952. (SCPC)

[105] John M. Swomley Jr., letter to Charles Walker, Jul. 3, 1952. (SCPC)

[106] Charles Walker, letter to John Deschner, Jul. 10, 1952. (SCPC)

[107] Miriam Pennypacker, "Minutes of the Executive Committee of the Phila. Fellowship of Reconciliation, Jul. 14, 1952. (SCPC)

[108] Ibid.

[109] Bayard Rustin, memo, New York FOR, Oct. 20, 1952. (CCW)

[110] Ibid.

[111] James H. Duckrey, President of State Teachers College, Cheyney, PA, letter to Charles Walker, Dec. 8, 1952. (SCPC)

[112] John Swomley, letter to E. A. (Red) Schaal, Dec. 29, 1952.

[113] E. A. (Red) Schaal, letter to John Swomley, Dec. 24, 1952. (SCPC)

[114] A Quaker boarding school a few miles from Cheyney.

[115] Charles Walker, letter to George Houser, Jan., 1953. (SCPC)

[116] Ibid.

[117] Jervis Anderson, *Bayard Rustin: Troubles I've Seen*, (New York: Harper Collins, 1977), 153–165.

[118] Ibid.

[119] A.J Muste, letter to Charles Walker, Feb. 24, 1953. (SCPC)

[120] Anderson, *Bayard Rustin: Troubles I've Seen*, 150.

[121] Ibid., 74, 164.

[122] Charles Walker, letter to Bayard Rustin, Mar., 1953. (SCPC)

[123] Charles Walker, "Report of the Executive Secretary to the Executive Committee, for the meeting of Monday, Mar. 9, 1953." (CCW)

[124] George Fox, quote written in Charles Walker's handwriting in his collection of papers. (CCW)

[125] Charles Walker, "On Pacifism," from his personal papers, Cheyney, PA, 1950s. (CCW)

[126] Ernie Lefever, letter to Charles Walker, 1950s. (Donated to author by E. Lefever)

[127] The first African American to receive (1950) the Nobel Peace Prize.

[128] Charles Walker, memo to A. J. Muste, Apr. 22, 1953. (SCPC)

[129] Mohandas, K. Gandhi, "The Doctrine of the Sword," article in *Young India* (India, Aug. 11, 1920), 3. (CCW)

[130] Marian Walker, interview with author, June 4, 2009.

[131] Ibid.

[132] Charles Walker, memo to George Walton, Aug., 12, 1953. (SCPC)

[133] Ibid.

[134] William Willoughby, letter to Charles Walker, Sept. 7, 1953. (CCW)

[135] Helen Corson, "Minutes of the Executive Committee, Phila. FOR," Sept. 14, 1953. (CCW)

[136] Charles Walker, flyer "Let's Talk It Over," Sept., 1953. (SCPC)

[137] Charles Walker, letter to Edwin Randall, Nov. 11, 1953. (SCPC)

[138] Charles Walker, memo to John Swomley Dec. 1, 1953. (SCPC)

[139] Helen Corson, "Minutes of the Executive Committee, Phila. Branch, FOR," Dec. 8, 1953. (CCW)

[140] Charles Walker, memo to George Houser, Oct. 26, 1953. (SCPC)

[141] Charles Walker, "Remarks By Charles Walker," at A. J. Muste Commemorative Meeting, NYC, Dec. 8, 1985, 1. (CCW)

[142] Ibid., 2.

Chapter 7

[1] Charles Walker, "Lessons from the Civil Rights Movement," monograph for Center For Conflict Resolution (Haverford College, Haverford, PA, 1973). (CCW)

[2] Ibid.

[3] John Swomley Jr., "Non-Violence and Racial Conflict," Fellowship of Reconciliation paper, Feb., 1954. (SCPC)

[4] Charles Walker, post card mailed from FOR, Feb., 1954. (SCPC)

[5] Helen Corson, Sec., (submitted) "Minutes of the Executive Committee of the Fellowship of Reconciliation- Phila. Branch," Feb. 8, 1954. (SCPC)

[6] Helen Corson, memo and Pledge Sheet to Present and Former Members of the Executive Committee, Phila. FOR, "Regional Office Proposals and the Present Situation," Feb., 1954. (CCW)

[7] Ibid.

[8] Memo to Present and Former Members of the Executive Committee, Phila. FOR, Re: Regional Office Proposals and the Present Situation, Feb., 1954. (CCW)

[9] Ibid.; "Minutes of FOR Executive Committee," Feb. 8, 1954; FOR Budget Proposal for Mar. 1 through Dec. 31, 1954. (SCPC)

[10] Charles Walker, letter to Bonnie Marshall, Apr. 14, 1954. (CCW)

[11] Charles Walker, "The Prayer of a Righteous Man," notes for a speech, date unknown, edited by author. (CCW)

[12] "Proposal for Christian Pacifist Work in the South," FOR paper, unsigned, 1954. (SCPC)

[13] Charles Walker, "Lessons From the Civil Rights Movement," monograph written for Center For Conflict Resolution, (Haverford, PA, Haverford College, 1973). (CCW)

[14] Wikipedia, *Gebhart v. Belton*, notes on Louis Redding's part in B*ulah v. Gebhart,* civilrights.org/education/brown/belton.html (Mar. 31, 2105).

[15] "Pro's and Con's on Peace and War," FOR pamphlet. (CCW)

[16] Charles Walker, "Report of the Executive Secretary to the Executive Committee," FOR Phila., May 10, 1954. (CCW)

[17] Charles Walker, "Report of the Executive Secretary to the Executive Committee," May 17, 1954. (SCPC)

[18] *The Mind of Gandhi,* eds. R.K. Prabhu and U.R. Rao, (Ahemadabad-380014 India: Printed and Published by: Jitendra T. Desai, Navajivan Mudranalaya, 1960).

[19] *Young India,* magazine, a weekly paper or journal - in English published by

Mohandas Gandhi from 1919 to 1932 (India, NY: May 6, 1926).

[20] Charles Walker, unpublished paper "Toward an Understanding of Meditation," date unknown. (CCW)

[21] Charles Walker, letter to Dr. A. C. Baugher, President, Elizabethtown College, Jan. 13, 1954. (SCPC)

[22] Helen Corson, Sec., "Minutes of the Executive Committee, FOR- Phila.," Apr. 12, 1954. (CCW)

[23] Charles Walker, "Mr. Average Citizen Views the News," radio show script, WCOJ, Oct. 3, 1954. (CCW)

[24] Charles Walker, "Mr. Average Citizen Views the News," radio show script, WCOJ, Oct. 3, 1954. (CCW)

[25] Charles Walker, "Bryant Bowles in Action: An Eyewitness Account," FOR report, Oct., 1954. (CCW)

[26] Ibid.

[27] Charles Walker, "Report of the Executive Secretary to the Executive Committee," FOR, Oct. 11, 1954, 2. (CCW)

[28] "Effects of Hurricane Hazel in Canada," http://en.wikipedia.org/wiki/effects_of_Hurricane_in_Canada, (May 6, 2015).

[29] Charles C. Walker, "Condensation of the chapter on Family Devotions in Ferre's *Strengthening the Spiritual Life*" (New York: Harper Bros, 1951).

[30] Charles Walker, "Report of the Executive Secretary to the Executive Committee," Oct. and Dec. Meetings, 1954. (CCW)

[31] Charles Walker, "Report of the Executive Secretary to the Executive Committee," FOR, Oct. 11, 1954, 2.

[32] Ibid.

[33] Ibid.

[34] Lyle Tatum, "Lyle Tatum Coordinating National Conference Travel," Jul., 1955. (CCW); minutes of the National Council of the FOR, May 1955, 6. (SCPC)

[35] Glenn Smiley, "Letter to a New FOR Secretary," letter to Charles Walker, June 6, 1955. (SCPC)

[36] A. J. Muste, letter to Friends, June 29, 1955. (SCPC)

[37] Glenn Smiley, memo to John Swomley, Apr. 1, 1955. (SCPC)

[38] Lyle Tatum, "Lyle Tatum Coordinating National Conference Travel," Jul., 1955. (CCW)

[39] William Walker, interview with author, Aug. 5, 2001.

[40] Tatum, "Coordinating National Conference Travel," (Jul. 1955). (CCW)

[41] Charles Walker, "Reflections on a Summer Abroad," Oct., 1955. (CCW)

[42] Walker, "Mr. Average Citizen Views the News," script for Sept. 25, 1954. (CCW)

[43] Walker, "Reflections on a Summer Abroad," Oct., 1955. (CCW)

[44] Ibid.

[45] Ibid.

[46] Ibid.

[47] Charles Walker, "What Would You Do If...?" *Pacifist Notebook*, FOR newsletter, Phila., PA. (CCW)

[48] "Emmett Till: Biography," murder victim/civil rights figure, Answers.com/topic/Emmett-Till, (Dec. 8, 2009).

[49] Walker, "Mr. Average Citizen," radio script November, WCOJ, Coatesville, PA, 1955. (CCW)

[50] Ibid.

Abbreviations Appendix

Abbreviation	Explanation
AFSC	American Friends Service Committee archives at Friends Center, Philadelphia
CCW	Charles Coates Walker personal papers
CORE	Congress of Racial Equality; refers CORE Archives at the University of Wisconsin
CPP	Convention People's Party
CPS	Civilian Public Service
E-A to the Fifth Club	Ethereal Agglutination of Agnostic Adherents to Ascetic Agamy
FMS	Friends Medical Society
FOR	Fellowship of Reconciliation
FPC	Friends Peace Committee
IV-F	or 4-F, not qualified for services in the armed forces
NAACP	National Association for the Advancement of Colored People
NAAWP	National Association for the Advancement of White People
NALC	Negro American Labor Council
NCC	National Council of Churches
NSBRO	National Service Board for Religious Objectors
NUL	National Urban League
PPC	Poor People's Campaign
PYM	Philadelphia Yearly Meeting

SAFE   Save a Friend in Europe

SCLC   Southern Christian Leadership Conference

SCM   Student Christian Movement

SCPC   Fellowship of Reconciliation Archives, Swarthmore
                        College Peace Collection at Swarthmore College

SNCC   Student Nonviolent Coordinating Committee

SVM   Student Volunteer Movement

UN   United Nations

USSR   Union of Soviet Socialist Republics, or Russia at the time

YMCA   Young Men's Christian Association

YWCA   Young Women's Christian Association

Index

A

Africa, 79, 91, 105, 226, 227, 240–43, 247, 254, 255, 294, 296
Albright, Mai, 35, 145
Albright, Pearl, 35, 36, 145, 270, 279
Albright, Rhea, 35, 145
Alexian Brothers Hospital, 135, 136
American Anti-Slavery Society, 40
American Friends Service Committee (AFSC), v, vi, 116, 159, 166, 167, 169, 170, 176, 178–82, 184, 186, 190, 192, 193, 216, 219, 244, 247, 270, 271, 301
Amish, 13, 33, 37, 45, 46, 53, 91, 108, 171
Ammon, Christine Walker, 15, 279
Ammon, Warren, 18, 34, 279
Anthony, Susan B., 168
Arch Street Meeting House, vi
Arnold, Benedict, 48
Avery, Chel, vi

B

Bagley, Edythe Scott, i, iv, vi
Bair, June, 38
Baker, Viola, vi
Berberian, Harry, 66
Bethany Biblical Seminary, 66, 79, 111, 132, 281
Birmingham, AL, 2, 8, 273
Blackburn, Bill, 172
Blackburn, Molly, 176, 288
Bleecher, Ellen, 243
Bleecher, Harry, 264
Blood, Peter, vii
Booth, John Wilkes, 31
Boulding, Kenneth, 96
Bowles, Bryant, 261–64, 266
Brethren, Church of the, 44–47, 51, 61, 66, 74, 77–79, 81, 110, 111

Brinton, Joseph, 41, 280
Brinton, Joshua, 280
Bristol, Jim, 203
Brotherhood Month, 213, 214
Brotherhood Pledge, 213, 214
Bryn Gweled, 222
Buchanan, James (President), 17
Buck, Pearl, 229, 230
Bulah v. Gebhart, 258
Bunche, Ralph, 249

C

Cadbury, Henry, 180–82
Candles, The, 74, 75, 85, 148
Cary, Stephen, 109
Center For Conflict Resolution, 254
Chester, PA, 195, 209
Cheyney College, 223, 244, 250
Cheyney, PA, 4, 10, 192, 194–96, 205, 216, 221, 250
Chmielewski, Wendy, vi
Christian Century, 271
Christiana Resistance, 27–31, 39–41
Civilian Public Service (CPS), 94, 100, 106, 108–17, 120–22, 131–35, 149, 301
Clarkson Anti-Slavery Society, 40
Clarkson, Thomas, 280
Clemson Gang, 277
Close family, 208
Coates, Charles, 20, 41, 280
Coates, Lee, vi
Coates, Levi, 41, 279
Coates, Lindley, 39, 229, 279
Coates, Mary Elizabeth (Molly) Kreider, 20, 145
Coates, Moses, 48
Coates, Robert, 145
Collins, Doug, 128
Communism, 204, 219

Concord Friends Meeting, 161, 207–9, 218, 222, 224

Congress of Racial Equality (CORE), ii, v, vi, 5, 8, 9, 11, 123–26, 132, 133, 141, 165–67, 171, 172, 196, 201, 213–15, 227, 249, 286, 292, 301

Convention People's Party (CPP), 226, 227, 301

Cooper, Jeremiah, 41, 279

Cooper, Truman, 41, 280

Corson, Helen, 297–99

Coulson, Ross, vii, 83, 90

Crozer Theological Seminary, 11, 209–11, 224

D

Day, Curtis, 57, 81, 149

Detzer, Dorothy, 197

Dickenson, Joseph, 279

Disney, Stan, 57, 83, 90

Dockhorn, Robert, i, vi

Dockhorn, Wayne, 242, 256

Douglass, Frederick, 30

Dutch Reformed Church, 96, 225

E

E-A to the Fifth Club, 50–52, 55–57, 68, 69, 76, 79, 301

Earle, Thomas, 40

Ebersole, Mark, 68

Edwards family, 208

Edwards, Ruth, 83, 224

Elizabethtown College, vi, vii, 44–46, 49, 55, 74, 77, 84, 86–90, 115, 147, 148, 185, 220, 251, 283

Emerson, Ralph Waldo, 37, 38

Etonian, The, 57, 280

Etownian, The, 62, 71, 80, 82, 88

Ewbank, John, vii, 185, 186, 222, 242, 251

Exman, Eugene, 179, 187, 188, 205, 242

F

Farmer, James, 8, 9, 96, 110, 111, 123–26, 133, 141, 190, 213, 214, 245, 286, 292

Fellowship House of Philadelphia, 211, 218

Fellowship of Reconciliation (FOR), v, 61, 91, 93–97, 110, 117, 119, 121, 123–26, 133, 141, 157, 159, 160, 165, 166, 169, 171, 182, 183, 189–93, 196–205, 209, 210, 213–18, 220–25, 227, 228, 231, 232, 234–49, 251–56, 258, 259, 264, 266–68, 270, 271, 301

Fisher, Bernice, 124

Fox, George, 164, 208, 247

Freud, Sigmund, 103, 232

Fridinger, Wilmer, vii, 54–56, 62, 64, 73, 79, 83, 85, 90

Friends. See Quakers

Friends Medical Society, 239, 245, 301

Friends Peace Committee, 237, 252, 301

Frysinger, William, vii

Fulford, Dawn, 240, 243

G

Gandhi, Mahatma, 11, 97–99, 124, 125, 129, 133, 184–86, 198, 201, 202, 209, 211, 235, 236, 239, 241, 248, 249, 254, 257, 259, 272

Gap, PA, vi, 13–17, 21, 24, 27, 33–35, 39, 41, 42, 45, 46, 48, 53, 58–60, 66, 73, 76, 83, 84, 91, 102, 108, 109, 117, 134, 136, 150, 189, 191, 198, 199, 222, 277

Garrison, William Lloyd, 40

Gibbons, Daniel, 40, 279

Gibran, Kahlil, 74

Glass, John, 49, 51, 52, 57, 61

Gorsuch, Dickenson, 279

Gorsuch, Edward, 29, 31

Gorsuch, Tom, 31

Graham, John, 279

Great Depression, 23–25, 32, 36, 45, 53, 60, 73, 78, 81, 85, 92

Gregg, Richard, 96, 126
Griffith, John, vii, 128–32, 166, 202
Groff, Elsie, 84, 93, 112, 122, 145, 156, 170, 175, 180
Groff, Isaac Brenneman (Marian's grandfather), 92
Groff, Raymond, 84, 92, 93, 102, 112, 156, 180
Guideposts Magazine, 274, 275
Guthrie family, 230

H

Hagner, George, 256
Hall, Francis, 231
Hanway, Castner, 29, 30
Harris, Karen, vii
Hartsough family, 208
Henderson Place, 53, 58, 60, 73, 102, 108, 150, 151, 280
Hendry, Clara, 279
Hentoff, Nat, 211
Herr, Aaron, 49, 50, 51, 57, 61
Herr, Arline, 38
Herr, Coach Ira, 85, 149
Hetzel, Theodore, iv
Holderith, Bill, 128
Hood, Caleb, 40, 41, 280
Hood, John, 41
Hood, Joseph, 41, 280
Hood, Thomas, 41, 280
Hope College, MI, 96, 225
Horning, Harry, 82
Houser, George, ii, vi, 124, 133, 141, 165, 172, 190, 192, 196, 201, 204, 214, 222, 227, 245, 252
Houser, Hank, 192
Huxley, Aldous, 108

J

Jack, Homer, 124, 172
Jackson, Charles, 41
Jackson, William, 280
James Family, 208
James, Robert, 204

Jane Addams House, 198, 255
Jesus, v, 72, 95, 97, 104, 105, 121, 137–39, 185, 192, 208, 218, 225, 257, 265, 275
Johnson, Mordecai, 210, 218, 292
Jones, E. Stanley, 96
Just War Doctrine, 47

K

Kang, Kilsoo Ken, 237
Karsner, Joseph, 237, 238
Keneagy, Carolyn Neuhauser, 22, 277
King, Coretta Scott, i, iv, vi
King, Martin Luther, i, iii–v, vii, 7, 8, 10–12, 209–11, 218, 224, 272, 273, 275
Korean War, 213, 221, 223, 235, 237, 254
Kurkjian, Amy, 243
Kurkjian, Ernest, 203, 256

L

Lakey, George, vii
Lancaster County, PA, iv, 13, 25, 34, 38, 41, 91, 188
Lawson, James, i, vi, 160
Lee, General Robert E., 31
Lefever, Ernest, iv, 46–52, 55–58, 61, 63, 66–69, 71–81, 85, 111, 132, 133, 148, 164, 184, 185, 199, 200, 221, 248, 251, 282
Lefever, Margaret, iv
LeFevre, Isaac, 48
Lester, Muriel, 96, 139
Lewis, Elijah, 29, 30
Lewis, John, i, iv
Logan, James, 14
London, Dan and Maggie, 14
London, Ed, 27–32, 39
Longstreth, Emily, 202, 217
Longstreth, Walter, 202, 203

M

March on Washington, iii–v, 1–12, 273

Markey, Charlotte, 83, 90
Marshall, Joy, 239, 240
Martin, Don, 279
McCorkel, Roy, 96, 203
Mendenhall, Isaac & Dinah, 279, 280
Mennonites, 45, 46, 48, 70, 109
Methodist Church, 14, 41, 47, 70, 86, 94, 96, 102, 105, 128, 130, 133, 162, 179, 192, 196, 198
Miner, Mary, 204
Montgomery Bus Protest (Boycott), 8, 210, 211, 272, 273
Moore, Charles, James, Joseph & Jeremiah, 41, 280
Mr. Average Citizen, 159, 249, 252, 255, 260–64, 266, 272, 273, 300
Muste, A. J., iii, 95–97, 97, 101, 124, 133, 134, 160, 169, 178, 182, 185–87, 190, 193, 202–4, 209–11, 218, 220, 223, 225, 226, 234–37, 241, 245–49, 252, 268, 270, 271

N

NAACP, 5, 263, 301
NAAWP, 262–64, 301
Naegle, Walter, vii
National Council of Churches (NCC), 9, 10, 301
National Urban League (NUL), 5, 301
Negro American Labor Council, 5, 301
Nehru, Jawaharlal, 11, 219, 221
Neuhauser, Don, 279
Nevin, Ethan, 247
New York University, 165, 168
Niebuhr, Reinhold, 127, 199
Nkrumah, Kwame, 226, 227
Nobel Peace Prize, 180–83, 297
nonviolence, iii–v, 3, 4, 7, 8, 11, 12, 96–98, 101, 124–26, 165, 166, 178, 184, 185, 186, 201, 202, 209, 211, 212, 218, 219, 225, 234, 236, 237, 241–43, 246, 247, 249, 255, 258, 259, 268, 272–75

O

Ooiman, JoAnn, 209

P

pacifism, 8, 47, 56, 58, 63, 64, 67, 68, 93, 96, 103, 104, 106, 107, 111, 118, 124–26, 128, 129, 133, 163, 164, 186, 188, 197, 199, 202, 204, 209–11, 220, 221, 225, 234, 236, 238, 244, 246, 250, 260
Pacifist Notebook, 271
Palmer family, 208
Paradise High School, 33, 37
Parker, William, 28–31, 39, 42
Parmer, Charles, 37, 190, 193, 211–13
Paul, Alice, 168
Peacemakers, 177, 178, 186, 188, 268, 288, 289
Pearl Harbor, 102, 105, 111, 141
Pearson, Dr. William, 90
Pendle Hill, PA, vi, 220
Penn, William, vi, 14, 15, 46, 48, 70, 108, 136, 168, 177, 178, 189, 207, 209, 228, 229
Petersburg Penitentiary, VA, 123, 126, 134, 135, 166
Philadelphia, iii, 2, 3, 99, 101, 108, 126, 190, 191, 201, 228, 229
Pickett, Clarence, 159, 180, 247
Pownall, Levi, 28, 29, 279
Pownall, Sarah, 28, 29

Q

Quakers (Friends), iii–v, 8, 10, 12, 14, 29, 30, 37, 39, 40, 41, 45–47, 60, 101, 107, 109, 116, 167–69, 178, 180–82, 189, 202, 204, 207–9, 218–21, 225, 228–30, 237, 258, 275, 279, 296
Quakertown, 238

R

Raitt, John, 172, 235, 238–40, 288

Randall, Ed, 249

Redding, Louis & Ruth, 258, 298

Reeder, Allen, vi

Rehobeth, 158

Repenning, Betsey, 224

Richland Friends Meeting, 238

Ridenbaugh, Lowell, vii, 80, 83, 90, 115, 116

Robinson, Jackie, 183

Rockel, Charles, 216

Russia, 67, 68, 91, 97, 103, 106, 114, 137, 163, 177, 184, 193, 213, 219, 293, 302

Rustin, Bayard, iii, 2, 97, 125, 131, 133, 141, 159, 165, 172, 177, 190, 196, 201–4, 209, 218–20, 223, 226, 229, 232, 241–43, 245, 246, 288, 294

Rutenber, Culbert, 238, 239

S

SAFE, 193, 302

Salisbury High School, 37, 146, 279

Savery family, 208

Schaal, Red, 203, 244

Scott, General Winfield, 17

Seneca Falls, NY, 168

Shank, Margaret Rice Good (Grandmother), 122, 207, 265

Sharp, Gene, 192

Shaw, Irwin, 236, 237

Shaw, Lillian H., 238

Shearer, Dr., 168, 170, 173, 174

Shirk, Ray and Dorothy, 279

Simmons, Pauline, 279

Smiley, Glenn, iii, 242, 258, 259, 267, 268

Smith, Allen, 280

Southern Christian Leadership Conference (SCLC), 5, 302

Speakers Bureau, 207

Springfield State Hospital, 112–15, 119

Steere, Douglas, 96

Stevens, Thaddeus, 40

strike, 101, 124, 131, 132, 215, 225–27, 259

Student Volunteer Movement (SVM), 232, 302

Supreme Court rulings, 116, 171, 219, 254, 258, 262

Swain, Thomas, vi

Swarthmore College Peace Collection, v, 190, 289, 302

Swomley, Jim, 192

Swomley, John, 96, 133, 169, 190–93, 195, 196, 199, 201–4, 216, 241, 244, 245, 254, 255

T

Tanguy, PA, 194, 205, 207, 221, 224, 228, 230–32, 243, 249, 264, 265, 293

Tatum, Arlo, 198, 290

Tatum, Lyle, vii, 256, 290

Thomas, Cherian, 236

Thomas, Norman, 96

Thompson, Ralph, 279

Thoreau, Henry David, 37

Thornton, PA, 222, 230

Thurman, Howard, 218, 292

Till, Emmet, 255, 272

U

Underground Railroad, vi, 39–42, 229, 279

United Nations, 140, 162, 178, 207, 213, 302

V

Valley Forge, PA, vi, 14, 158, 189

Vlastos, Gregory, 125

W

Walker, Allan, vi, 10, 154, 206, 208, 217, 223, 251, 259, 265

Walker, Anthony, 25

Walker, Asahel, 279

Walker, Brenda, i, iii, iv, 10, 153–55, 153, 175–77, 181, 184, 189, 203, 206, 208, 223, 251, 259, 265, 274, 275, 281

Walker, Charles
  as conscientious objector, 67, 68, 94,
    100, 105, 108–10, 112, 113, 120,
    126–32, 136, 141, 167–69
  March on Washington, involvement
    in, iii–v, 1–12, 273, 276
  pacifist views of, 8, 47, 63, 64, 68, 91,
    93, 95, 97, 98, 104–8, 117–19,
    124–26, 128–30, 163–64, 176, 188,
    193, 194, 197, 199, 204, 205, 220,
    221, 234, 235, 238, 239, 244, 247,
    248, 260
Walker, Charles, writings
  "The Prayer of a Righteous Man",
    256–58
  "A Discipline for Peacemakers", 137–
    40
  "Captive of the Spirit", 162–64
  "Conciliation and Direct Action: A
    Time for Collaboration", 180, 289
  "Cryme in Rhyme", 127, 128, 131,
    132, 167
  "Lessons from the Civil Rights
    Movement", 254, 298
  "On Leaving CPS", 121, 122
  "Pacifism Confronts a World at
    War", 91, 117–19
  "Peace Talk", 63, 67, 68
  "Saga of a C.O.", 112, 113, 123, 136,
    167
  "The Impact of Gandhi on the U.S.
    Peace Mvmt.", 125, 209, 286
  "The Man of Montgomery", 8, 11,
    276
  "The March on Washington", 1–5
  "The Prayer of a Righteous Man",
    298
Walker, Gloria, vi, 10, 155, 260, 265
Walker, Isaac, Jr. (great-grandfather), 28,
    39, 277
Walker, Isaac, Sr. (great, great
    grandfather), 14
Walker, James Madison (Charlie's
    grandfather), 14, 25, 42
Walker, Joseph, 14, 59, 117, 136, 145
Walker, Larry, vi, 10, 141, 142, 152, 153,

158, 165, 167, 170, 173, 175, 177, 181,
    184, 189, 203, 206, 208, 221–23, 251,
    259, 265, 276, 285, 287
Walker, Lewis, 14, 158, 189
Walker, Marian, i, iv, 69–71, 79–87, 89–
    103, 106–17, 119–23, 145, 146, 148,
    150–53, 156, 158, 164–68, 170–76,
    180–86, 188, 189, 191, 194–96, 199,
    200, 204–8, 216, 217, 219–24, 228,
    230, 231, 238–43, 249–51, 256–59,
    264–68, 276, 283
Walker, Mina, 13, 15, 16, 19–22, 25–27,
    31–37, 39–46, 53, 58, 66, 79, 89, 102,
    103, 105, 108, 133, 134, 136, 137, 144,
    145, 158, 180, 191, 194, 265, 269, 280
Walker, Valerie, vi, 10, 154, 155, 232,
    243, 249, 251, 259, 265
Walker, William, vi, 19, 21, 23, 25, 32,
    36, 39, 43, 44, 53, 58–60, 66, 102,
    155, 268–70
Walker, Winnie, vi, 10, 119, 120, 133–36,
    140–42, 152–54, 165–67, 170, 171,
    173–77, 181, 184, 189, 203, 206, 208,
    221–23, 240, 251, 259, 265, 288
Walton, George, 203, 251, 255, 256, 297
West Chester, PA, 156, 195, 218, 223,
    230, 258
Westtown Friends School, 10, 195, 221,
    222, 245
Whitson, Thomas, 40
Wikipedia, 274
Will, Herman, 179, 182, 196
Willoughby, George, vii, 198, 266
Willoughby, Lillian, vii
Willoughby, William, vii, 49–52, 54–56,
    61, 65–74, 76, 77, 79–81, 83, 85, 88,
    89, 148, 220, 221, 228, 251, 297
Wilson, Bob, 230
Wilson, Charles, 73
Women's International League for Peace
    and Freedom (WILPF), 197, 198, 268
World War I, 33, 62, 93, 116
World War II, 8, 91, 135, 140, 169, 213,
    219, 236, 238, 254
Worst, Ida, 279

Y

Yates, Howard, 264
YMCA, 58, 65, 67, 69, 164, 167, 184, 191, 198, 204, 302
YWCA, 69, 85, 167, 200, 204, 302

Z

Zimmerman, Mildred Coates, 22, 35, 37, 58, 145

59995509R10179

Made in the USA
Middletown, DE
13 August 2019